PLAINS

T0246068

John R. Wunder, *Series Editor*

Also in the series:

Route 66: A Road to America's Landscape, History, and Culture, by Markku Henriksson

Ruling Pine Ridge: Oglala Lakota Politics from the IRA to Wounded Knee, by Akim D. Reinhardt

A Sacred People: Indigenous Governance, Traditional Leadership, and the Warriors of the Cheyenne Nation, by Leo K. Killsback

A Sovereign People: Indigenous Nationhood, Traditional Law, and the Covenants of the Cheyenne Nation, by Leo K. Killsback

Trail Sisters: Freedwomen in Indian Territory, 1850–1890, by Linda Williams Reese

Urban Villages and Local Identities: Germans from Russia, Omaha Indians, and Vietnamese in Lincoln, Nebraska, by Kurt E. Kinbacher

Where the West Begins: Debating Texas Identity, by Glen Sample Ely

Women on the North American Plains, edited by Renee M. Laegreid and Sandra K. Mathews

THE
FALLS OF
WICHITA
FALLS

AN ENVIRONMENTAL
HISTORY OF THE RED
ROLLING PLAINS

JAHUE ANDERSON

TEXAS TECH UNIVERSITY PRESS

This book is typeset in Adobe Caslon Pro. The paper used in this book meets the minimum requirements of ANSI/NISO Z39.48-1992 (R1997). ⊗

Designed by Hannah Gaskamp
Cover design by Hannah Gaskamp

Library of Congress Cataloging-in-Publication Data

Names: Anderson, Jahue, author. Title: The Falls of Wichita Falls: An Environmental History of the Red Rolling Plains / Jahue Anderson. Other titles: Plains Histories. Description: Lubbock, Texas: Texas Tech University Press, [2023] | Series: Plains Histories | Includes bibliographical references and index. | Summary: "An environmental history of the Red Rolling Plains of Wichita Falls, Texas, detailing the region's Progressive Era land ethics, water management, boom-and-bust oil towns, and natural resource allocation"—Provided by publisher.
Identifiers: LCCN 2022032884 (print) | LCCN 2022032885 (ebook) |
ISBN 978-1-68283-156-4 (paperback) | ISBN 978-1-68283-157-1 (ebook)
Subjects: LCSH: Natural resources—Texas—Wichita Falls Region. | Biotic communities—Texas—Wichita Falls Region. | Wichita Falls Region (Tex.)—Environmental conditions.
Classification: LCC F394.W6 A64 2022 (print) | LCC F394.W6 (ebook) |
DDC 976.4745—dc23/eng/20220715
LC record available at https://lccn.loc.gov/2022032884
LC ebook record available at https://lccn.loc.gov/2022032885

Printed in the United States of America
23 24 25 26 27 28 29 30 31 / 9 8 7 6 5 4 3 2 1

Texas Tech University Press
Box 41037
Lubbock, Texas 79409-1037 USA
800.832.4042
ttup@ttu.edu
www.ttupress.org

To Uncle David
for inspiring an interest in the environmental history of
Wichita Falls.

CONTENTS

ILLUSTRATIONS

ACKNOWLEDGMENTS

My maternal grandmother Ami (Jo Ella Hearne) married Harry L. Banks Jr. and he brought her to Wichita Falls. It was his hometown, where he grew up with five sisters and a brother all raised by his mother and a hardworking father, Harry "Lee" Banks Sr. My great-grandfather, Lee Banks, worked on the oil rigs as a roughneck in Wichita County, where he lost a finger. For many years, they lived in a tent as the oil boom city grew to meet the demands of its new occupants.

Through hard work (blood, sweat, tears, and a finger) and perseverance, they prospered and their descendants, including me, call Wichita Falls their hometown. Both of my grandfathers served in World War II. My paternal grandfather, Eargle Anderson, married Juanita Tucker and after the war they landed at Sheppard Air Force Base on the outskirts of Wichita Falls. My "Greatest Generation" grandparents birthed my "Baby Boomer" parents in the 1950s. My parents met in the 1970s and by 1979, just before Terrible Tuesday (which featured an F4 tornado that destroyed the city of Wichita Falls), I came into the world. I register all this to emphasize my deep attachment to the place. I acknowledge these ancestors and Wichita Falls and its sometimes dangerous, but mostly beautiful, big blue skies.

Growing up on a twelve-acre plot of land in Lake Arrowhead Ranch Estates during the 1980s, I became interested in why people settled in Wichita County. At the time, I didn't realize that my family's own history revealed several clues. Every school day, my mother, Allison Anderson, a kindergarten teacher and dedicated educator, drove my brother, Micah Anderson, and me into the city of Wichita Falls for school at Episcopal Elementary. On the twelve-mile ride, I pondered why people settled on these pumpjack-filled, cattle-laden, mesquite-infested red plains. Why here? Did the wheels fall off the wagon? Did they get stuck in the red mud? I can't stress enough the redness. When my brother and I got muddy or swam in the regional lakes, the waters stained our shorts a deep red.

My grandparents, Eargle and Juanita Anderson, sparked an interest in history. My history teacher at Episcopal, Margaret Aldridge, fueled that love of history. More importantly, she inspired me and gave me a love for historical storytelling. But the greatest storytellers were my father, Steve Anderson, and my uncle, David Anderson. They are masters of the great Texas yarn. I acknowledge their influences on my storytelling abilities. Moreover, I want to acknowledge Uncle David's help and encouragement on this particular project. In fact, he helped me identify the topic for this monograph. I would like to thank David, Debbie, and Matt for their continued support and help exploring the rich history of Wichita Falls and its red rolling plains. They've literally brought me books and documents found in this work.

At Midwestern State University, Dr. Kenneth Hendrickson mentored and showed me the realities of an academic life. At the same time his work on the local history of Wichita Falls and the region aided this study. At the University of Texas, Karl W. Butzer inspired an interest in the intersection of geography, archeology, and history. At graduate school at Texas State University, Dr. J. Frank de la Teja focused these interests and steered me to Texas environmental history. He helped me begin the scholarly path for this particular study. At Texas Christian University, Dr. Todd Kerstetter directed important research and writing on the topic. Drs. Benjamin Tillman, Rebecca Sharpless, Gregg Cantrell, Ken Stevens, and Susan Ramirez read, edited, and helped me to improve the manuscript. I would also like to acknowledge the input, critiques, and edits of Dr. Christopher Morris. He challenged me to improve several sections of this work.

I would like to especially thank the support offered by the Formby Research Fellowship at the Southwest Collection. With its aid, I was able to spend a summer in the Southwest Collection at Texas Tech University. In Lubbock, Texas, I benefitted from the knowledge and help of Monte Monroe, Randy Vance, and Diane Warner. In fact, I would like to thank and acknowledge all the archivists and librarians who aided in my research for this book. I found myself engaging with staff members in archives, libraries, and museums across the states of Texas and Oklahoma, including the National Archives (Fort Worth), Dolph Briscoe Center for American History (Austin), Texas General Land Office (Austin), Museum of the Great Plains (Lawton), Moffett Library at Midwestern State University (Wichita Falls), and the Wichita County Archives (Wichita Falls).

Most important, I want to thank my family, Ryan and Emma, and especially my wife, Kelly McMichael, for her support. Dr. Kelly McMichael is not only my partner but also a top-notch Texas historian, scholar, and editor. Without her love and support, this book would not exist.

THE
FALLS OF
WICHITA
FALLS

INTRODUCTION

I n the spring of 1886, storm waters swelled in the Big Wichita River, breaking the dam near downtown Wichita Falls, spilling wreckage downriver and leveling the waterfalls.[1] Both settlers and historians lamented losing the falls, the very place-name of Wichita Falls. Local settler Aaron Dodson wrote, "[T]he dam went out with the first head rise and the rock and force of the water leveled the falls." In her "Historical Sketch of Wichita Falls," Mrs. A. H. Carrigan related that "old Mr. [J. A.] Foreman, sanguine as to the possibility, endeavored to put in a water mill" but afterwards, the flood debris erased the falls, "dividing asunder the high-sounding name of our city." Historian Johnnie Morgan lamented the falls were "destroyed by the washing out of a dam built by ambitious waterpower enthusiasts and the filling of the riverbed below the falls. Thus was wiped away what promised to be natural scenic view that might have been a pride to us now, especially since from them we get part of our name." The history of the erasing of the falls highlights a major theme in water development at the turn of the twentieth century—schemes to improve human conditions through conservation and efficiency often failed.[2] This monograph is the tale of natural limitations to those human schemes and the lack of knowledge about the local environment that doomed the Big Wichita Valley irrigation projects and other developments in Wichita Falls to

Irrigation promoter Joseph Kemp (1923) served as president of the board of Wichita County Water Improvement District No. 1. (Photo courtesy of the Southwest Collection/Special Collections Library, Texas Tech University)

failure and sometimes to catastrophic failure like that of the washing out of the falls in Wichita Falls.

Since the 1880s developers had neglected natural conditions as they attempted to populate sections of the Southern Plains. In the Big

Wichita Valley, for example, city builders celebrated man's conquest over nature and natural resources, especially its waters, fossil fuels, and grasslands. Joseph Kemp promoted reclamation and conservation and envisioned the Big Wichita River Valley as the "Irrigated Valley." But Wichita Falls water developers and city boosters like J. A. Foreman and Joseph Kemp faced serious ecological limitations and political obstacles in their efforts to conquer water, accomplishing only parts of their grandiose vision. Most of the water projects in the valley never met the expectations of the boosters.

City boosters were local capitalists seeking to improve the economic position of their towns and regions and included men like Joseph Kemp in Wichita Falls and Buckley B. "Captain B. B." Paddock of Fort Worth.[3] Throughout the Gilded Age and Progressive Era, regional boosters gathered at area chambers of commerce to plan for future development, propagating their agendas through regional newspapers. In reality, Paddock and Kemp had misguided if not outdated visions of yeoman farmers inhabiting the Big Wichita Valley. They believed that farmers would benefit from their wise planning. Businessmen understood water to be the basic resource for supporting economic development: agriculture, towns, and industry depended on water. City builders in Northwest Texas claimed an ability "to conquer nature" and "reclaim the desert," converting nonproductive lands into bountiful fields and cities. In the Wichita Valley, people built systems to water their farmlands and livestock. They piped water to industries and towns and foresaw more "upbuilding" in the valley, the seemingly natural progression of economic development on the Texas Rolling Plains. And that interpretation of events is how many early historians recorded irrigation and agricultural development—as another step toward modern civilization.[4]

Under closer examination, the people of the Wichita Valley made water a commodity to be exploited. And when the farmers dug irrigation ditches and tilled their fields, the inexperience with watering the land caused severe environmental problems. Water quality and poor drainage proved to be the important and overlooked issues. The Big Wichita's saline waters, caused by the local Permian red beds and gypsum, created significant problems for irrigation systems, for the land, and for the people in the valley.[5] Many environmental consequences went unforeseen for decades. Yet the damaging effects of saline water and poor drainage slowly destroyed the boosters' dream of an agrarian Eden.

Historians, including Frederick Jackson Turner and Walter Prescott Webb, fostered these narratives of hydraulic civilizations watering arid plains. At the turn of the twentieth century, historians like Turner wrote about Anglo-Saxon males taming the frontier and bringing civilization to the plains.[6] On the Texas plains, Walter Prescott Webb endorsed the conquest-oriented model but questioned parts of the Turnerian vision, arguing for the environmental impact of human settlement.[7] Webb pulled from the theories of geographer Ellen Semple, who popularized environmental determinism. She argued that the environment was the prime force for historical change.[8] Many historians, including Webb, subscribed to environmental determinism, and they applied it to the North Texas plains.[9] Webb, "an exemplar of the southern plains water craze," epitomized the deterministic approach to plains history, writing in *The Great Plains*: "[T]he scarcity of moisture is the subject that furnishes the greatest amount of thought and talk: in fact it is the crux of the whole problem of conquering the Great Plains."[10] Webb and the generations before and after him saw water as the basic "problem" or determinant that stood in the way of settling the Southern Plains.[11] Regional historians followed in Webb's footsteps with similar deterministic approaches to water history, applying the paradigmatic framework to the North Texas plains.[12]

Only a handful of American naturalists and European intellectuals challenged this perspective. Over time, critics slowly brought about a growing awareness of the assault on nature by advocating the rejection of materialism and utilitarianism.[13] Many European intellectuals argued that modern capitalist societies divorced the individual from nature, creating a situation in which nature itself became a commodity ripe for exploitation.[14] According to this critique of private water development, both human culture and the natural world suffered great harm. From the 1960s to the 1980s many historians pointed to the Dust Bowl as validation for this argument.[15] In this revisionist vein a "new western history" emerged. From this standpoint "New Environmental Historians," such as Donald Worster, provided new perspectives on water history.[16]

Worster's pivotal work *Rivers of Empire* transformed the study of water resources from determinism to an environmental declensionist approach. As contended by Worster, bureaucrats and agriculturalists converted river valleys into agricultural empires through a process of ecological intensification to extract more and more economic yield. Large amounts of exploration, capital, and labor enabled a "hydraulic society" to control populations by harnessing wild rivers and harvesting the river's wealth.[17] Worster challenged the positivist outlook with a declensionist approach, ascribing dust storms and environmental degradation to exploitative capitalistic forces. More recently some environmental historians have questioned parts of both of these ideas. Geoff Cunfer in his book *On the Great Plains* claimed that both Webb and Worster are "ideologically driven" and lack "rigorous empirical analysis." According to Cunfer, humans negotiated with nature as one of the many contending forces shaping the Great Plains.[18]

Most environmental historians can agree that human development resulted in an overbuilt landscape that lacked concern for natural rhythms and with an intolerance for the limits of the rivers. Many historians have focused on river valleys and water resource developments in the American West, and there have been some who have focused specifically on Texas and the Southern Plains.[19] As posited in Stephen Bogener's *Ditches Across the Desert: Irrigation in the Lower Pecos Valley*, irrigation boosters and federal reclamation efforts did not meet Gilded Age and Progressive Era expectations.[20] And James Sherow's *Watering the Valley: Development along the High Plains Arkansas River, 1870–1950* echoes themes and developments in the Pecos and Big Wichita River Valleys. In all these river basins, speculative booster projects caused environmental degradation, which in many ways outweighed economic benefits.[21] When this perspective is applied to the plains of Northwest Texas, a compelling portrayal of the valley's development unfolds, offering a more rigorous assessment of the environmental consequences of human interaction with the landscape. The process of bringing irrigation to the Big Wichita River Valley fits into the national model of watering the West. The process, however, ignored knowledge of the local environment, which was "key to making complex social and ecological systems work."[22] In this case, the national model disregarded water quality, and when quality became the local issue, the national model failed the locality.

The Falls of Wichita Falls explores the environmental history of the late nineteenth and twentieth century Red Rolling Plains. The work moves chronologically out from the development of Joseph Kemp and Frank Kell's business empires. Their railroads and agribusiness connected the hinterlands of Northwest Texas and Southwest Oklahoma, making Wichita Falls a regional hub. The ecological ramifications of tying the hinterlands to the city are explored through Teddy Roosevelt's wolf hunt in Frederick, Oklahoma Territory, at the beginning of the century. The book begins with the wolf hunt in the "Big Pasture" and concludes with a discussion of the "Indian casinos" in those same pastures. It observes the washing out of the falls of Wichita Falls in the 1880s and the rebuilding of new falls by the 1980s. This work follows the oil boom as it transforms the Red Rolling Plains, which in due course bust as drought crushed the region, leaving behind dust and ghost towns. The book reveals the human relationship with the environment and the ways people of the Red Rolling Plains have made sense of their natural world.

In chapter 1, a history of President Theodore Roosevelt's wolf hunt in the "Big Pasture" (near Frederick, Oklahoma) establishes a baseline ecology for the succeeding chapters and explores rural-urban and predator-prey relationships and the ecological consequences of those relationships. The chapter also explores the land ethics of President Roosevelt, the wolf catching homesteader Jack Abernathy, Comanche headman Quanah Parker, city boosters Kemp and his brother-in-law Frank Kell, small-scale rancher and lawman Capt. Bill McDonald, and large-scale cattlemen W. T. Waggoner and S. Burk Burnett while analyzing the interactions between these individuals and their respective groups.[23]

The second chapter moves to the Texas side of the Red River on the Big Wichita River tributary during the Gilded Age and Progressive Era (1880–1930). From the washing out of the falls of Wichita Falls on the Big Wichita River during the Gilded Age (1870–1901) to the massive reservoir and irrigation systems of the late Progressive Era (1901–1930), city boosters strove but failed to improve human conditions.[24] Chapter 3 explores the oil boom of the war years (1912–1945) and the stress placed on the water systems of the Big Wichita River by increasing population pressures. The dreams of an "irrigated valley" gave way to a cultural landscape of oil derricks, military installations, suburbs, and a complex system of reservoirs and pumping stations built on the Little Wichita River to bring water to people living in the Big Wichita River Valley. The chapter describes the first "inter-basin" or basin-to-basin water transfer system in the state of Texas. The City of Wichita Falls pumped and still pumps waters from the Little Wichita River Basin (an entirely separate watershed) into the Big Wichita River Basin where Wichita Falls sits on the muddy red Big Wichita River.[25]

Chapter 4 depicts the boom-bust cycles of the postwar years. It reveals how failed ideologies, dysfunctional administrations, and poor leadership played roles in environmental crises since the 1950s. Oil booms gave way to busts and ghost towns while waves of droughts and tornadoes plagued the Red Rolling Plains. Despite the problems, growth of military infrastructure in the American West expanded after World War II and Wichita Falls (home of Sheppard Air Force Base) and Lawton (which houses Fort Sill Army Base) continued to draw people to the region.[26] The final chapter examines the recent past and the cultural landscape of "Indian casinos." The Indian casino represents an important juxtaposition to the "cowboy myth" of rugged individualism.

The complex history of the region has been oversimplified and shrouded by such myths, which muddies the historical reality and allows dated and destructive ideas and policies to remain popular today.

CHAPTER 1

WOLF CATCHER

S ome histories oversimplify the effects of the iron horse, arguing railroads were harbingers of "civilization" that led to erasure of wilderness. Even while it was often scapegoated as the final death knell for wolves, bison, and Plains Indians, early historians recorded the railroad's "progress" and "advancements" as part of an unstoppable and inevitable "manifest destiny." In its wake, the wild things—bears, bison, wolves, and Comanches—faded at the onslaught of the railroad's "civilizing" influence. In reality, the story of the ecological consequences wrought by railroads is much different, richer and more complex, than the simplified and dangerous myth of "manifest destiny."[1] At these Red River borderlands the narrative of railroad development includes railroad boosterism, Plains Indians change and continuity, cattle baron cronyism, homesteaders clamoring for opening of lands, agribusiness expansion, Texas and Oklahoma state politics, and the growing power of the federal government. Fortunately, these complex relationships can be illustrated through the lively story of President Theodore Roosevelt's railroad trip to and wolf hunt in the Big Pasture.

By the turn of the twentieth century, the railroad firmly tied Wichita Falls to its agrarian hinterlands and initiated a process of transforming the Red River borderlands into a landscape dominated by commercial agriculture (primarily grain production). On the plains of Southwestern Oklahoma (previously Indian Territory), there existed a process of agrarian colonialism similar to the description found in Timothy Bowman's *Blood Oranges: Colonialism and Agriculture in the South Texas Borderlands.* Whereas the Rio Grande Valley in *Blood Oranges* saw Anglos transform the region from that of a culturally "Mexican" space, with an economy based on cattle, into one dominated by commercial agriculture focused on citrus and winter vegetables, the Anglos of North Texas transformed Southwestern Oklahoma Territory from that of a culturally "Plains Indian" space, with an economy based on cattle, into one dominated by commercial agriculture focused on grain production.[2] Both spaces—the Rio Grande River Valley and the Red River Valley—can be considered borderlands and both spaces experienced parallel transitions from livestock to agriculture production around the same time.

The grocer and railroad developer Joseph Kemp provides a perfect example for this transformation in the Red River Valley. He arrived in Wichita Falls in 1883, the year after the Fort Worth and Denver Railroad (FW&D) completed the track from Fort Worth to Wichita Falls.[3] Kemp owned wholesale and retail grocery businesses selling goods to the residents of Fort Sill in Indian Territory, the Plains Indians, the ranchers in Wichita County, and the citizens of Wichita Falls. Although the Red River divided Indian Territory (Oklahoma) from North Central Texas, neither the political boundary nor the river restricted trade or other human endeavors. Commerce and people flowed freely across the Red River and throughout the Red Rolling Plains.

Ultimately through his railroad promotions, Kemp helped to make Wichita Falls the commercial hub of the region. Kemp's most important contribution to the Wichita Falls economy came when he chartered the Wichita Falls Railway Company in 1894. His company connected Henrietta to Wichita Falls in 1895 and, in doing so, connected the Missouri–Kansas–Texas Railroad (MKT) to the Fort Worth

Wichita Falls city booster Frank Kell (1924) served as director of the Wichita Falls Chamber of Commerce during the 1920s. (Photo courtesy of the Southwest Collection/Special Collections Library, Texas Tech University)

and Denver Railroad (FW&D) via Wichita Falls. It meant Henrietta dawdled while Wichita Falls boomed. After Kemp's success with the connection between the FW&D and the MKT, his brother-in-law

Frank Kell saw opportunity in Wichita Falls and purchased the Wichita Valley Mills Company.[4]

Frank Kell married Lula Kemp (Joseph Kemp's sister) and they settled in Wichita Falls in 1896. Kell became more than part of the family—he became Kemp's longtime business partner in the milling and railroad industries. In Kemp and Kell, the direct link between railroad developments and agribusiness on the Red Rolling Plains becomes abundantly clear. Together the brothers-in-law embarked on an ambitious plan for railroad promotion in the region that made their mills and real estate the center of economic activity. By 1905, when Frank Kell expanded his milling business by purchasing a mill in Vernon, the Wichita Valley Railroad, Wichita Falls Railway, the Wichita Falls and Southern Railway, the Wichita Falls and Oklahoma Railway, and the Wichita Falls and Northwestern railways acted as arteries and veins extending out from a hub in Wichita Falls into the grain and mineral producing regions of Northwest Texas and Southwest Oklahoma.[5]

Together Kemp and Kell transformed the Red River borderlands cultural landscape through their railroads and agribusiness. When they learned the President of the United States Theodore Roosevelt planned to visit their part of the red earth to hunt wolves and coyotes, it is not hard to imagine that Kemp and Kell were ecstatic. Although Kemp and Kell voted as Democrats and the president was a Republican, they all three embraced the political label "progressive." The *Dallas Morning News* reported it "is well understood from . . . J. A. Kemp and Frank Kell that the President will stop at Wichita Falls *en route* to Vernon."[6] The paper also expected large crowds since people from Archer City, Seymour, and the other towns in the surrounding area were coming to Wichita Falls to see President Roosevelt. For Kemp and Kell, the crowds meant money for their railroads and the headlines meant national promotion for the city of Wichita Falls.[7]

The following not only tells the story of Roosevelt's wolf hunt and his presidential visit via the railroad to the area, it attempts to build a baseline of the region's ecology. The succeeding chapters display the changes and continuities in relationships between predator and prey, between human and environment, between plant and animal species, between urban railroad hubs and rural producers, and between Plains Indians, homesteaders, and ranchers. With its gallery of bigger-than-life characters, Teddy Roosevelt's wolf hunt provides a vehicle for introducing the various forces at play in the region and exploring how those forces interacted with one another.

THE WOLF HUNT

On a sunny day in April 1905 at two o'clock in the afternoon, the presidential train pulled into the depot of the little settlement of Frederick, Oklahoma Territory. The train carried President Theodore Roosevelt and his retinue of followers, including a personal security guard, Texas Ranger Capt. Bill McDonald.[8] The people of Frederick erected a bandstand, where the city mayor made introductions to an estimated crowd of six thousand gathered for a glimpse of the president. Cavalrymen from Fort Sill, located about forty-five miles from Frederick, secured the town and helped patrol the perimeter of the hunting grounds so that the president might have an uninterrupted hunt, free of uninvited guests. An oversized crowd had gathered in the town of Frederick and the president worried that "curious citizens" might spoil his hunt.[9] From the grandstand, he asked the citizenry for "four days' play. I hear you have plenty of jackrabbits and coyotes here [and] I like my citizens, but don't like them on a coyote hunt. Give me a fair deal to have as much fun as even a President is entitled to."[10]

Huge crowds had thronged rail stations in Texas at Fort Worth, Wichita Falls, and Vernon en route to the hunting grounds near Frederick. At Wichita Falls, crowds rushed as the train came to a standstill, where one report cited that people were "trying to climb over one another, it would seem—to get near the President."[11] Four Secret Service men attempted to quell the crowd as they tried to catch a glimpse of the man. When President Theodore Roosevelt appeared with Texas Ranger Capt. Bill McDonald, however, the crowd quieted. The people of Wichita Falls knew Capt. Bill McDonald and immediately followed his orders. According to McDonald's biographer, "Roosevelt marveled at the way McDonald handled the large crowds in Wichita Falls and Vernon, providing instant order in the chaotic rushes at the rail stations."[12] At Vernon the hunting party took the train to Frederick, Oklahoma Territory, in Comanche County, and from the bandstand in Frederick the president and his group rode a distance of twenty-five miles to the hunting camp.[13]

That evening at the campground near the Deep Red, Theodore Roosevelt prepared to explore the Red River Valley and hunt the "Big Pasture"—the southwestern edge of the territory that had been recently carved out of Indian Territory and renamed Oklahoma Territory. Roosevelt had been to the territory once before, soon after accepting the Republicans' vice-presidential nomination to serve under President William McKinley. Roosevelt campaigned for President McKinley's reelection bid in 1900 under the direction of the famed campaign manager Marcus Alonzo Hanna, crossing the American heartland and stopping in Oklahoma City for a Rough Riders' Convention in July 1900. In 1905 Roosevelt returned to Oklahoma Territory as president and "in favor of immediate statehood" for the territory.[14] He brushed off interest in the politics of statehood on this visit, however, claiming instead that he was ready for a few days relaxation, gearing up for what would become a historic "wolf hunt" in the Big Pasture.[15]

Teddy Roosevelt's wolf coursing on the Red Rolling Plains tells an interesting story of how humans perceived and negotiated their relationship to the environment. President Roosevelt and the men who attended the wolf hunt viewed the plains environment in very different terms and with varying land ethics. Among the men who gathered with President Roosevelt for his trip were wolf catcher and lawman John R. Abernathy, Texas Ranger captain and small-scale rancher from Wichita County Capt. Bill McDonald, "two old-style Texas cattlemen" Capt.

Samuel Burk Burnett and W. Tom Waggoner, and Comanche head-man Quanah Parker, described at the time as "now painfully teaching his people to travel the white man's stony road."[16] The varying land ethics of these men, alongside Roosevelt's own views of nature, explain much about Progressive Era perceptions and misperceptions of the environment.[17]

Earlier in the week, President Roosevelt had attended another Rough Rider reunion in San Antonio, Texas, again reliving and celebrating the glory of the Spanish-American War campaigns. Col. Cecil Lyons, who planned the president's trip to Texas, previously witnessed John "Jack" Abernathy's "Phenomenal Prowess as a Wolf Catcher" and knew that the president's admiration for "pluck and originality" made him "desirous" to witness Abernathy's performance.[18] Fort Worth native and fellow Rough Rider Sloan Simpson also plied the president with stories of Abernathy's wolf-catching escapades in 1903 at a White House dinner. The president believed Simpson had exaggerated Abernathy's exploits, but now Lyons's tale seemed to confirm Simpson's account. Roosevelt was an avid hunter and after hearing stories from Simpson and Lyons of Abernathy's ability to catch wolves using only a gloved hand, he was eager to meet the man. Moreover, Roosevelt wanted to go on a hunting trip with Abernathy with the promise of an opportunity to witness "Catch 'Em Alive Jack" in action.[19]

Colonel Lyons, in charge of planning the president's itinerary in Texas, called Jack Abernathy to Fort Worth in February 1905, giving the twenty-eight-year-old the power to select an exclusive site for the wolf hunt. When people heard of Abernathy's hunt, many towns across Texas and Oklahoma courted Abernathy and encouraged him to have the hunt near their town. The *Frederick Enterprise* wrote, "Influential men of these towns tried to bulldoze Mr. Abernathy in the hope of having the hunt take place in their town," and many attempted to bribe him.[20] There is no evidence to indicate that Kemp or Kell attempted to bribe Abernathy, but it does not seem unlikely. Abernathy "spurned" the bribes and "was determined that the hunt should occur in the place best adapted." According to a local newspaper account, "The President wanted to hunt wild wolves and these would hardly be found in abundance in old settled communities . . . and even if they were, there would be very little sport in trying to catch them where a fence would block the way every few minutes." The Frederick, Oklahoma, newspaper reported that, "Fortunately for Frederick, the gateway to the greatest hunting ground in all America lay but four miles to our [Frederick's] east."[21]

Ecologists describe the environment of the Big Pasture as bluestem–grama and mesquite-buffalo grass prairies, that at the turn of the twentieth century consisted of, among various other species, the interplay of prairie dogs, birds of prey, rattlesnakes, canines, livestock, mesquite trees, humans, and bluestem, grama, and buffalo grasses.[22] President Roosevelt described the land and environs in *Scribner's Magazine* in November 1905:

> The [wolf] coursing was done on the flats and great rolling prairies which stretched north from our camp toward to the Wichita Mountains and south toward the Red River. There was a certain element of risk in the gallops, because the whole country was one huge prairie-dog town, the prairie dogs being so numerous that the new towns and abandoned towns were continuous with one another in every direction. . . . Stunted mesquite bushes grew here and there in the grass . . . [and] as always in prairie dog towns, there were burrowing owls and rattlesnakes.[23]

Roosevelt added, "Cottonwood, elm, and pecans formed a belt of timber along the creek . . . [and] Cardinals and mocking birds—the most individual and delightful of all birds in voice and manner—sang in the woods."[24]

The canines on the Red Rolling Plains shared a long co-evolutionary history with humans. In terms of human history, the relationship is so old it possibly predates human use of fire as a tool.[25] Yet wolves as predators in Euro-American societies came to traditionally symbolize cunning, evil, and wickedness. They have been represented in centuries of literature and historical texts as the products of uncivilized and untamed wilderness. The "Big Bad Wolf" image threatened the wolves' ability to survive in the midst of increasing human settlement.[26] Environmental historian Dan Flores wrote about American cultural perceptions of wolves as "any animal that's regarded as a threat to little girls, cuddly lambs, and Santa Claus has a definite spin problem."[27] Wolves hunt, kill, and feast on other animals. They like freshly killed mammal flesh and really prefer large mammals to smaller ones.[28] Roosevelt expressed these Euro-American sentiments, "the ravages of [the] . . . grim . . . wolf, which, wherever it exists in numbers is a veritable scourge to the stockmen."[29]

What Roosevelt did not understand at the time and what we are still learning today is that the wolf is a "keystone" species and/or an "apex" predator. A keystone species is a predator whose removal will allow for growth in a prey population. For example, the prairie dogs that were once prey experienced population growths with the disappearance of the wolf. The story of the environmental history of the wolf on the Red Rolling Plains *is* about "trophic cascades." Trophic cascades are ecological processes that start at the top of the food chain and travel down. In the case of the plains environment, wolves, as a keystone species, changed the behavior of other predators, including coyotes and wild cats. In turn, this shaped the behavior of prey, like prairie dogs and deer. For example, the deer that visited creeks and rivers for a drink had to be cautious of lurking predators. Fear among prey created what ecologists have called a "landscape of fear." Deer left to their own devices overbrowse or overuse areas near creek and river bottoms caus-ing erosion of the banks. So not only do the wolves kill prairie dogs, deer, and bison, but also they give life to many other plants and animals on the banks of the river by limiting the numbers of browsing deer and foraging mammals. The wolf's predatory behavior ensured regeneration of vegetation and woodlands near riverbeds.[30]

The presence of beavers and wolves in the Red Rolling Plains eco-system made for a unique landscape. The beaver acted as an important intermediate trophic-level herbivore that thrived in the riverine environments. Rivers lined with denser vegetation and woody patches allowed beavers, fish, and other aquatic animals to live in the pools created by the beavers' dams. Appreciative waterfowl filled the beaver ponds while smaller mammals found habitat in the dense vegetation around the pond. The Red Rolling Plains ecosystem—where uninhabited by humans—was a teeming landscape with much biodiversity. A large population of smaller mammals meant other predators could benefit from the "landscape of fear," notably coyotes and bears, which ate the smaller mammals.

Wolves could not kill every deer, bison, or prairie dog, but they did force them to avoid areas where they could get trapped by a predator, particularly valleys and gorges. Fear of the apex predator—the wolf—changed the behavior of the prey. Thus the "landscape of fear" created by the presence of predators—especially wolves—changed physical geography. Stabilization of river and creek banks meant rivers meandered less, formed deeper pools, and saw less erosion. Channels also narrowed, which meant more wildlife habitats. Mix in beaver dams that pooled water and the Red Rolling Plains landscape looked much different than it does today. Wolves and beavers functioned as "ecosystem builders," both then and now. The wolves killed coyotes and other smaller predators, which meant more badgers, rabbits, and small mammals, normally eaten by coyotes. Plus, the presence of more mammals meant more bears. Without wolves and beavers as ecosystem builders, the ecosystem changes significantly. At transition zones, such as between the Red Rolling Plains and the Western Cross Timbers, losses in biodiversity could especially become significant without these ecosystem builders present.

There is no doubt that mammals—predators and herbivores—played a critical role in the Red River environment that existed before the twentieth century. Bears, beavers, prairie dogs, badgers, wolves, and numerous other mammals made the Red Rolling Plains their home in the centuries before the arrival of the homesteaders. The loss of these mammals and the reasons behind that loss have been oversimplified. Many historians claim they had been hunted out of existence. Although partly true, this explanation does not fully grasp the ecological dynamics at work. The study of the natural dynamics of predator-prey relationships has been developing slowly since the late 1990s when scientists started reintroducing wolves back to their natural environments. As of yet, wolves have not been reintroduced to the Red Rolling Plains in a systematic way. Recently, however, small numbers of wolves reintroduced in Yellowstone National Park transformed its physical geography and allowed for what conservations called a "rewilding" of the land. It allowed for scientists to watch the process of keystone species ecosystem builders and trophic cascades in real time. Scientists witnessed the "landscape of fear" in action and the rehabilitation of diverse ecosystems.[31]

Canines, wild and domesticated, have been part of the plains ecosystem since before the arrival of Europeans. Before the Plains Indians made use of the Old World horse, they used their domesticated dogs to haul equipment. In many cases their domesticated dogs aided in the hunt for game. The wild canines, especially the wolf packs, followed herds of buffalo across prairies while coyotes were left to scavenge or hunt smaller mammals. George Catlin, a naturalist painter, portrayed Southern Plains wolves in his 1830 writings and art. Most famously, he depicted a wolf pack preying on a bison. The wild canines ranged in size from the larger timber wolves, weighing more than one hundred pounds, to the smaller coyotes, weighing twenty-plus pounds. The smaller coyotes coexist in the shadows of human settlements more easily than the larger wolves because of their size and innate ability to steer clear of humans, especially wolf catchers like John Abernathy.[32]

Progressive Era hunters searched the plains for wolves and coyotes to make the region "safe for civilization." Sometimes the newspapers and various writers from the wolf hunt, including Abernathy and Roosevelt, used the terms coyotes and wolves interchangeably. Science, however, clearly defines coyotes (*Canis latrans*) as a different species than the wolf (*Canis lupus*). It does appear there were both coyotes and wolves to be hunted in the Red Rolling Plains region based on the weights and descriptions given by the attendees of the hunt. Abernathy, for example, tracked down a black wolf that "baffled all efforts at capture, and has probably been chased more miles in the last three years than any other wolf in this country."[33] In an interview with the *Dallas Morning News*, Abernathy explained, "For several weeks before the President arrived he [Abernathy] scoured the country, capturing wolves to be penned up and turned loose when the President arrived."[34] One of the largest was a "lobo wolf which weighed nearly 120 pounds, and which stood three and one-half feet high."[35] *Canis lupus* (wolves) weigh in anywhere from eighty to 120 pounds or more.[36] *Canis latrans* (coyotes) weigh in between fifteen and forty pounds or more.[37]

Although newspapers reported that Abernathy would release the penned wild canids before the hunt, ultimately President Roosevelt refused to hunt the large wolves held in captivity, demanding to "catch wild ones." Abernathy's large confined wolves, therefore, stayed in captivity. In fact, Abernathy kept many of the captive wolves and coyotes at his home in Frederick. Oddly, Abernathy claimed in an interview with the *Dallas Morning News* that a tornado struck the kennels at his home in Frederick and "one of the cages . . . was picked up, wolf and all, and carried a distance of fifty yards."[38] The caged wolf survived this particular cyclone, but the wild wolves ultimately would not survive the colonization of the Red Rolling Plains. Wolves had hunted the bison but with the disappearance of the ancient herds of wild shaggy beasts, the wolves turned their predatory ways on the cattle of the Texas cattlemen. For the cattlemen, their cattle were worth more than a wild beast on the plains—cattle were a commodity and an investment to be protected. To safeguard their profits, cattlemen hired wolf catchers like Abernathy. These wolf hunters caged and poisoned wolves. Some like Abernathy kept a few of the wolves and made pets of them but ultimately, the wolf would be fully eradicated from the Southern Plains by 1924 and only the coyote remained to fill and, in some cases, overfill the undomesticated canine niche left behind.[39] The coyotes hunted the smaller mammals and targeted calves and fawns, but their jaws limited the size of their prey. Thus, the ranchers killed coyotes, even though the coyotes did not create the same havoc on herds as wolves because of their smaller size.

One such wild canine emerging in the last one hundred years since the hunt to fill the niche left behind by wolves appears to be the coywolf (*Canis latrans var.*), the *var.* in the Latin species name standing for "variant." Thus technically, the coywolf would be a coyote variant. But some in the field now suggest the designation *Canis oriens*, which indicates a new and independent species, the argument being that the coywolf is more wild dog and wolf (60 percent) than it is coyote (40 percent). Where bounties and poisons "dewolfed" areas one hundred years ago, this new canine the coywolf—which falls between the sizes of coyotes and wolves (between thirty and fifty pounds)—alongside the coyote appears to be filling the modern wild canine niches left behind by the wolf. Stephanie Rutherford describes coywolves as "opportunistic omnivores, with the ability to eat deer (because of their larger jaws) or urban compost." They hunt in packs like wolves but show a coyote's fearlessness and/or curiosity towards humans and their urban spaces.[40]

Interestingly, on Teddy Roosevelt's wolf hunt, it appears they hunted both coyotes and wolves. Perhaps there existed a hybrid at this time, but the coywolf does not appear to be one of the wild canines hunted in 1905. Hunters, however, did use domesticated canines to locate and chase the wild canines. Roosevelt himself noted, "In chasing the coyote only greyhounds are used," making the hunt a very fast-paced sport.[41] Forty greyhounds ran down most of the wild canines, but some staghounds and long-eared deer or fox hounds did special work.[42] Hunters mounted on horseback sprinted behind their hounds, forcing the wild canines to face off with the purebred domesticated dogs of the professional wolf hunters. Most professional "wolfers" preferred to poison or trap the wild canines, but some hunted them with greyhounds and shot the wild canines from horseback. Abernathy, who hunted from horseback, rode his "famous horse" Sam Bass, chasing behind his pack and leaping off his horse when the canines faced off, catching the wolf in an instant by the jaw.[43]

Writing of Abernathy's wolf-catching technique, Roosevelt explained that Abernathy rode his horse until the greyhound forced the wild canine to face off. At that point, "Catch 'Em Alive Jack":

> leaped off and sprang on top of the wolf. He held the reins of the horse and thrust the other, with a rapidity and precision even greater than the rapidity of the wolf's snap, into the wolf's mouth, jamming his hand down crosswise between the jaws, seizing the lower jaw and bending it down so that the wolf could not bite him.[44]

Once subdued, the canine "seemed to resign itself to its fate."[45] One time, after Abernathy captured a wolf in this manner, the group stopped to be photographed. In the description of the now famous photograph of the hunt it reads "taken immediately after a quick catch made by Jack Abernathy with his bare hands. The wolf shown above was alive and unhurt."[46]

According to those in attendance, Teddy Roosevelt was one of the only riders who kept pace with Abernathy, following closely behind on Tom Burnett's huge cutting horse at "full gallop." One breakneck chase covered ten miles of open plains. Abernathy, with the president in the rear, raced for miles after the wild canine before it faced off with domesticated dogs. Roosevelt found the hunt and Abernathy's athleticism exhilarating, claiming "this beats anything I have ever seen in my life, and I have seen a good deal."[47] According to historian Brian Lee Smith in his article "Theodore Roosevelt Visits Oklahoma," "To Roosevelt, Oklahoma represented the last frontier to be conquered, and the frontier atmosphere allowed him to pursue the strenuous, active life he enjoyed most."[48]

In the 1890s historian Frederick Jackson Turner wrote that a civilizing Euro-American society conquered nature on the "frontier."[49]

Roosevelt, who wholly subscribed to Turner's "Frontier Thesis," wrote his *The Winning of the West* in that same vein.[50] His speech in Oklahoma City in 1900 centered on the theme of growth and territorial expansion and praised the Oklahomans for "settling and developing" the "frontier." Roosevelt's Anglo triumphalism over nature and native peoples became apparent when he stated, "You of Oklahoma formed . . . because you came here not seeking ease, but out of labor to rest in splendor and in triumph."[51] His speechmaking at the grandstand in Frederick in 1905 struck on these themes as well. He bellowed, "ever since the [American] Revolution we have been making new states [and] now we are about at the close of this period." Rallying the people around his Panama Canal scheme and playing on their sympathies to expand and conquer "uncivilized" regions, he exclaimed, "You don't think I should be quiet while the American people are being held up. We want our right not as a favor, but as a right."[52]

The *Frederick Enterprise* wrote that the president "first beheld the beautiful panorama of virgin prairie, without a sign of civilization," believing what geographer William Denevan called the "Pristine Myth."[53] According to this perception, the New World was pristine, virgin wilderness, which made the agency or even existence of American Indians inconsequential. Despite Paleo Indians, Comanches, Kiowas, and Wichitas making use of the Big Pasture, often burning the prairies, hunting wild game with horses, establishing powerful trade networks, and—by the reservation and allotment periods—running and leasing large herds of livestock on the plains, Anglo-Americans still saw, or at the very least portrayed, virgin wilderness ready to be opened to white settlement.[54]

Roosevelt's son Kermit Roosevelt amplified this myth, stating in his introduction of Abernathy's book, "In the newly opened frontier, the wild life is the first to vanish. It has been able to exist alongside primitive man with his spear and arrow and trap [but] . . . With the advent of the civilized settler . . . change has become rapid." The homesteaders and President Roosevelt viewed Oklahoma Territory as "untrodden wilderness" ripe for conquest. The demise of the wolf symbolized a progression to this "civilization," creating a "civilized frontier." Theodore Roosevelt, like his son Kermit, presented the idea that "settlers were at their wits' ends how to deal with the pests" and that eventually through traps, poison, and hound hunts the "vermin" were being more effectively killed.[55]

Also, the president rode into the area on an iron horse—the train—which some thought illustrated "progress," too. Perhaps more accurately, the railroad represented the direct link to national and international markets for a region transforming into mono-crop agriculture production. Kemp and Kell understood that link and could envision the transformation afoot. It is quite possible that Roosevelt could see that vision as well. For most folks, however, the agricultural transformation of Southwestern Oklahoma would only become clearer in the next decades as ranchers and farmers slowly transitioned to meet the demands of the new markets created by the railroad linkages. On this particular trip, Roosevelt ostensibly disavowed interest in the future and in politics, but continuously he politicked from his mobile bully pulpit. Moreover, Roosevelt's conservationism was refracted through the ideas of scientific management and technology. His idea of conservation did not mean saving some of nature from the onslaught of exploitative capitalism. It meant close examination of resources managed efficiently by highly trained bureaucrats. It meant making nature more productive and efficient so that it could better support a capitalist structure. This meant removing the wolf so that profitable ungulates—cows—could be safe from predation.[56]

More importantly for Roosevelt on this day was the fact that John Abernathy caught wolves with his bare hands. That fact captured Roosevelt's imagination. Abernathy impressed Roosevelt at the hunt, catching nine of the seventeen wolves brought in by the wolf-hunting party.[57] Abernathy had been a professional "wolfer," poisoning two hundred to three hundred wolves a year in the 1890s on the XIT Ranch.[58] As reported in the *Frederick Enterprise*, his talent emerged from "this age of specialists" where Abernathy "has been making the art of wolf caching a study."[59] Roosevelt claimed Abernathy's techniques to be very "mechanical." Roosevelt, like Abernathy, made the hunt in itself a scientific endeavor, carefully measuring weights and lengths of the captured wild canines, sending "skins and skulls to Dr. Hart Merriam, the head of the [United States] Biological Survey" for further study.[60]

Roosevelt idealized Abernathy because he embodied the conqueror of the plains, a man leading a strenuous and exuberant life. Roosevelt believed that a white man living on the threshold of the "frontier" brought with him civilization and through arduous activity tamed and settled the wilderness for those who followed. Abernathy, also a law-man, used his efforts to bring order to nature and society, which is abundantly clear in his autobiography, *"Catch 'Em Alive Jack": The Life and Adventures of an American Pioneer*. Not only did Abernathy trail predatory animals, he trailed criminals. Whereas Roosevelt idolized the wolf-catching Abernathy as a modern lawman, he romanticized the Texas cattlemen, especially W. T. Waggoner and Tom Burnett. They too represented the myth of the individualistic spirit of western progress.

But there were real signs of strain between the cattlemen and the home-steading lawmen. An interesting story from *"Catch 'Em Alive Jack"* illus-trates the dichotomy that existed between homesteaders and cattlemen. Abernathy wrote of the preparations for the wolf hunt and his run-in with:

Tom Burnett, son of Burke [*sic*], who was to take part in the events of the third day, was one of my most bitter and determined rivals. His attitude recalled a near fight he and I had in a saloon in Wichita Falls. After the President first wrote me about staging the wolf hunt, Tom Burnett had wired me to meet him in Wichita Falls. I met Tom in the saloon and we talked it over. Tom wanted me to have the chase on the Burke [Burnett] Ranch near Electra, Texas, but I refused. He offered me one thousand dollars. I told Tom, in refusing the offer, that this was a lot of money—a mighty sum to me, a poor boy from Oklahoma—but that, if we held the race on the Burnett Ranch, our lives would be endangered by the mesquite bushes which covered the ranch. I pointed out that we had open prairie [without fences] in the Big Pasture, making it much safer for the race.[61]

The cattlemen had wanted to host the president's hunt on their ranches, a sure sign of national prestige. Abernathy selected the Big Pasture in present-day Tillman and Comanche Counties because it contained 480,000 acres of open range, much better suited for a wolf hunt.[62] Plus the Big Pasture leased by the Waggoner and Burnett families from the Comanches allowed the ranchers to technically host the hunt.[63] A great deal of hostility existed between homesteaders, like Jack Abernathy, and large-scale North Texas ranchmen like Tom Burnett and W. T. Waggoner. It should be noted that in terms of the ecology of the ranches, wired fences and mesquite overgrowth had made it impossible to safely and effectively hunt for wolves. A wolf could easily escape if the horseman constantly had to divert for fences and mesquite overgrowth. Cattle defecating mesquite beans on fenced-in ranches helped to create these problems with the mesquite overgrowth.

The Texas cattlemen maintained "a very profitable association" with the Kiowa and Comanche during the 1880s and 1890s. Historian William T. Hagan in his article, "Kiowas, Comanches, and Cattlemen, 1867–1906," explained how Texas cattlemen "at the peak of their operations" gained access "to two million acres of range land at bargain rates." Between 1885 and 1906 "grass money" annuities—money obtained through livestock leases—put more than an estimated $2,000,000 into the Indian economy and untold amounts into the coffers of Texas cattlemen.[64] And the land remained somewhat free of mesquite because it had not been fenced in, allowing the cows to graze more like the bison. More importantly, it kept the cows from defecating mesquite seeds in concentrated pastures and thus causing the mesquite overgrowth.[65]

Modern range management science indicates that the Red Rolling Plains grasslands were free of brush when dominating grasses had the strength to hold the lands against invaders. When livestock crowded ranges and ate down the best grasses first, the lower-class plants, which succeeded them, were not strong enough to hold off aggressive brush and tree invaders. Since the mesquite infestations began, millions of acres of brush and trees have been hand-grubbed, bulldozed, plowed, sawed, cabled, doused with kerosene, and sprayed from the air. For many years, kerosene dousing provided the most thorough and cheapest kill for mesquite. The more costly cabling of mesquites consists of double cables attached to two tractors. Tractors drag the cables between them, pulling over trees and brush. The continuous battles against mesquite infestation raged for decades and still rage because nature spreads the mesquite back across the pasturelands at a rapid clip. Mesquite seed spreaders included cattle, horses, mules, goats, deer, peccaries, cottontail rabbits, jackrabbits, and coyotes. Hundreds of domesticated animals, wild animals, and birds eat and spread mesquite seeds. The mass invasion of undesirable woody plants onto millions of acres of range lands in Texas and Oklahoma constituted and still constitutes a major economic and conservation problem.[66] The issues with mesquite foreshadowed future environmental problems with the irrigation projects in the region by putting on display the constant battles with the unanticipated consequences of human environmental alterations.

By 1905 the Waggoner family ranched land in a broad area of the western portion of North Central Texas and Southwestern Oklahoma, including the land leased from the Comanche in Southern Oklahoma. The land in Southwestern Oklahoma did not suffer from the mesquite overgrowth because it had not been disturbed to the extent it had been in North Central Texas. In Texas, Waggoner properties spread throughout Wichita, Wilbarger, Baylor, Knox, Foard, and six other North Texas counties.[67] The town of Electra, named after Waggoner's daughter, emerged as a settlement in northwest Wichita County with houses and a store the Waggoner family built for the employees of the westward growing ranch.[68] John Hirshi, an early settler, recalled, "They used to call the place 'sidetrack B' but after Waggoner got here, he named it Electra for his daughter."[69]

The other large-scale cattle baron who attended the wolf hunt was

William Thomas (W. T.) Waggoner participated in the wolf hunt with President Theodore Roosevelt and established the Red River Three-D Ranch in Wichita County eight miles north of Electra, Texas. (Photo courtesy of the Southwest Collection/Special Collections Library, Texas Tech University)

Burnett family patriarch Samuel Burk Burnett. The fifty-six-year-old Burnett and retired Lt. Gen. S. B. M. "War Bonnet" Young followed behind the hunting party in a buggy.[70] Samuel Burk Burnett

(1849–1922), a native of Missouri, had brought a large herd to Denton County, Texas, and then to Wichita County by the 1870s.[71] As his cattle business blossomed, he bought banks in Fort Worth and married Ruth Lloyd, daughter of a wealthy banker, solidifying his elite status. While the marriage to Ruth and the business partnership with the Lloyd family later dissolved, Burnett maintained his economic status and influence among the elites of North Texas.[72]

In Washington, DC, Burnett and President Theodore Roosevelt formed a friendship that preceded the wolf-hunting trip in 1905. During the hunt Roosevelt called the ranch town in northern Wichita County, Burk-Burnett. He later suggested to the United States Post Office that the little town be named after the host of his wolf hunt. The Post Office obliged, naming the town Burkburnett.[73] Roosevelt claimed, "Burnett's brand, the Four Sixes has been owned by him for forty years"[74] and stated, "Men like Burk Burnett and others came out here when this was a frontier, into these lands of the Indian and the buffalo, and then made ready the way of civilization that we now see before us, great is our debt of obligation."[75] Early historians echoed this sentiment, arguing Burnett "prepared the way for our present civilization of the Great West."[76] According to such interpretations, the cattlemen were brave forerunners to civilization.

Now that the supposed "civilization" arrived on the Red Rolling Plains, changes were afoot. The year after the hunt, in 1906, the government opened the Big Pasture to homesteaders. Once the Big Pasture was broken up into homesteads, the North Texas cattlemen looked to West Texas for land to ranch on a large scale. They found their new headquarters in West Texas towns like Guthrie and westward up onto the far reaches of the Big Wichita and Brazos Rivers and into the Panhandle. Thus, it is no surprise that so much hostility existed between the large-scale cattlemen and homesteaders like Jack Abernathy and Bill McDonald. Although they did not see eye to eye, the ranchers and homesteaders both viewed their settlement and agro-ecological processes as inevitable progressions in civilization.

They saw private ownership and the capitalist economy as the road to that progress.

Quanah Parker, who also attended the 1905 hunt (with his three wives and at least two children in tow), saw the situation in a very different light. President Roosevelt viewed Quanah Parker as a "Progressive" Indian, one who now followed the "white man's road"—a road that meant private ownership of square allotments, farming individual parcels, and individually participating in the market economy. At Roosevelt's inaugural parade in Washington, DC, the president chose Quanah Parker to ride in the ceremony because Parker was one of "the most publicized Indians in the United States."[77] When President Roosevelt saw Quanah Parker among the crowd gathered at the grandstand on his first day in Frederick, he singled the Comanche headman out and shook his hand, stressing, "we are one people and one country." He informed the onlookers, "I am glad to see Quanah Parker here, who has done so well with his farm. One thing of which I am proud is that I have tried to give a fair deal to every man. Give the redman the same chance as the white. This country is founded on the doctrine of giving each man a fair deal to see what there is in him."[78]

Quanah Parker took the chance while the president was in the Big Pasture to express some of his grievances and highlight some of his people's problems. Obviously, Parker made an impression upon Roosevelt. The president wrote the commissioner of the Bureau of Indian Affairs (BIA) and insisted that he visit the Kiowa Agency at Anadarko, where the Kiowa, Comanche, Apache, and Wichita reported to their agent James F. Randlett. Roosevelt wrote the BIA commissioner that "My sympathies have been much excited and I have been aroused by what I have seen down here, and I am concerned [about] the condition of these Indians and the seeming helplessness of their future."[79] Although Parker got the ear of President Roosevelt and excited his sympathies, ultimately Congress preferred to follow the interests of their constituents, the land-hungry homesteaders, instead of the interests of a minority group of Plains Indians.

Homesteaders demanded the Big Pasture be thrown open to settlement immediately. The local Frederick newspaper reported, "If the Big Pasture remains open the President will return here to hunt. If it is thrown open to settlement Frederick and the entire south-west portion of the country will receive a boom that will go far towards making its success assured."[80] Although Roosevelt enjoyed the strenuous life and idealized the cowboy camps, this "frontier"—the Big Pasture—was closing. United States Congressman John Hall Stephens accompanied Roosevelt by train to Vernon, Texas, where Stephens returned to his family and home.[81] It is not certain if Stephens had the ear of Roosevelt on the train ride from Frederick, Oklahoma Territory, to Vernon, Texas, across the Red River, but "early in 1906 Stephens' bill to open the 480,000 acre Indian [Big Pasture] tract . . . [at] $1.50-an-acre minimum," was introduced in the United States Congress. Initially, President Roosevelt met the bill with a veto threat. He said if the congressmen did not rewrite the bill to include better terms for the Plains Indians, he would veto it. Congress rewrote the bill, this time with a $5-an-acre minimum, and with Roosevelt's signature, his wolf-hunting grounds opened for white settlement.[82]

Roosevelt had personally helped close this "frontier" known as the Big Pasture through hunting and policymaking. In fact, he felt that he had personally helped make it safe for "civilization." Roosevelt made this clear when he wrote in *Scribner's Magazine* about his exploits killing rattlesnakes, coyotes, and wolves.[83] The other members of the hunting party recounted Roosevelt's stubbornly persistent attempts to clear the land of deadly predators. Texas Ranger Capt. Bill McDonald, for example, recalled when the hunting party came upon a coiled rattlesnake on a prairie dog hill, the president saw it and got down from his horse with his quirt—a small rawhide riding whip—in hand. With the security detail watching in astonishment, the President of the United States approached the coiled rattler, which struck at him. Roosevelt stepped aside and struck the snake with the quirt over and over again, eventually crushing the head of the rattlesnake. Later Roosevelt repeated the rattlesnake killing performance. That night, Captain McDonald hid

Roosevelt's quirt because he found the act too risky for a president. Roosevelt grumbled so much about the missing quirt the next morning that McDonald finally had to admit to taking it. He told the president that he worried he would be snake bit.[84]

Unfortunately, the president failed to realize the selective killing of predators unbalanced the ecosystem. Wolves, bears, and other mammals disappeared. Afterwards, the prairie dogs and their attendant flea populations exploded. Rattlesnakes grew fat off their prairie dog prey. Deer and cows, without predators, ate away at the vegetation on the riverbeds causing serious erosion, eradicating habitats for smaller mammals. Fenced-in cows grazed and defecated mesquite beans on concentrated plots of land, conveniently spreading seed and fertilizer, which started a plague of mesquite overgrowth. Despite frenzied attempts to eradicate rattlesnakes, fat diamondbacks still slithered over the red plains, eating large numbers of rodents found in the pastures.

When Roosevelt concluded his hunt, the campers returned to Frederick. The townspeople expected another speech, but Roosevelt had other plans. The *Frederick Enterprise* reported, "The reception committee were seated in the grandstand while Cong. John H. Stevens [*sic*] was addressing the crowd as the president and his party mounted on their chargers rode into town." The presidential hunters rode past the grandstand "in true cowboy style . . . on a run . . . like a whirlwind" through town directly to the train.[85] Roosevelt sent a messenger back to the grandstand that informed the people that he would address the crowd from his rear-end platform on the train, making a farewell speech from his moving pulpit. It seems some of the townspeople were dismayed that Roosevelt did not formally speak to the crowd from the grandstand, choosing instead the back of a train: "the president dressed in his brown trousers and hunting jacket appeared like a private citizen out for a hunt."[86] After the Oklahoma Territorial Gov. Thomas B. Ferguson introduced the president to the crowd, the president simply thanked the crowd for not interfering in his hunt. The "citizens" had left him alone to hunt, and Roosevelt thanked them for their courtesy.[87]

The different groups represented in the wolf hunt included home-steaders, cattle barons, Comanches, and local, state, and federal officials. Kemp and Kell interacted with these various groups while promoting Southwestern Oklahoma and Northwestern Texas. Kemp and Kell established the Wichita Falls and Northwest Railway Company of Texas in September 1906. Its Wichita Falls and Northern Railroad line reached into the grain-producing hinterlands of Southwestern Oklahoma. It connected Wichita Falls, Texas, to Wellington, Oklahoma, tying Southwestern Oklahoma's farmers to Kemp and Kell's railroads and mills. In 1911, the MKT purchased Kemp's railroads and in 1928 Kell sold his mills to General Mills. But before they sold out to these mega-corporations, Kemp and Kell interacted with farmers, cattlemen, and government officials on a regular basis. In the same ways the farmers cultivated the land, Kemp and Kell cultivated relationships with these different groups, especially the government officials like Congressman Stephens.

Kemp also interacted regularly with the cattle barons (especially with the Waggoner and Burnett families), not only on water issues but also because there was a direct interrelationship between agriculture and livestock. In fact, in 1905 Kemp delivered a program at the Fort Worth Stock Show entitled "Co-Relation of Agriculture and Live Stock Industries."[88] The ranching ecology of the Plains Indians and cattle barons competed with the grain-producing homesteaders, but more often than not they complemented one another and would do so increasingly as farmers grew feed and hay, irrigated those feed crops, and watered cows with water from Kemp's irrigation projects. More importantly, Kemp, Kell, and the ranchers discovered oil production to be more profitable than the cattle that grazed their real estate and pastures and eventually, banking, oil leases, water rights, and grazing leases tied the city boosters and cattle barons together more so than railroads in the next two decades.

The cattle barons shared a close relationship with the Plains Indians because of the history of profitable cattle leases. With the Big Pasture broken up into homesteads, the cattle barons moved onto the western reaches of the Texas Panhandle. Burnett, for example, moved his headquarters from Burkburnett west to Guthrie, Texas. It appears Burnett had the closest relationship with Quanah Parker. Quanah Parker does not represent the entirety of Plains Indians views. In fact, those views vary from group to group. Kiowa views, for example, may differ significantly from the Comanche. And even within Comanche groups, opinions and views varied significantly. But generally, it can be said that most Plains Indians hoped to stall the opening of the Big Pasture and generally agreed with Quanah Parker's view on the taking of Indian lands, "that the country should be opened now is too quick."[89] Kemp and Kell's agricultural empire rested on the opening of these Indian lands. Thus, the relationship between Parker and Kemp and Kell makes for an interesting story, as does the relationship between homesteaders and Plains Indians. Unfortunately, Kemp and Kell viewed Parker more as a relic of the past than as a living man with agency. It was fine for the Comanche headman to lead a parade or attend an important event in Wichita Falls or Fort Worth, but his role was to be strictly ornamental. Homesteaders viewed the Plains Indians as romanticized representations of a mythic past rather than as living, breathing minority populations with important local environmental knowledge.

The ways in which Kemp and Kell interacted with homesteaders like Jack Abernathy and Bill McDonald seem to be more subtle and nuanced and thus much more interesting than the transactional and business interactions between Kemp and the cattle barons. Generally, men like Kemp and Kell viewed the homesteaders more as customers. They were not competition or business partners because the homesteaders lacked the capital and connections. Instead, the working and middle-class farmers sought loans from banks owned by Kemp, Kell, and Burk Burnett. Abernathy, who lived on a farm in Frederick, Oklahoma, and McDonald, who owned a small ranch in Wichita County, fit squarely into the types of middle-class farmers and ranchers: selling cattle at local sale barns, producing crops for Kell's mills, purchasing groceries at

Kemp's stores, and making deposits at Kemp and Kell's banks. Most of these middle-class ranchers and farmers go down in the history books as a faceless mass. They toiled in the worlds envisioned by Kemp and Kell. But some stood out because of their extraordinary deeds.

In the case of John Abernathy, at first it was wrestling, which led him to the skilled art of wolf catching and then on to fame as a US Marshal. Capt. Bill McDonald fits into this same mold. Without his exploits as a Texas Ranger, Bill McDonald might be best described as a small-scale livestock rancher in Wichita County. But after their deeds as lawmen became known, these middle-class men achieved some level of historical noteworthiness. In this specific case, Roosevelt reinforced their notoriety (despite their class, or perhaps because of it) by putting them in positions of authority because of their prowess and abilities. But other than as novelties, Abernathy and McDonald do not share in the success of men like Kemp and Kell. In fact, Abernathy appears to be the perfect example of middle-class novelty, a skill that he passes on to his children Louis "Bud" Abernathy and Temple "Temp" Abernathy, who at ages ten and six years old (without adult supervision) made in 1910 a horseback trip from Frederick, Oklahoma, to Manhattan, New York, to greet Roosevelt after he returned from a hunting trip in Africa. Abernathy and McDonald might have mastered the art of storytelling and self-promotion, but Kemp and Kell surpassed them when it came to economic wealth and real political power.[90]

Political and socioeconomic power seem to be the point of Kemp and Kell's projects, more so than the success of any one individual project. As will be seen in the following chapters, some of their projects succeed while others fail catastrophically. The fact that Kemp and Kell could foster so many projects—successes and failures—reveals the scale on which they operated. Plus it underscores the close relationship they had with local, state, and national officials and between investors and business leaders, especially the Wichita Falls Chamber of Commerce. In Richard White's *Railroaded*, he points out that the traditional view of transcontinental railroad promoters was in the "realm of individualism, not of the state and corporations." But after an expansive financial exploration of the transcontinental railroad companies, White challenged and convincingly disproved that individualistic idea and found that in reality, these companies were public/private enterprises entwined with the state. It would be the same for city boosters and local railroad promoters Kemp and Kell. Historians perceived them as successful individuals, but in reality their success hinged on public-private partnerships. Those private-public entanglements will become clearer in the next chapter.

CHAPTER 2

THE IRRIGATED VALLEY

T he main concern on the Red Rolling Plains was lack of
water due to drought. Normally during dry spells, the
Wichita Valley Railroad brought drinking water into
Wichita Falls from Seymour, Texas (located on the upper
Brazos River). Hawkers sold the Brazos water by the glass
to paying customers near the rail station.[1] In extreme cases, the Wichita
Falls city boosters became more creative. For example, in 1912 Joseph
Kemp and seven other men shot eight hundred dollars' worth of dynamite into the sky to try and bring rain to the farmlands surrounding
Wichita Falls.[2] Boosters raised funds by public subscription, purchased
6,000 pounds of dynamite, and detonated it in intervals during the
day in an attempt to spur the sky into action.[3] No rain came from the
venture, but such subscriptions and community efforts were common
when trying to bring water to Northwest Texas.

Droughts and floods always loomed, which initiated the first local
calls for water reclamation and flood control. Reclamation and irrigation
for many like Kemp and J. S. Bridwell served as the answer to remedy

their "aridity problem." The Wichita Falls Chamber of Commerce wrote to Texas Gov. William P. Hobby in 1918 that their region needed "immediate relief for the drought region of Texas." Their solutions included a constitutional amendment that allowed bonds for the purpose of building dams and irrigation networks.[4]

Unfortunately, the boosters did not recognize that in the Big Wichita River Valley water quality, and not water quantity, would cause greater future problems. Some might argue that it is anachronistic to look back on these people and condemn them for not understanding the nuances of their environment. The water quality issue, however, was well known by this time. US Army explorer Capt. Randolph Marcy identified the water quality issue in the early 1850s. Although the exact scientific causes for the brine waters went unknown for several decades, people knew that water was below drinking standards. In 1852, for example, Marcy found "the water in the mainstream . . . brackish and unpalatable."[5]

The Big and Little Wichita River Valleys run through the Rolling Plains and Western Cross Timbers regions, and underneath the earth, geologic history reveals marine and freshwater deposits formed during the Permian period, which lasted from 290 to 248 million years ago.[6] During the Permian, inland seas covered extensive portions of Oklahoma and Texas. At the end of the Permian, the seas receded leaving behind extensive deposits of marine evaporates or salt, which created a gypsum-laden stratum underneath the earth.[7] The ancient Permian geologic formations underlie the region's profitable relationship with oil and conversely its problematic relationship with water. The forks of the Big Wichita River became highly saline because of the soluble evaporates in the Permian red beds.[8] Due to the salts in the red earth drained by the Big Wichita River basin, the river and groundwater contained high quantities of dissolved solids, particularly sodium chloride, which limited usefulness of water supplies for agricultural, industrial, and municipal uses.[9]

City boosters focused more on the issue of water quantity and ignored the issue of water quality because this is the way conservation projects were conceived by engineers and technocrats at the time. For the most part it was believed that fresh rainwater would fill the reservoirs and dilute the salt content. On average, the Big Wichita and Little Wichita River Basins received twenty-four to twenty-eight inches of rainfall a year. Historical precipitation patterns, however, indicate erratic rainfall.[10] Drought-like conditions and hundred-degree days, followed by sporadic days of torrential and damaging thunderstorms—including flash floods and tornadoes—might occur in a regular season of weather.[11] Boosters wanted to figure out a way to better control rainfall distributions since thunderstorm activity caused precipitation to fall at high intensity rates. Planners solved the issue of water availability with dams and reservoirs. What the rainwater and dams could not solve was the water quality issue, especially during periods of low rainfall when the water in the mainstream remained highly saline.[12]

The boosters promoted engineering and science to overcome their particular problems, or what historian Samuel Hays called "conservation and the gospel of efficiency."[13] The Wichita Falls *Record News* claimed the "progressive" Kemp "helped to rear an empire out of the wastelands of Northwest Texas, and earned . . . the title . . . 'the father of irrigation in Texas.'" A preacher of conservationism, Kemp participated in politics from the local to national level, serving in state and national irrigation associations, conservation congresses, business committees, and on local water improvement district boards.[14] For Kemp, conservation and reclamation were one and the same. To reclaim waters meant to conserve them for future use. Conservation also implied efficient future use of resources. It meant good water, hunting, and fishing for future generations. The idea of conservation held significant political and scientific ground during the twentieth century. But economic reasoning really dominated Progressive Era thought. Neither altruistic nor environmental, conservation rewarded entrenched business interests. The conservation Kemp wished to assert on the Big Wichita Valley was really order: Kemp wanted to make order out of the North Texas environment; he wanted an orderly process for water allocation and distribution. Perhaps one could call it altruism because water development meant economic growth. Put in a more accurate context, the record indicates Kemp ignored the natural limitations in the Big Wichita Valley and fostered development in the city and outskirts of Wichita Falls to ultimately bolster his own economic interests.[15]

But Joe Kemp cannot be characterized simply as a greedy capitalist who wrecked the environment. The Kemps fostered the Wichita Falls community's music, arts, and educational facilities. And despite Kemp's cultural gifts to the city, his business interests rested with the fate of the area's agribusiness. Kemp started in the grocery business, purveying nature's commodities to the people. He understood well the relationship between good crop seasons and grocery sales receipts. The same heavy rains that washed out the falls in 1886 meant fat cattle and green pastures. The family continued to prosper during the 1890s, their general store doing a large share of business with people in town, the neighboring countryside, and nearby Fort Sill.[16] The town of Wichita Falls, a new railhead on the edge of Indian Territory near Fort Sill, attracted Indian traders, farmers, and ranchers. The market for groceries in Northwest Texas continued to grow with the population. The farmers who shopped at Kemp's grocery store described the difficulty of raising crops in Wichita County's dry environment and erratic climate—years of drought followed by years of intense rainfall. Farmers with bumper crops meant money to spend on groceries, whereas years of drought meant fewer goods sold.[17]

Seeing crop failures in 1895 due to continued drought, Kemp watched merchants and farmers "battle against nature."[18] He pondered how conditions might be improved. How could the erratic climate that caused an unstable economy be better controlled? How could a water system be overlaid atop the landscape to provide a more orderly distribution of water to the farmers, ranchers, and townspeople? Kemp believed "conserving" floodwaters behind dams would not only protect property during rainy years but also retain the "precious water" for drought-stricken ones.[19] By the 1890s Kemp had settled on the solution to the region's unreliable water supply problem: reclamation and conservation.

Inspiration struck after Henry Sayles, an attorney and newspaper editor and fellow Northwest Texas booster from Abilene, Texas, gave a paper on irrigation at a bankers' association meeting in Galveston. Sayles had traveled to California and Colorado to learn about irrigation and reclamation of arid lands and reported back on the profitability of western irrigation projects. Newspapers across Texas published the paper, which attracted Kemp's attention. Kemp immediately hired an engineer and made a trip up the banks of the Big Wichita River. The engineer located the best site for a reservoir—a point where the bluffs along the river came close enough together to make damming a relatively simple task. Better water distribution could be made possible by storing the storm and floodwaters of the Wichita River and releasing them when farmers needed water for crops. Irrigation engineer James Schuyler, "an eminent authority on irrigation," investigated Kemp's early Big Wichita River irrigation plans and claimed it would succeed as a "safe and sound enterprise." Kemp, however, knew he could not pull together sufficient private capital to meet the great expense of damming the Big Wichita River. Kemp could envision the project; he just needed a tax-supported municipal bond to fund it.[20]

Since Reconstruction, Texans increasingly feared speculators. Many Texans believed promoters had failed to deliver on municipal bond issues in the past. The state, leery of such municipal bonds, outlawed them in its constitution in 1876. Although Kemp easily found irrigation authorities like Schuyler to endorse the Big Wichita Project, the actual political atmosphere in Austin, Texas, remained hostile for such projects and bond issues. Also by the 1890s, Texans divided along geographic lines on the issue of water resources. In West Texas, farmers clamored for irrigation but because the area was sparsely settled, congressmen representing the western farmers had little voice in the Texas Congress. And in East Texas, flush with water and people, lawmakers determined to oppose any constitutional amendments that helped create dreaded bond issues. The first attempt by Northwest Texans to amend the constitution in 1896 failed, and the effort failed again in 1899.[21] Additionally, Texas's state constitution of 1876, which the *Handbook of Texas* calls "adequate for a rural people engaged principally in subsistence farming, but not for an urban-industrial-commercial society," seemed to the boosters "prohibitive"; the "many requirements and limitations on both state and local governments" made water development restrictive. Boosters and irrigators found the state government entrenched and outdated.[22]

On the national level, politics took on another level of complexity and consequently brought certain disadvantages to the state. United States authorities insisted on more centralized control of public lands and water resources through either the Bureau of Reclamation or the Army Corps of Engineers, but since Texas owned its public lands, the issue remained moot.[23] The federal government wanted to focus on public lands within its jurisdictions, and Texas stood outside of that. For the moment, the federal government seemed uninterested in Northwest Texas.

Yet success stories emanating from western irrigators in Nebraska, Colorado, California, and especially Utah inspired Kemp and his brother-in-law Frank Kell to continue their dreams of an irrigated valley. Several Northwest Texas boosters toured irrigation farms in the American West and reported back to Texas on the benefits. Kemp and Kell, who read books that dealt with exploration, railroads, industry, commerce, and history, also read extensively about Brigham Young and Mormon irrigation farmers in Utah.[24] In 1897 Joseph Kemp met with "the lion" Henry Sayles at the Driskill Hotel in Austin. From Abilene, Sayles faced the same state legal obstructions as Wichita Falls. The two men agreed there needed to be a constitutional amendment that would allow them to set up irrigation districts, "as has been done in California, Nebraska, and other states."[25] West Texas boosters pulled together and pushed harder to get an irrigation amendment.

After Kemp and Sayles met with Gov. Charles Allen Culberson

and members from both chambers of the Texas Congress (members sympathetic to the West Texan concerns), Henry Sayles framed an amendment. Sen. W. W. Turney of El Paso introduced the amendment. Kemp pontificated to the Texas Senate, "Gentleman, with irrigation in West Texas, the population of our state would soon be doubled, millions would be added to our taxable values, myriads of opportunities opened up to willing hands and the investment of capital and such general industrial revival as would mean a new era." Kemp argued that the state would benefit from the development of West Texas and that such development augmented tax revenue. Making order out of drought-stricken West Texas and turning water resources into commodities meant more tax income and boundless opportunities for the state.[26] For Kemp, this amendment to the Texas State Constitution of 1876 would allow local bond issues for tax-supported projects and bring irrigation to the "wastelands" of West Texas. A handful of West Texas congressman like John H. Stephens supported adoption of the amendment.[27] Despite his grand speech to the Texas Legislature, Kemp found many of the Texas lawmakers difficult to persuade and the whole process laborious and unrewarding. The amendment process remained slow, and many Texans remained unconvinced.

With public funding for the Big Wichita River Project seemingly out of reach, Kemp explored private financing in the form of a mutual stockholding company. He courted eastern investors, but they wanted too much in the way of compensation. Instead, Kemp turned to Texas private investors and decided to fund a smaller project on Holliday Creek. Kemp called the water situation in Wichita Falls "pressing" and since Congress "thwarted" his public bond efforts, he organized private investors for the lake and irrigation project on a smaller-scale reservoir to be called Lake Wichita. Thus, Kemp worked on a smaller, privately funded project on Holliday Creek while at the same time continuing his push for a larger, publicly funded project on the Big Wichita River.

In 1902, privately owned irrigation projects watered lands around the state, from Del Rio and San Antonio to the San Saba, Colorado, and

Brazos valleys. From irrigation systems in El Paso, Big Bend, and the Pecos Valley to the Port Arthur Irrigation Company in the rice paddies of Texas's Gulf Coast, private irrigation continued to grow in popularity. Kemp, with the legal restrictions blocking municipal bond issues, turned his full attention to bringing outside capital and investment to Wichita County, as had been done in these other parts of the state.[28]

Kemp persuaded Henry Sayles and Galvestonian financiers Isaac Herbert Kempner and Morris Lasker to invest funds in his private water and irrigation project. Wells, windmills, and small stock tanks could no longer provide for a growing town population. The privately owned Highland Lake Wichita Irrigation and Water Company constructed the Lake Wichita dam and reservoir to function as a private municipal water and power supplier and irrigation system. A dam of earth, nearly thirty-five feet high and 8,800 feet across Holliday Creek, created a reservoir that Kemp estimated would "irrigate 4,000 to 8,000 acres."[29] The company financed the construction ($175,000) of the dam and reservoir and purchased the 4,000 acres to be irrigated by the project. Water came to the city of Wichita Falls but it came with an additional monthly water bill for the people. For Kemp, the Lake Wichita Irrigation Company meant more than increased profit for his electric, water, wholesale grocery, and real estate interests. It was a model to hold up for political change at the state and federal levels. Kemp with "beautiful photographs of Lake Wichita" at hand impressed gatherings of businessmen, statesmen, and bureaucrats.[30]

The political momentum in Austin and Washington, DC, had stalled for public projects but Kemp proceeded through private ventures to carve up land and waters. In 1903 he traded his wholesale grocery business to C. C. White for Cherokee County School Lands in Wichita County. He sold the lands and bought others. The land business proved promising and profitable—more so than the grocery business—especially if irrigation would increase its value. Experienced irrigators from Colorado bought some of his tracts on the Lake Wichita Project in 1903, giving land seekers proof that the project had merit.[31]

While Kemp's private venture developed, he continued to press for a publicly funded project. On November 8, 1904, developers persuaded the legislature to submit the constitutional amendment again. This time, Wichita Falls waged a more systematic campaign. Kemp and his associates prepared all types of publications explaining the amendment and its importance to West Texas. Numerous citizens of Wichita Falls spent time making speeches to help inform voters of the need for a constitutional amendment. Citizens wrote letters and cards to Texas representatives. So many letters accumulated it took several days before enough money could be collected for stamps to mail them. This time the amendment passed and was put into effect December 29, 1904. But the amendment overcame only one obstacle standing in the way of allowing bond elections. Other hurdles still blocked the bond issue due to the "convoluted" nature of the state constitution.[32]

The 1904 amendment set the groundwork for providing for the creation of irrigation districts in Texas. Kemp explained it this way in 1917 when pressing for another state amendment that "[t]he great difficulty in the way of the development of the natural resources of Texas now is that bonds amounting to only one-fourth of the assessed valuation of the property can be issued. The unimproved property is of small value. Therefore the law absolutely prohibits the improvements. It is absolutely necessary that we have this amendment adopted."[33] The Texas government since then has twice completely reenacted the law, with the latest revision made in 1917. In other words, Kemp got part of what he wanted in 1904, but he would not get everything he needed from the state until 1917, and not everything he needed from the federal government until 1919. In 1917, the governor of the state of Texas, William P. Hobby, framed the water conservation issue as a wartime measure and finally state legislators agreed through the amendment to fully allow the creation of districts for the purposes of conservation, reclamation, and irrigation. To fund and maintain these districts, the state allowed the reclamation and conservation districts to issue bonds.[34]

Developing publicly funded water projects required that the boosters turn to politics to alter the cultural landscape. Stockholding companies could only function on a small scale in the Wichita Valley, whereas water districts funded by bond elections offered boosters a larger scale for development, especially for those boosters like Kemp who were highly invested in the lands to be irrigated.[35] For men like Kemp, the process of turning "wilderness" into irrigation tracts did not require knowledge of local ecology. It required outside experts, such as engineers and scientists, who applied irrigated landscapes over placid nature. Boosters focused more on legal restrictions than natural conditions. And engineers saw the landscape in terms of mathematics, moving water commodities through man-made plumbing systems.[36]

In 1918 Kemp informed local businessmen of a bill introduced into the United States Congress that permitted the federal government to take securities of an irrigation company, or district, or any other reclamation district that might be formed, and against that issue their bonds, which would make available funds for large conservation projects. Kemp explained, "this means we could secure an adequate water supply for a city of 100,000 people; and could cheaply irrigate 100,000 to 150,000 acres of land here at a cost of two or three million dollars." Kemp asked that the chamber of commerce support the bill "vigorously." He encouraged every man in Wichita Falls who knew a member of the Unites States Congress to address a letter to him asking support for the bill. The Wichita Falls Chamber of Commerce agreed and sent Kemp and Judge Edgar Scurry off to Washington, DC, to lobby for the bill.[37]

Wichita Falls, and notably Pecos, Texas, which proposed a reservoir that included 150,000 acres for irrigation in the Pecos River Valley, secured unanimous consent from the US Senate Reclamation Committee and approval by the secretary of the interior for the Chamberlain Bill. The bill provided means for federal assistance in "financing worthy irrigation projects." The bill allowed the government to underwrite irrigation and reclamation bonds issued by local-level water districts. It was important because it made the funding of the

Streetcar unloads at 8th Street and Indiana Street in Wichita Falls on Armistice Day, November 11, 1918. (Photo courtesy of the Southwest Collection/Special Collections Library, Texas Tech University)

project possible. In September, Kemp returned from Washington and eagerly spoke of irrigating the country in a short time by damming the Big Wichita River.[38]

In 1919 after a prolonged drought gave the Wichita Falls territory another "unpleasant object-lesson on the subject of water supply,"[39] residents prepared to organize water improvement districts. In order to get the irrigation project underway, local businessmen needed a petition to be sent to the Wichita County Commissioner's Court. The petition claimed the establishment of a Wichita Water Improvement District was a necessity "because the lands included in the boundaries are very productive when irrigated."[40] The Big Wichita Project, an ambitious plan, would greatly increase the population and wealth in the county, plus give the city of Wichita Falls another source of water.[41] The commissioners, with the required petition now in place, set the date for the bond election.

Most people spoke positively of Kemp and the project. According to a Chamber of Commerce pamphlet entitled "Where Today's Dream is Tomorrow's Achievement," Kemp the "pioneer, banker, land-owner and city builder of Wichita Falls" would build a "great dam across the Big Wichita River . . . for the impounding of torrential waters in a mammoth reservoir."[42] Articles claimed the project assured ample irrigation for farmlands suffering during dry seasons. Kemp, with his stellar reputation and countless assurances, urged businessmen to work for the success of the irrigation project and to personally "see ten voters each . . . to make sure that they went to the polls and voted for the creation of the district."[43] Furthermore, the Wichita Falls Chamber of Commerce Irrigation Publicity Committee authorized spending whatever money was deemed necessary for ensuring the success of the election.[44]

People believed Kemp. There seemed to be no reason not to trust the wealthy banker. In the summer of 1919, a Wichita Falls citizen could stroll through downtown, catch the street railway car, pass irrigated fields, and arrive at the Lake Wichita pavilion. At the resort the citizen could enjoy a baseball game at the 4,200-seat ballpark, take a leisurely cruise across the lake, or enjoy dancing to national-touring music acts. Joseph Alexander Kemp promoted, invested in, and in some cases completely funded all of these projects. He developed the community's infrastructure and reservoirs and commodified its land and water. Since 1883, Kemp involved himself in waterworks, electricity, churches, traction trolleys, roads, grocery stores, rail lines, banks, libraries, parks, apartment buildings, hotels, housing subdivisions, mills, factories, ice houses, and irrigated farmlands, among other projects.[45] Joseph Kemp influenced community decision-making processes that shaped the Big Wichita River Valley.

On October 1, 1919, the Wichita County commissioners sent on the required petition to the State Board of Water Engineers to appropriate waters from the Big Wichita in compliance with state water laws (H.R. No. 237). On November 15, 1920, the Board of Water Engineers in Austin, Texas, held the mandatory public hearing. Afterwards, the state granted the right of irrigation on 92,327 acres of land and the right to the area municipalities to appropriate water resources from the Big

Wichita River. Authorities called an election on May 31, 1920, on the question of making the said district a Conservation and Reclamation District. The proposal carried and was legalized under the revised amendments of 1917.[46]

The reservoir and irrigation system formed the first locally organized tax-supported project of its kind in the state and it took acts of the Texas and US legislatures to ensure its establishment. It also took the votes of local citizens in the district. Voters believed the $4 million bond issue not only enabled expansion of irrigated acreage but also covered the reservoirs, the main expenses of the project. The reservoirs would provide municipal drinking water and control floods. The Wichita County Commissioners Court officially created the Wichita County Water District on December 29, 1919. The district encompassed 15,543 acres, including the city of Wichita Falls. On December 31, 1919, the first meeting of the irrigation directors was held. The directors nominated Kemp president.[47]

Texas law sets up water districts like school or road improvement districts. The people owned the project itself and managed it by an elected board of directors. Local tax collectors declared land within the district either irrigable or non-irrigable, with irrigable lands being valued more and thus taxed more. Although the bond might appear as an act of local autonomy in the community, the bonds authorized by the election in 1920 for $4,500,000 matured serially, spanning a period of years to 1950, drawing six percent interest semiannually. The district paid both principal and interest on the bond to Hanover National Bank in New York City, tying this part of Texas to East Coast capitalists for the next three decades.[48]

The directors of the Wichita County water district awarded the contract to the W. E. Callahan Construction Company of Dallas. Within thirty days the company began transforming the Wichita River with drag lines, shovels, tractors, wagons, elevating graders, blade machines, pile drivers, and trucks, constructing bridges, roads, and camp buildings. A thousand men labored to finish the Big Wichita Project. After hydraulic dredges lifted dirt from the reservoir sites, rainwater slowly filled in behind the dams. The actual construction of the project took four years to complete. The larger storage reservoir and dam received the place name Lake Kemp, in honor of Joseph Kemp. By 1924 Lake Kemp became the largest man-made reservoir in the state, seven times larger than Lake Worth near Fort Worth. Waters impounded at Lake Kemp released slowly into Lake Diversion. At Diversion Dam, spillway waters were diverted either into the Wichita River or to the main irrigation canal and to laterals through rural fields.[49] The inhabitants of the Big Wichita Valley believed they had tamed the rampaging river, conserving its water and putting in place irrigation networks through which its veins flowed the red waters of the Big Wichita River.[50] At the end of 1925 farmers irrigated 19,825 acres and in 1931, irrigated acreage expanded to 30,195 acres.[51] Boosters celebrated their perceived conquest over nature. For many the water meant "permanent and lasting prosperity."[52]

At the same time Kemp served as president of the water district, he also presided over the Texas Conservation Congress, arguing much work still remained to perfect the irrigation laws of semi-arid West Texas. He claimed such bond elections would not be wholly sufficient for future developments. Kemp informed gatherings of irrigationists that it was impossible to reclaim vast areas in West Texas river valleys and make them highly productive by relying solely on local bond issues and those who lived in local districts. Local people could not accomplish bigger projects without aid from the state and federal governments. Kemp chided Texans that they "could go much further in supporting irrigation."[53] The association lauded amendments to the constitution as progress and warned members to "be on guard to the end that nothing be done that will handicap progress now being made."[54]

Kemp convinced many community leaders around the state of conservation's benefits, holding up the Big Wichita River Project as a template for what could be done on other waterways. From 1922 to 1927 Kemp called the Big Wichita irrigation project an "outstanding" conservation and flood control achievement. In Brownwood, Texas,

Spillway construction at Lake Kemp c. 1920. (Photo courtesy of the Southwest Collection/Special Collections Library, Texas Tech University)

Ariel view of Lake Diversion Dam and irrigation gate. (Photo courtesy of the Southwest Collection/Special Collections Library, Texas Tech University)

Boating on Lake Kemp. (Photo courtesy of the Southwest Collection/Special Collections Library, Texas Tech University)

Hydraulic gates delivered water from the Wichita County Water Improvement Districts to the fields. (Photo courtesy of the Southwest Collection/Special Collections Library, Texas Tech University)

Carrot field irrigated by Wichita County Water and Improvement District canal system. (Photo courtesy of the Southwest Collection/Special Collections Library, Texas Tech University)

Map of the irrigated valley. (Map by Tracy Ellen Smith)

The Wichita Falls Chamber of Commerce displays produce from the Wichita County Water Improvement Districts' irrigation system. (Photo courtesy of the Southwest Collection/Special Collections Library, Texas Tech University)

Kemp said Wichita Falls had been built because "water of inexhaustible quantity" had been secured through the building of "great dams" and by opening dry lands to cultivation. Kemp argued that Brownwood could be built into a "great city" too, especially if the people could secure an "abundant water supply." Kemp insisted that water for irrigation and municipal purposes could be secured by building the newly proposed dam near Brownwood.[55] The *Dallas Morning News* reported that if Kemp and his associates could accomplish reclamation and conservation projects often "at a tremendous cost and still make a profit, think what we can do under favorable conditions." The paper concluded, "The truth is that water conservation is of State-wide interest."[56]

Underneath the rosy exterior, the Wichita County water district started to have problems. At first it had funding, taxation, colonization, and marketing problems. Soon boosters discovered they needed a larger capital outlay to complete the dams and irrigation improvements. In order to meet the additional financial need, the Wichita County Commissioners Court initiated another bond election ($1,570,000) creating Wichita County Water Improvement District Number Two on December 29, 1920.[57] Also, many landowners protested the new classification of their lands as irrigable and therefore subject to higher taxes. Many believed portions of their land should be reclassified as non-irrigable. Even water district vice president T. B. Noble complained that lands he owned were wrongly classified as irrigable. He stated, "It has occurred to me that you have evidently used some land down near the River that is impractical to irrigate, otherwise you could not have arrived at a total so large as this."[58] And irrigated lands needed settlers—citizens that would till the land, pay taxes, and generate the revenue needed to run the project.[59]

The Chamber of Commerce envisioned "desirable and efficient farmers," working small intensive twenty to forty acre tracts and dotting the valley with "commodious, comfortable country homes."[60] At first boosters looked locally for settlers but due to low numbers of interested farmers, they expanded the search nationally.[61] Reports from the Chamber's Valley Development Committee indicated visits to recruit farmers on irrigation projects in California, Kansas, Illinois, New Mexico, Colorado, Utah, Idaho, and Arizona.[62] Actually getting irrigation farmers to move to the Big Wichita Valley proved extremely difficult. Eventually the colonization program presented a "grave situation." The developers confronted "the absolute necessity" for some plan to subdivide land for sale and control land prices within reasonable limits. To the flabbergasted members of the Wichita Falls Chamber of Commerce, colonization was unfinished business, and the development and settlement of irrigated lands by experienced farmers constituted a "paramount duty." Many suggested advertisements in magazines and newspapers, particularly to poultry raisers, dairymen, and irrigation farmers.[63] Even if settlers could colonize the valley, they still needed markets for their crops.

Marketing farm produce persisted as another major problem. Commissioners and agents sent out by the Chamber of Commerce to identify potential markets reported back that they were unable to develop any market outlets and that national and state markets were glutted. On top of that freight costs had risen. Both issues reduced profits.[64] The commissioner believed a growers' association should be formed at once to manage these matters in the future. In response, the Valley Development Committee proposed organizing a corporation known as the Wichita Valley Marketing Company for the purpose of buying, grading, and selling regional farm products.[65] For years the questions of taxation, funding, colonization, and marketing perplexed the boosters.

Developers also found the natural limitations of agricultural expansion in the Big Wichita River Valley. The impacts from natural conditions started to emerge by the late 1920s. Irrigators realized the valley had poor drainage on farmlands. No irrigation farmer wanted poorly drained lands because it could cause a host of problems, from germination issues to rot. An objective appreciation of the connection between poor drainage and lack of interested settlers eluded the promoters. For the Wichita Falls Chamber of Commerce, the solution was not better drainage, which would be "expensive," but rather more marketing to potential colonizers.[66] For the most part, Wichita Falls and the surrounding area had plenty of water. The major flaw in the promoters' vision was that it ignored, or never acknowledged, water quality and the saline water's effects upon poorly drained soil. The environmental consequences included seepage, salting of soils, and weed infestations.

After Kemp's death in 1930, criticism of the project emerged more frequently. Kemp died before it became apparent that the water quality issue would cause the project to fail. He had lived until 1930, seeing more than 33,000 acres under the ditch and the foundation laid for development of the entire 105,000 acres. But the development of those 105,000 acres would never occur, and Kemp's conquest would remain incomplete.[67]

Many experts such as Col. E. S. Nettleton of Denver, Colorado, a federal expert on irrigation, visited Wichita Falls and North Texas as the amendment vote approached. These experts had claimed it did not matter how fertile the soil or what kind of climate but that the one factor of utmost importance was moisture, making sure dams conserved water for future use during dry times. According to Nettleton, the factors that contributed to a successful irrigation system were capacity of the water supply, cost per acre of land, and annual expenses for maintenance and distribution. Thus the engineers and developers overlooked the two most important factors for success in the Big Wichita Valley: drainage and water quality. Applying a general model—a model that did not include knowledge of the local environment—to the Big Wichita River Valley grossly failed to meet the real social needs of the Wichita Falls community.[68]

Margaret Lee Morgan's "The History and Economic Aspect of the Wichita Valley Irrigation Project," written in 1939, revealed the Big Wichita River's water carried large quantities of salts, but found that the final effects of this fact would take some time to determine. Although Morgan could not determine the long-term environmental impacts in 1939, she did reveal dissent from the accepted triumphal narrative often printed in newspaper articles and Kemp hagiographies. For example, Tom F. Hunter, who owned real estate in Wichita County, sharply criticized the water development project as "short of the dreams" of Joseph Kemp. Hunter believed the development not worth the millions of dollars it cost to build. Future Wichita Falls mayor W. B. Hamilton, from the viewpoint of a real estate man, criticized the valuation of property in the city of Wichita Falls by the irrigation district as "too high." He believed owners paid too great a tax for the benefit derived by the owners of real estate in Wichita Falls.[69]

By 1951, newspaper editorialist John Gould, who published the "Furthermore and However" column in the *Wichita Falls Daily Times*, detailed the criticisms in connection with its water supply. "A great many Wichitans believe that the Lake Kemp undertaking as a whole was a mistake," wrote Gould, arguing the Lake Kemp water was of "unsat-isfactory quality" for municipal and irrigation purposes. Land priced too high was another error, claimed Gould. "There were Wichitans, including Kemp, who tried to develop a system of agriculture that could make the irrigation project pay its way," but Gould reasoned: "It can be said . . . that they never succeeded."[70]

In 1939 Margaret Morgan speculated about the environmental, social, and economic consequences of the Big Wichita River develop-ment. She knew the water in the Big Wichita River, ranging in color from chocolate-red to chocolate-brown, contained gypsum and salt.[71] What scholars have learned since 1939 is that the main sources of these salts emanate from saline springs located along the North, Middle, and South Forks of the Big Wichita River. Use of saline waters from the Big Wichita River caused environmental, social, and economic problems. In more severe cases, high levels of sodium caused "crusting" of the soil that affected seed germination and oxygen and nutrient levels. Often water evaporated leaving "a whitish powdery substance"[72] on the surface. Public health standards, set by both the state and federal government, define saline water "as water containing more than 1,000 parts per million (ppm) of dissolved solids." In 2002, for example, water analyses from Lakes Kemp, Diversion, and the Bradford irrigation canal found total dissolved chlorides at 2751 ppm and total chlorides at 1064 ppm. The water from Lake Kemp and Lake Diversion by 2002 still did not meet public health water standards.[73]

The social and economic context for the development phase (1917–1925) of the irrigation project came during a time of relative prosperity but the economic situation abruptly changed after 1926, as indicated by the failure of the farm colonization project and the crisis that existed in the marketing and selling of produce from the irrigated Wichita Valley. Additionally, real estate and oilmen came into conflict with the interests of the water district and irrigation farmers. Many of the area oilmen opposed watering lands. Oil interests and large landowners wished to retain lands for oil leasing rather than "block them up into small farms."

For this reason historians and locals cited the oil boom "as one of the reasons for the partial failure of the irrigation system."[74] Although the political obstacles could be navigated, the lack of knowledge of the natural conditions forced the boosters up against the natural limitations. While the livestock industry survived and the oil business thrived in the decades following the Progressive Era, the dream of idyllic irrigated farmsteads slowly disappeared. The continued belief that scientific and technological expertise could solve the problem, however, remained, and still remains.[75]

CHAPTER 3

BOOMTOWN

Oil field town in a blood red sky
way out here that sun takes a long time to die.
—HOUSTON MARCHMAN, "WICHITA FALLS," 2000[1]

I n 1940, film operators projected *Boom Town* onto big screens
across the nation. Starring Clark Gable and Hedy Lamarr
and based on a *Cosmopolitan* article titled, "A Lady Comes to
Burkburnett," *Boom Town* featured two wildcatters (played by
Clark Gable and Spencer Tracy) striking out for riches in the
oil fields of Burkburnett, Texas. Like the films that romanticized the
cowboys of the Texas Plains, *Boom Town* sensationalized the individualism and ruggedness of early twentieth century wildcatters. *Boom
Town* "espoused all the virtues of unbridled capitalism," "lamented the
restrictions imposed by governments," and took its "characters from
hardship to success, back to poverty, and on to great riches."[2] The history
of Burkburnett includes the boom-bust cycles, environmental scars, and
a revealing cultural landscape left behind by "unbridled capitalism."[3]

The oil boom on the Red Rolling Plains spanned two decades (1901–
1921) and featured three booms: Petrolia, Electra, and Burkburnett.
These booms, historian Kenneth Hendrickson wrote, "laid the

Panoramic view of the Burkburnett, Texas, oil field. (Photo courtesy of the Southwest Collection/Special Collections Library, Texas Tech University)

Roughnecks pose for a photo on Clayco No. 1 on April 1, 1911. L–R: Hal Hughes; unknown; Woody; Dad Massingill. (Photo courtesy of the Southwest Collection/Special Collections Library, Texas Tech University)

Electra Townsite opening in October 1907. (Photo courtesy of the Southwest Collection/Special Collections Library, Texas Tech University)

Burkburnett Townsite oil field. (Photo courtesy of the Southwest Collection/ Special Collections Library, Texas Tech University)

Smoke shrouds the Burkburnett Townsite oil field. (Photo courtesy of the Southwest Collection/Special Collections Library, Texas Tech University)

Smoke, open pools of standing oil, high-priced town lots, and fast-paced development transformed the landscape in Burkburnett, Texas. (Photo courtesy of the Southwest Collection/Special Collections Library, Texas Tech University)

groundwork for the growth of an industry that was to be a main feature of the North Texas economy for a half of a century to come."[4] The search for oil began in 1901 in Clay County and eventually led to the development of the Clay County Oil Company or "Clayco" in 1903. The next year, Frank Kell's Wichita Oil Company developed the Henrietta-Petrolia Field in a more systematic way that extended the search for oil from Clay into Wichita County. A settlement called Oil City, later called Petrolia, sprang up on a spur rail line through the area. Close to Petrolia, John D. O'Donohoe staked the Dorthulia Dunn No. 1, which was the first gusher in the Petrolia Field. Then west of Petrolia, in the Electra oil field in 1911, free-flowing wells gushed. One well, Clayco No. 1, sprayed oil into nearby stock tanks and overflowed into a nearby creek. By World War I, Electra produced 100,000 barrels per day. Burkburnett, located north of Wichita Falls in the northern part of Wichita County, struck black gold in 1912 at the oil field called "old Burkburnett." Then, in 1918 in the middle of the Great War (World War I), wildcatters discovered a massive underground pool at another oil field called "Burkburnett Townsite," producing as much as 7,500 barrels a day and making many millionaires. Exploration and rapid expansion of the oil industry by 1919 (known as the Northwest Extension) had brought tremendous wealth and a wide array of commercial endeavors throughout Wichita County.[5]

Oil boomtowns needed two resources: oil and water. The old adage that the two do not mix might sound cliché, but it is true in the Big Wichita River Valley where its salty waters are a byproduct of its Permian rocks. In 1910, Wichita County had a population of around 16,000 people. By 1920, there was a 353 percent increase to 73,000 thirsty folks. Growth brought new problems for sustaining large populations in a semi-arid environment, especially because the largest city had only a small reservoir on Holliday Creek filled with fresh drinking water (Lake Wichita) and two reservoirs (Lake Kemp and Lake Diversion) on the Big Wichita River filled with salty water.[6] Alongside growth related to the oil industry, the landscape ballooned with military bases and housing for military personnel. With its blue skies and flatlands, Wichita County made a perfect training ground for pilots. Between 1917 and 1919 at the height of the Great War, the Army Air Corps operated Call Field as a training facility. It housed 3,000 people and several planes in forty-six buildings. In 1918, officers at the Army air base asked the Wichita Falls Chamber of Commerce to improve the water quality and drainage.[7] Officers lodged complaints about health issues, which in turn became national security concerns.[8] Such grievances from military personnel and citizens led the president of the Wichita Falls Chamber of Commerce to say, "the [water] situation required thoughtful and careful consideration at once."[9]

Unfortunately, a solution would take forty years. In those four decades engineers developed an inter-basin (or basin-to-basin) water transfer system to meet the needs of the plains community. The community now included oil producers, a military-industrial complex, and a large military and civilian population. Lake Kemp and Lake Diversion did not meet drinking water safety standards due to salinity in the Big Wichita River Valley. Therefore, another system to water the population living in the Big Wichita Basin had to be developed. The City of Wichita Falls secured water appropriation rights to the drainage of a neighboring river basin—the Little Wichita River. Dams and reservoirs (Lake Arrowhead and Lake Kickapoo) built on the Little Wichita River Basin bring water into the Big Wichita River Basin. The system constitutes the first basin-to-basin (inter-basin) transfer system in the state of Texas.

Throughout the four decades it took to build the basin-to-basin water transfer system, boom-bust cycles played out on the Red Rolling Plains. Through the ups and downs of the Great War, Roaring Twenties, Dirty Thirties, World War II years, and the postwar period, the local, state, and federal governments got more involved, relieving struggling farmers and indebted irrigation districts. Ironically, the same Permian-age rocks that housed the profitable fossil fuels spoiled the local water supply with chlorides. The local government in the Big Wichita Valley hired drainage engineers and soil scientists; the state paid for water engineers to run tests on saline waters; and the federal government sent in various agencies to fund restoration projects and desalinize waters. Significant federal aid came to the Red Rolling Plains in the twentieth century, beginning in the 1930s with New Deal programs (specifically the Reconstruction Finance Corporation, Civilian Conservation Corps, the state Public Works Administration (PWA), and the Works Progress Administration). The New Deal brought financial relief, saving the Wichita County irrigation project from economic disaster. New Deal programs also funded recovery of some of the salted lands. But the aid came with strings attached in the form of more control exerted from the federal government. Eventually, the Army Corps of Engineers exerted tremendous control through its flood control programs and the Red

River Chloride Project that sought to desalinize the waters of the Big Wichita River. Plus, the State of Texas exerted more authority over local water resources through regulatory agencies, including the Texas Water Rights Commission, Texas Water Development Board, Red River Authority (RRA), and the Texas Parks and Wildlife Department (TPWD).[10]

By the late 1920s, Joseph Kemp and Frank Kell's dreams of an agricultural Eden in the "irrigated valley" had petered out, replaced by a cultural landscape of oil derricks, military installations, and livestock. With the new reality in place, local county water districts faced lawsuits, tax collection problems, and bond debts. In 1926 the Wichita Falls City Council hired Dr. T. U. Taylor, Dean of the Engineering Department at the University of Texas, to make a survey and report on the water problems of the county. Ironically, Taylor's report called for another local bond election to fix drainage and water problems.[11]

The city delayed, knowing such a bond election would be unpopular. Delay caused the issue to become even more acute and problematic. According to local records, from 1928 to 1929 farmers asked for "crop damage" payments caused by alkaline water, "which payment was refused."[12] City authorities feared that if they made payment on a claim it would open the floodgate to more claims and financially ruin the water district. In Margaret Morgan's 1930s interview with district attorney A. H. Britain, Britain admitted, "Farmers have brought suits claiming that their lands had become water-logged. The district, however, has never had to pay a cent for damages of any kind as it has always been proved that carelessness and inexperience with water application were the reasons for this water-logging."[13]

At the same time, the local newspaper downplayed the water problems in the 1920s because the owner of the Wichita Falls *Daily Times*, Rhea Howard, was a major proponent of irrigation and a member of the water improvement board of directors. In a newspaper article titled "Irrigation and Irrigation System One of City's Great Achievements: Low Water Charges, Fertile Land and Steady Development Point to Future Wichita Valley Prosperity," Howard anticipated "extensive development in coming years."[14] And even when the *Dallas Morning News* reported in 1925 that "the only doubt expressed by experts about the success of the Lake Kemp project was the quality of the water . . . containing gypsum," most local newspapers continued to promote the water districts.[15]

But real ecological factors had concrete economic ramifications. By 1930 a Wichita Falls Chamber of Commerce report found that in order to improve community business "the drainage problems of the Wichita County Water Improvement Districts [WCWID]" needed "prompt action." Poorly drained lands and poor water meant that the colonization of lands could not continue as farmers could not be encouraged to own farms.[16] Plus, litigation finally came to a head in a suit filed in the District Court of Wichita County, Texas, styled *Mrs. J. M. McGrath v. Wichita County Water Improvement District No. One* (No. 21501-B). The case asserted that water from the districts' canals adjacent to and near McGrath's farm escaped from and seeped into and upon her land so as to "materially damage" the land.[17] The water districts authorized manager G. A. Remington and attorney A. H. Britain to settle the case out of court and "to try to agree on a price with Mrs. McGrath" for the settlement.[18]

By 1931, local water districts could no longer ignore water quality issues and keep them out of the courtroom.[19] After community meetings, the board of directors decided to employ a drainage engineer.[20] His investigations led to a report that included field investigations of the lawsuit claims.[21] Drainage engineers, engineering reports, drainage construction projects, and organization of drainage districts had been unforeseen consequences of the increasingly complicated water quality issue.[22] Plus, these expenses meant landowners paid higher taxes.[23] Despite enthusiasm from farmers, land developers, and the water district for another local bond election, the citizenry could not be motivated to vote for higher taxes and bond debt for better drainage. City boosters could no longer sway taxpayers to vote for local bonds, especially as times became leaner in the 1930s.[24]

By 1932, economic issues compounded the water quality problems. The Wichita Valley Development Association called it an emergency "condition . . . a serious deterrent to the development of our Irrigated Valley and the prosperity of our community."[25] Once the water districts realized that there was not enough money to complete necessary drainage projects, they also realized there was a serious need to refinance the original bond debt.[26] Due to poorly drained lands, the farmers produced little in the way of profits or revenue to pay taxes.[27] Several attorneys appeared before the water district board regarding delinquent taxes and complained about the tax classifications of their clients' properties.[28]

Since a local solution to the water problem was impossible, leaders looked to Washington, DC, and President Franklin D. Roosevelt's New Deal for assistance.[29] The Wichita Falls Chamber of Commerce and the water districts wrote a letter to Julian Montgomery, acting state engineer for the Public Works Administration, endorsing an application for drainage funds.[30] Ultimately, relief came in the form of a loan of $580,000 from the Reconstruction Finance Corporation (RFC) (officially the Levee, Irrigation, and Drainage Division of the RFC pursuant to the provisions of the Emergency Farm Mortgage Act of 1933).[31] Federal mandates associated with the loan called for liquidation of delinquent tax rolls and refinancing the debt. Taxpayers had lands reappraised, changing acreage within the district from irrigable to non-irrigable. Re-categorization relieved farmers straddled with tax debts and refinancing the debt saved the district from financial ruin.[32] In 1935, WCWID got another loan from the PWA to do drainage work, which completed the much-needed drainage system.[33]

With federal aid came federal oversight and bureaucracy.[34] The chief of the RFC interceded in questions of local taxation and operating measures,[35] hiring drainage engineers, ditch tenders, attorneys, a superintendent, an auditor, two tax collectors, a stenographer, a Diversion Lake caretaker, a Lake Kemp caretaker, a deputy assessor, blacksmiths, truck drivers, foremen, teamsters, laborers, and team camp watchmen needed to upkeep and complete projects.[36] Then in 1939, the United

States acquired "real property for . . . a rural rehabilitation project . . . for resettlement purposes" in Wichita County.[37] In theory it meant more farmers on irrigated lands.

The development of the Big Wichita River was not unique in attaining federal aid. On the Brazos River, the Public Works Administration and the Reconstruction Finance Corporation helped to complete the first dam in 1941. The Lower Colorado River Authority, Guadalupe-Blanco River Authority, and the Brazos River Conservation and Reclamation District all required federal aid to complete similar projects. In fact, most Texas river valley "development" depended on the federal government.[38] Unlike for some of the other Texas rivers, though, water quality in the Big Wichita River Valley threatened its "development."[39]

Six major salt springs emit water from gypsum cliffs on the north bank of the upper Big Wichita River. The springs here flow at a rate of about two cubic feet per second and produce about 195 tons of chloride per day. The large dissolved solids and chlorides emanating from these springs caused humans in the valley to avoid drinking the Big Wichita's water. Somehow, Wichita Falls city boosters convinced people that capturing water behind dams would dilute the saltwater enough for the water to be filtered and used for drinking. It is true that the salty water could become diluted enough to be less noticeable when rainfall was high. At low flows and high rates of evaporation, however, the water became more saline. During hotter and drier months, when the water was most needed, it reached its highest salinity levels.[40]

Ultimately, Lake Diversion and Lake Kemp failed to meet public health standards for drinking water.[41] The reservoirs failed as domestic and industrial water supplies as well.[42] The corrosive action of the water damaged agricultural equipment, industrial and municipal water-treatment facilities, piping systems, water heaters, and other household appliances.[43] Owners of public laundromats reported that the water not only harmed their machines but also decomposed the fabric of their patrons' clothes. Gardeners in the Big Wichita Valley claimed the water from Lake Kemp was unfit for growing gardens or greenhouse plants. And local beauticians complained about the damaging effects of the water on ladies' hair.[44]

Some people did find uses for the salty water, including Ohioan Louis Bromfield, an agriculturalist and author, who started a Malabar Farm in Wichita County.[45] Bromfield found that highly salt-tolerant crops such as alfalfa did well with saline irrigation.[46] Alfalfa required more water than most crops because of its rapid growth and number of cuttings. As long as the alfalfa's root zone drained adequately, irrigation water containing appreciable salt could be used without killing the crop.[47] State agricultural experimental stations also found Bermuda grass did well with salty water.[48] Also, livestock fared better with saline water than did crops or humans. Experiments indicated that livestock tolerated a relatively high number of dissolved solids, as much as 10,000 ppm.[49] Ranchers watered livestock directly from irrigation canals until the water district ordered ranchers to construct tanks or stock ponds in the 1950s.[50]

Thus, the irrigation project had changed its mission from vegetable and common crops to salt-tolerant crops and pasturage.[51] Common crops, such as cotton and sorghum that only need about fourteen inches of rain, produced lower yields due to the heavy salt content.[52] In fact, as irrigation farmers applied water, evaporation caused the loss of the water and the salt remained, sometimes visibly, on the soil.[53] Moreover, salty water robbed the topsoil of its capacity for supporting healthy vegetation, with salt cedars thriving in such conditions and taking over some large tracts.[54]

Still, many believed technology and more federal aid could solve the water quality issue. Politically, World War II presented new ways to attain federal aid. Flat pastureland north of Wichita Falls attracted Maj. Gen. Rush B. Lincoln, commander of the US Army Air Corps Technical Training Schools, to Wichita County.[55] Rancher J. S. Bridwell sold three hundred acres of his cattle ranch to the federal government for one dollar, sealing the deal with Major General Lincoln for a World War II flight training facility. Construction began June 12, 1941, and was completed October 17. The government named the training facility Sheppard Field, in honor of Texas Sen. John Morris Sheppard. At war's end in 1945, the base reached peak strength of 46,304, making it the largest concentration of air corps troops in the world.[56] Later Sheppard Air Force became a North Atlantic Treaty Organization (NATO) air training facility.[57] In 1940 the population of Wichita Falls was 45,112. By 1964, Wichita Falls grew to 107,000.[58] Building Sheppard Air Force Base significantly augmented the population of the city of Wichita Falls and Wichita County.[59] With population increases in Wichita County came greater demands on the municipal water supply.

Fortunately for Wichita County, the acquisition of Sheppard Air Force Base meant their water problems now became pertinent political issues linked to national security. Not only did Wichita Falls' citizens complain about being forced to drink salty water, but now airmen made formal complaints to Washington, DC. Before its construction, authorities at Sheppard Air Force Base extracted promises from the City of Wichita Falls that the city would supply "essential support items" to the base, including water, electricity, and gas. By war's end Sheppard had become a behemoth, supporting thousands of family quarters, an eighteen-hole golf course, swimming pools, bowling alleys, and miles of paved airfields. Training pilots for World War II and the Cold War required large amounts of good quality drinking water.[60]

As a result, the city restricted water usage from Lake Wichita, guarding access to the better-quality drinking water from the Holliday Creek watershed. During a drought the water supply in Lake Wichita got so low the city cut off the water for irrigation from Lake Wichita to the Lake Wichita irrigators and instead turned to salty Lake Kemp water. According to irrigation farmers, the Lake Kemp water "was so much salt and mineral content that it ruined the land and killed the produce." The farmers sued the city "because the truck growers were supposed to have permanent water rights to Lake Wichita."[61] Mayor W. E. Fitzgerald testified in the case brought against the city by the farmers, arguing that under no circumstances could the city furnish landowners water for irrigation from Lake Wichita because the supply was not sufficient for the city of Wichita Falls, the Sheppard air field, and irrigation all at the same time. Despite the mayor's testimony, the judge ruled in favor of the farmers. The judge determined the farmers had prior appropriation rights to Lake Wichita water. Wichita Falls, like Los Angeles and Phoenix, had become a lesson in the dangers and unintended consequences of developing an arid southwest. Good drinking water was scarce, and a dammed creek and the Big Wichita's salty irrigation water could no longer sustain a modernizing society.[62] Local businessmen viewed the municipal water problem as a fundamental handicap to more growth. The Wichita Falls Chamber of Commerce called for a "practical and speedy solution."[63]

Under the Mississippi River Control Act of May 15, 1928, the federal government made a survey of the Red River and its tributaries "with a view of improvement for navigation in combination with flood control, power development and irrigation."[64] Plans for hydroelectric plants on Lakes Kemp and Diversion never came to fruition because engineers found that the salty water would ruin the generating plants.[65] The Big Wichita River had proved inadequate to meet the power production and drinking water needs of a growing city and its air base.

With population pressures in mind, water district attorney A. H. Britain and Mayor W. B. Hamilton travelled to Washington, DC, and sought more federal aid. The two local leaders presented a plan and program for placing Lakes Kemp and Diversion under the federal flood control system. In this way the water district wanted to obtain federal aid to refurbish their water system.[66] Aid at first appeared imminent, but the battle for funding turned into an uphill struggle when R. W. Knight, manager of the Wichita Falls Chamber of Commerce, regretfully reported back to Wichita Falls that "various and sundry parties in Washington," which included the US Army Corps of Engineers, "were likely to give an adverse report" on the Big Wichita River Project. The federal engineers argued there was no precedent for including the Big Wichita River improvements into a federal flood control plan. Knight recommended that WCWID join with the Wichita Falls Chamber of Commerce and employ a professional lobbyist, Roy Miller, to be sent to Washington for a period of three years. All agreed on sending the lobbyist to DC, where Miller expressed the developers need and want for federal aid to congressmen and senators.[67]

Ironically, Wichita Falls had the largest water supply in proportion to population when compared to any other city in the United States. In fact, the population of Wichita Falls had access to an immense quantity of water ample for a city of half a million people stored in three lakes: Wichita, Kemp, and Diversion. But the water in the two largest lakes, Kemp and Diversion, proved unfit for use. These facts made Miller's lobbying efforts nearly impossible when trying to convince federal authorities to fund more development on the Big Wichita River Valley.[68] Most congressmen thought in terms of quantity and did not consider quality. They balked at the idea of increasing the quantity of water in Wichita County. The irony runs deep, considering how Joseph Kemp's promotion of "the Beneficent Results of Plenty of Water" later hindered federal lobbying efforts.[69]

In the neighboring basin—the Little Wichita Basin—water proved to be of "excellent quality," especially when compared to the Big Wichita River. This fact had been known for a long time. In the 1850s Capt. Randolph Marcy jotted down that the Little Wichita River water had "a slightly brackish taste, but is palatable." Ecological historian Del Weniger was right when he found the "Little Wichita River was apparently a very different sort of stream" than the Big Wichita. "The Little Wichita was smaller," Weniger wrote, but made "an especially agreeable stream for this area, which probably explains the location of the major Indian settlements we know were upon it." In the Little Wichita River, concentrations of dissolved solids registered at less than 250 parts per million (ppm) at Henrietta and less than 200 ppm upstream. In comparison, the water of the Big Wichita River averaged more than 2,000 ppm dissolved solids. After being denied funds for improvements on the Big Wichita, the city completed a $3,000,000 project on the Little

Wichita River. This included the building of Lake Kickapoo in the 1940s. William Hamilton served as mayor of Wichita Falls from 1944 to 1948, and his chief campaign promise and mayoral accomplishment was construction of Lake Kickapoo to serve the drinking water needs of Wichita Falls and Sheppard Air Force Base. Engineers located Lake Kickapoo, with a capacity of 106,000 acre-feet, ten miles northwest of Archer City on North Fork Little Wichita River.[70]

The Texas State Board of Water Engineers authorized construction of Lake Kickapoo dam in 1944 and allowed for diversion of 40,000 acre-feet per year for municipal purposes. The local developers impounded waters in 1945 to form Lake Kickapoo. The reservoir, located thirty-two miles northeast of the city of Wichita Falls (in Archer County), was owned by the city. The city sold lots along the 3,000 acres of shoreline for recreational use.[71] Wichita Falls completed the municipal water pipeline from the lake to Wichita Falls and diverted water through it for the first time on September 24, 1947.[72] The City of Wichita Falls owned and operated Lake Kickapoo and Kickapoo Dam, which provided and still provides municipal water for the towns of Wichita Falls and Holliday.[73] The city named the reservoir Lake Kickapoo after the Kickapoo people and more specifically for the Kickapoo Creek, which empties its waters into the man-made lake.[74]

Before the creeks and rains filled Lake Kickapoo, Wichita Falls received its municipal water supply from Lake Wichita on Holliday Creek. When Lake Wichita ran low (and often it did) the city received water via the irrigation canal system from the Big Wichita River. The city then mixed the salty Big Wichita water with the Holliday Creek water, treated it, and piped water to residents. When the city completed Lake Kickapoo in 1947 on the Little Wichita River, Wichita Falls could now pipe better-quality water to the homes of its residents. Thus, the city pumped the precious commodity from the Little Wichita Basin into the Big Wichita River Valley. The basin-to-basin transfer of water resources required appropriative rights. The towns of Wichita Falls and

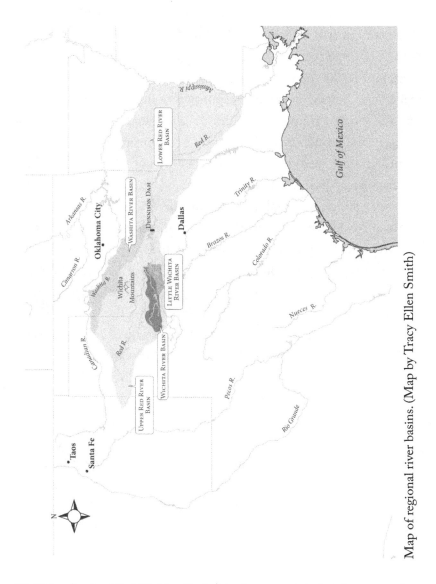

Map of regional river basins. (Map by Tracy Ellen Smith)

Holliday (in the Big Wichita Basin) had appropriated rights to portions of Lake Kickapoo (on a completely separate Little Wichita Basin) water supply. It was the first basin-to-basin or inter-basin system in the state of Texas. Although a costly enterprise, many hoped the basin-to-basin transfer model would be a template to solving water problems in other arid and semi-arid basins.[75]

In conclusion, an environmental history of the population boom in Wichita County is a story driven by three factors: oil, warplanes, and the politics of water pollution. In 1910, Wichita County had a population of around 16,000 people. By the 1940s, more than 100,000 residents made their homes in Wichita County. The demands of oil production and the new commercial endeavors associated with the petroleum industry, the growth of military bases and housing for military personnel, and the needs of agriculturalists were not met by the local Big Wichita River Basin. The man-made and "natural" pollutants in the river caused high water salinity. Due to federal intervention as a result of wars (World War I and World War II) and depression (New Deal), an environmental problem became a national issue. To provide water for the growing population, the City of Wichita Falls secured funding and water appropriation rights to the neighboring Little Wichita River Basin. Ultimately, waters from the Little Wichita Basin pumped into the basin of the Big Wichita. Spanning the course of forty long years, engineers developed the inter-basin (or basin-to-basin) water transfer system to meet the needs of modern-day Wichita County. In hindsight, starting with a conquest-oriented ideology first, based on technology and city boosterism, and attempting to mold it to the landscape rather than beginning with an understanding of the limitations of the local environment had proven damaging to the region's ecology and costly to Wichita County. The Wichita Falls Chamber of Commerce demanded a solution, but that solution took forty years to implement because of the underlying ecological limitations.

CHAPTER 4

THE LAST PICTURE SHOW

I'd play the Red River Valley
And he'd sit out in the kitchen and cry
And run his fingers through seventy years of livin'
And wonder, "Lord, has ever' well I've drilled run dry?"
   —GUY CLARK, "DESPERADOS WAITING FOR A TRAIN," 1975[1]

L arry McMurtry's novel, *The Last Picture Show* (1966), depicted a dying Red Rolling Plains town where a closing cinema rolled its last film, *Red River*, starring John Wayne. Peter Bogdanovich adapted McMurtry's novel into an Academy Award–winning film four years later. The narrative follows two high school seniors—Sonny Crawford and Duane Jackson—as they come of age in the early 1950s. The film brought to life the hard realities of the Red Rolling Plains in the mid-nineteenth century: dying rural towns, dusty hot streets, class conflict, and changing notions of masculinity. In black and white, *The Last Picture Show* paid homage to the Old West, but it was really about decline in a New West.

As illustrated by the themes of McMurtry's work, the environment bred uncertainty, violence, and hardships. One of those hardships was the drought of the 1950s, which is the dusty backdrop for the film's fictional protagonists.[2]

By the 1950s, the oil booms of the 1910s and 1920s had given way to busts and ghost towns—towns with names like Clara, Newtown, and Texhoma City.[3] Communities like the fictional town of Anarene, Texas, in *The Last Picture Show*, which was based on McMurtry's real-life hometown of Archer City, fell on hard times. Oil fields emptied, stores closed, and a record drought dried up the countryside. In the decline, depression, tragedy, and violence flowed like a river. And, even when boomtowns were at their height, as depicted in films like *Boom Town* and *There Will Be Blood* (based on Upton Sinclair's novel *Oil!*), greed and deception consumed boom and bust communities.[4] At one point, the violence even threatened to break out between states. At the height of the boom (1919–1920), twenty Texas Rangers took possession of a well on the southern bank of the Red River, which was owned by the Oklahoma-based Burke-Divide Oil Company. It led to a shootout between oil well security forces and the Texas Rangers and ultimately to the Supreme Court case *Oklahoma v. Texas* (1923).[5]

Folk singer Woody Guthrie, who was raised in an Oklahoma boom-town that went bust, wrote of his hometown Okemah:

> one of the singiest, square dancingest, drinkingest, yellingest, preachingest, walkingest, talkingest, laughingest, cryingest, shootingest, fist fightingest, bleeedingist, gamblingest, gun, club, and razor car-ryingest of our ranch towns and farm towns, because it blossomed out into one of our first Oil Boom Towns.[6]

It was a tidal wave of success, followed by a crushing bust that left the town on hard times or, as Woody put it, "busted, disgusted, and not to be trusted."[7] The inherent violence in economic uncertainty, however, paled in comparison to destruction caused by nature, which included tornado outbreaks, floods, droughts, fires, and in the case of Woody Guthrie's communities, oil booms, busts, and blinding sandstorms. In fact, Guthrie's terrifying experiences in Pampa, Texas, which included the Black Sunday Dust Storm on April 14, 1935, came to define his career with *Dust Bowl Ballads* like, "I Ain't Got No Home in This World No More," "Dust Bowl Refugee," and the apocalyptic "So Long, It's Been Good To Know Yuh" where he sang, "We talked of the end of the world." Add in social problems like addiction, toxic masculinity, suicide, and racial violence and the environmental history of the Red Rolling Plains becomes downright scary.[8]

Some argue that the harsh environment determined this violent outcome. Yet modern geographers, historians, and archeologists have refuted environmental determinism. Geo-archeologist Karl Butzer, with years of comparative studies of global communities in decline, found "environmentally grounded crises are culturally screened and per-ceived . . . with poor leadership, administrative dysfunction, and ideo-logical ambivalence . . . [all] endemic to the processes of collapse."[9] This is the case for the Red Rolling Plains. Failed ideologies, dysfunctional administration, and poor leadership played roles in its environmental crises. From the nineteenth century to the current day, the cultural per-ceptions of the landscape were based on ecological knowledge foreign to the region (usually based on river valleys with non-alkaline waters). The technocrats required knowledge of the local river's water and ecology, which they misunderstood, ignored, or intentionally covered up so that they could sell more real estate.

City boosters tried to establish a "hydraulic society" on the semi-arid Red Rolling Plains. They hoped to replicate irrigation networks of arid Utah. For the city boosters like Joseph Kemp, irrigation and the process of turning deserts into productive fields was demonstrative of civiliza-tion. Kemp, for example, saw:

history . . . repeating itself [in] Europe, Asia and Africa all working with one accord to reclaim the waste places and . . . ancient and erstwhile scenes of . . . harvests, bursting granaries and the varied charm and contentment of pastoral life, which to man of advanced thought offers the only remedy for the growing evil. . . . The conditions making irrigation desirable to the ancients exist to-day in both the old world and the new.[10]

A similar irrigation process could be traced back to the earliest civilizations and, in fact, building hydraulic societies in arid river valleys goes back to Mesopotamia and Egypt. A finer analysis of all these ancient and modern irrigation projects reveals the building of elaborate dams, reservoirs, and irrigation ditches. Construction and maintenance of such massive public works projects required laborers, engineers, scientists, bureaucrats, and priests (who gave the project legitimacy). Directing farmers and rivers maximized agricultural production. At the same time the process stripped farmers and communities of their local autonomy, "concentrating hegemony in fewer and fewer hands."[11] The ultimate outcome in Mesopotamia was a country "empty of people and lying in ruins" with "decrepit canals . . . dry and choked with silt, while a whitish alkaline residue lay everywhere on the soil." Mesopotamia "had fallen into the infrastructure trap, building a bigger and bigger water system until they could no longer keep pace with the ecological backlash they were creating."[12] The fate of the Tigris and Euphrates Rivers in the Mesopotamia Valley looks eerily similar to the story of the Red Rolling Plains, down to the "alkaline residue" on the soil. Moreover, the irrigation project inflated the demand for irrigation farmers. It was an inflation based on a nonexistent market. The city booster Joseph Kemp developed Wichita Falls and the point was development, not satisfying a demand for irrigation, which was purposefully inflated by the project itself. In other words, Wichita Falls also fell into the infrastructure trap.

Egypt's development was more sustainable than Mesopotamia or Wichita Falls because its bureaucrats heeded natural flooding cycles on the Nile River. On the other hand, the people of Mesopotamia, like the inhabitants of the Red Rolling Plains, tried to force its rivers to follow the dictates of ideology and technology. Similarly, the natural cycles of the Upper Red River and its tributaries, the Little Wichita and Big Wichita, experienced long periods of drought followed by intense thunderstorms and flash flooding. It was an erratic and unpredictable climate reminiscent of the Tigris and Euphrates Rivers. Interestingly, Mesopotamia—home of the Babylonian Code of Hammurabi, which included the well-known "eye for an eye" law—could have been as violent a place as the Red Rolling Plains. Erratic floods and droughts ravaged Mesopotamia in the same way that they tore through the Red Rolling Plains. Rapid changes in temperature with marked extremes (maximum temperatures of more than 100 degrees Fahrenheit are common in the summer), erratic rainfall, and violent downbursts meant that death from environmental factors or natural disaster was as common as death at the hands of another human.[13]

Drought scorched the Red Rolling Plains in 1870, 1885–1887, 1908–1912, 1915–1918, 1924–1925, 1933–1935, 1938–1940, 1950–1957 (Record Drought), 1961–1967, 1970–1971, 1988–1990, 1995–1996, 1999–2002, 2005–2006, 2007–2009, and 2010–2011. Usually, violent storms and flooding followed these long periods of drought.[14] On the Red Rolling Plains, tornado outbreaks occurred frequently. For example, just in the small settlement of Frederick, Oklahoma, tornadoes struck in 1908 killing a child, twisters zigzagged through the 1950s, and four confirmed tornadoes descended on the Frederick area on the same day in 1973, two of them striking the city and causing three million dollars of damage. In the city of Wichita Falls alone, large tornadoes (measured on the Fujita scale from F0 to F5) have been recorded in 1888 (F2), 1892 (F2), 1923 (F2), 1936 (F2), 1939 (F2), 1951 (F2), 1953 (F2), 1955 (F2), 1958 (F3), 1958 (F2), 1961 (F2), 1963 (F3), 1965 (F5), 1979 (F4), 1997 (F1), and 2001 (F1).[15]

The F5 tornado in 1965 killed seven and injured 111 people, causing more than ten million dollars in damage on the northwest side of Wichita Falls. On "Terrible Tuesday," April 10, 1979, at least eleven tornadoes struck the Red Rolling Plains in an event now referred to as the Red River Tornado Outbreak of 1979. First, sirens sounded in Vernon, Texas, as a tornado bore down on the southern part of town. In ten minutes, the F4 left eleven dead, more than sixty injured, and hundreds of homes destroyed. Witnesses described a "dark mass of clouds low to the ground" with "heavy rain, hail, and low cloud base."[16] This storm system skipped across the Red River and into Lawton, Oklahoma, spawning another tornado just after 5 p.m. Despite siren system warnings, the F3 left three dead and 109 injured in Lawton. Then, at 5:50 p.m. sirens blared over the city of Wichita Falls. At 6:15 p.m., with wind speeds in excess of two hundred miles per hour, three snaking funnel clouds merged into one massive F4—the twister killed forty-seven people, injured about 1,700 people, destroyed an eleven-square-mile area, and caused more than three hundred million dollars of property damage. At one point the tornado stretched one mile across the city, leaving behind a broad swath of death and destruction.[17]

Although death rained down from the sky on many occasions, most days on the Red Rolling Plains are clear with blue skies. These conditions, alongside flat topography, make it ideal for training airplane pilots. The United States government realized these ideal conditions with the Army Air Corps base at Call Field during World War I. Since then, the growth of the military-industrial complex on the Red Rolling Plains has been expansive and today includes the US Army base at Fort Sill and US Air Force base at Sheppard Field. Fort Sill came into existence in the mid-nineteenth century. Sheppard Air Force Base began as an Army Air Corps Base in World War II but now is a US Air Force base with a North Atlantic Treaty Organization (NATO) training facility for international pilots. These bases are economic pillars for their respective communities, Lawton and Wichita Falls, which are the largest cities on the Red Rolling Plains. Thus, the economic solution for the Red Rolling Plains literally came out of the clear blues skies. Interestingly, pilots at Sheppard and artillery units at Fort Sill are trained to rain down death from the sky. Did the environment determine the Plains to be the best place for pilots and gunners to train for such deadly missions? Or did the material cultural, the warplanes and artillery pieces, allow humans to perceive the landscape as such an ideal training space? There is no doubt that environmental determinism is flawed. Likewise, as there is no doubt humans perceived and still perceive the environment through a cultural lens, and it cannot be overstated that *Homo sapiens* are part of the environment and by no means masters over it.

From the 1950s to the present, once-irrigated farmlands transformed slowly into air fields and suburban Wichita Falls. The most striking example of this transition from agrarian to suburban landscape is seen in the story of Louis Bromfield and his Malabar Farm in Wichita County. According to historian Whitney Snow, Bromfield argued "agriculture could succeed in virtually any climate and soil if farmers would simply adapt rather than expending time and energy dreaming about what the land might be under different conditions." Snow brilliantly showed how "This romantic vision . . . came to an unpleasant end in the early 1950s when . . . [Bromfield] attempted to build a model farm near Wichita Falls, Texas." Louis Bromfield:

> hoped that the property might become a pilot farm that would dis-
> suade farmers from abandoning the land. Members of the Wichita
> Falls Chamber of Commerce (WFCC), however, had a different vision
> and imagined the farm as a grand tourist attraction that might serve to
> make the city famous and bring in revenue. These conflicting purposes,
> both of which depended on the stubborn soil and climate of Wichita
> County, resulted in an embarrassing failure.[18]

Some members of the Wichita Falls Chamber of Commerce still believed in Kemp's agrarian vision for the Wichita Valley and they learned again the environmental realities and consequences. Developers built suburbs atop the failed farms and salted acreages. The Wichita County water district attorneys in the 1950s, for example, advised the Federal Housing Administration (FHA) about waterlogged land conditions at the new Sunset Terrace subdivision, making clear that the land where the housing subdivision rested was a former irrigated area and the water district wished to be held exempt from liability and absolved of responsibility for future use of the land.[19]

The Record Drought of the 1950s compounded water salinity issues. Despite the addition of Lake Kickapoo as a water source in the 1940s, the supply of drinking water evaporated during the drought. As Sheppard Air Force Base, the city of Wichita Falls, and its suburbs like Holliday grew, the lakes emptied just as water engineers tried keep up with the growth. As a result, the water district hired a "Water Policeman" to apprehend persons guilty of water violations.[20] The water district discovered oilrig operators were using stock ponds filled with irrigation water. Once the district found out about the practice, and "since its origin is from irrigation canals," the district sent oil companies water bills.[21]

Literally thirsting for more water, the water district sent Rhea Howard to Washington to see if he could get government aid for another municipal freshwater water project.[22] As a result of Howard's proposal, in the 1950s the engineering firm Freese and Nichols of Fort Worth, Texas, submitted a report on the feasibility of the construction of another reservoir on the Little Wichita River in the vicinity of Windthorst, Texas.[23] Shortly thereafter the water district board submitted the required application for the appropriation of water from the Little Wichita River near Windthorst to the State Board of Water Engineers.[24] The Wichita Falls Chamber of Commerce Water Study Committee and the US Army Corps of Engineers engaged in a detailed plan and analysis of the cost of a new lake.[25] After considerable discussion both groups decided to employ Freese and Nichols for construction of the proposed new lake and a second inter-basin (basin-to-basin) watering system.[26]

The Texas Water Commission permitted construction in 1962. The permit allowed for the impoundment of 228,000 acre-feet with an annual diversion of 45,000 acre-feet for municipal use.[27] Freese and Nichols built Lake Arrowhead on the Little Wichita River for the

THE LAST PICTURE SHOW

city of Wichita Falls to accommodate their growing need for water.[28] Wichita Falls owned and operated Lake Arrowhead, located thirteen miles southeast of Wichita Falls on the Little Wichita River. In 1966 crews constructed pipelines and roads to Lake Arrowhead.[29] Oilmen and cattle ranchers had dominated this part of the lower Little Wichita River Valley and continued to do so. Lake cabins, cattle ranches, and oil fields encircled Lake Arrowhead, and oilmen erected steel derricks in the lake—fourteen in the middle—and used barges when the derricks required maintenance.[30]

Since the turn of the twentieth century, Wichita Falls has built five reservoirs to serve water needs. Lakes Arrowhead, Kickapoo, Wichita, Kemp, and Diversion act together as the modern sources of water to supply the city of Wichita Falls. Specifically, Lakes Kickapoo, Arrowhead, and Wichita provide the municipal drinking water supply. The salty lake water from Lakes Kemp and Diversion needs to be mixed with waters from the better-water-quality lakes to be used for industrial and domestic purposes. The irrigation system uses the saline waters directly from Lakes Kemp and Diversion mainly for livestock pasturage.[31] Once Wichita Falls had plenty of drinking water from its freshwater reservoirs on the Little Wichita River Valley, regional towns such as Archer City purchased water from Wichita Falls.[32]

Water pollution in these freshwater lakes now concerns not only the people of Wichita County but also those cities in other counties like Archer that purchase their drinking water from Wichita Falls. The five lakes in the area experience two forms of salt pollution: man-made pollution and "natural" pollution. Man-made pollution occurred primarily from improper disposal of saltwater produced by oil and gas.[33] Many oil producers disposed of oil-field brines in the subsurface, pumping them into the ground. Some used unlined surface pits for disposal and others just abandoned wells. Man-made pollution has contributed to overall deterioration of water quality in the basin, adding to the salinity problems. Storage of oil-field brine (underground saltwater left over after drilling) constituted a major problem in the Wichita County region and throughout the upper Red River Basin. Oil-field brines have contaminated portions of the Ogallala Aquifer in Carson, Gray, and Wheeler, and portions of groundwater reservoirs in Wheeler, Wilbarger, and Wichita Counties and numerous other areas. Saltwater from oil fields contaminated surface waters, too. Electra City Lake, for example, on China Creek, served as Electra's municipal water supply, but the water became too mineralized for drinking water standards because of contamination by oil field brine after the oil booms of the 1910s and 1920s. The people of Electra turned to another water resource, finding Camp Creek to be less polluted than China Creek. Man-made pollution from the oil fields forced Electra to locate a new municipal water supply and dam an entirely different creek.[34]

Many irrigation farmers claimed their lands had been salted out due to oil field saltwater pits. Farmers reacted to man-made pollution of ground and surface waters by trying to make an agreement with oil companies that oil operators would find a proper way to dispose of excess saltwater.[35] A committee found saltwater injection and water-flooding operations degraded ground- and surface-water quality.[36] The WCWID deemed it necessary to call a hearing before the Railroad Commission and other state agencies in charge of law enforcement of pollution laws to hold the oil companies liable and accountable.[37] The Railroad Commission held a hearing on oil and saltwater pollution for Wichita, Archer, Wilbarger, and Baylor Counties at Memorial Auditorium in Wichita Falls, Texas, in January 1953.[38]

Rhea Howard, director of the water district board and owner of the local newspaper, led this movement against man-made pollutants and carefully followed the developments of the committee investigating man-made pollution. The negligence of the oil and gas companies infuriated Howard. The newspaperman fumed at the idea that pollution of water in irrigation ditches and laterals and contamination of land in Wichita Valley came from oil field saltwater pollution. Howard regarded the matter as a progressive cause and personally requested a public hearing in Wichita Falls with the Railroad Commission, working to alleviate the condition as soon as possible.[39] The movement against man-made pollutants culminated in the early 1960s with the Red River Authority (RRA). The RRA tried to eliminate the practice of unlined surface pits in the watershed and combatted environmentally damaging oil field practices. The Federal Water Pollution Control Act of 1961, the Water Quality Act of 1965, and specifically the Oil Pollution Act, part of the Clean Water Restoration Act of 1966, helped to fund clean-ups and established some regulations on man-made water pollution.[40]

On the other hand, the "natural" pollution problem appeared to be much more complicated than the man-made one. By 1957, the US Public Health Services determined the causes of "natural" pollutants in the Arkansas and Red River Basins. The concept of "natural pollutants" is questionable because it infers nature pollutes itself. In reality, these salt waters are completely natural and it is humans that have determined that these natural salt waters are pollutants because the salt waters create adverse effects for humans trying to drink them. Despite the questionable and anthropocentric label, state agencies in the official reports refer to these salt waters as "natural pollution." Most sources of natural pollution occurred as saline seeps and springs that emitted from naturally occurring chlorides and sulfates. These saltwater springs emitted the principal "natural pollution" into the river systems. The US Public Health Services identified ten salt sources that collectively produced about two-thirds of the 3,450 tons per day of chloride that entered the Red River. Many of the sources emanated from the Big Wichita River watershed. In 1959, Congress authorized the Corps of Engineers to study and determine if the salt sources could be controlled.[41] After officials from Wichita Falls met with the US Public Health Department and the US Army Corps of Engineers in Dallas to discuss "natural salt pollution," Congress commissioned the Army Corps of Engineers to fight the saltwater conditions in the upper Red River Basin.[42]

The decision came just in time. The 1961 "Survey Report on Lake Kemp" by the US Army Corps of Engineers found Lake Kemp to be "a potential hazard to the valley below because of deterioration of the spillway and outlet works." The Big Wichita dams required complete reconstruction to make the facility safe for future operation. The corps determined rehabilitation feasible and in the public interest. In 1962 the Texas Water Commission and Texas Gov. Price Daniel endorsed the federal plan to rehabilitate the dams.[43] In combination with the flood control project, the Army Corps of Engineers initiated the natural saltwater pollution control project. The corps started the desalinization (or demineralization) program in the form of the Red River Chloride Project and the Texas State Legislature created the Red River Authority. The Red River Authority's role in the Red River Chloride Project was to ensure that the state employed the most "economical methods" to reclaim Red River water resources and make them available for "beneficial uses."[44]

Tom Foley, president of the Red River Authority, coordinated financial assistance from cities, counties, and political subdivisions within the upper Red River watershed to help institute the chloride project.[45] The Wichita County water district contributed $5,000 to the Red River Authority of Texas in an attempt to help the RRA work to end natural and man-made pollution.[46] Wichita Falls and the Wichita County Water Improvement Districts enthusiastically hoped work with the state-level RRA and the federal-level Army Corps of Engineers would edge the county closer to desalinization of the Big Wichita's waters, and many hoped that chloride control could make Lake Kemp water more productive for irrigation.[47]

The corps began work in 1962 at Estelline Springs, Texas. The Estelline Springs are saltwater springs on the Big Wichita River that escape from a highly saline Blaine Gypsum formation. Engineer surveys found waters from the Estelline Springs were not suitable for any kind of public water supply, far exceeding safety limits set up by the US Public Health Service. Estelline Springs directly affected the potential water supplies of the towns of Childress, Quanah, Vernon, and Chillicothe, Texas, and impacted downstream salinity levels for Holliday, Iowa Park, and Wichita Falls, Texas.[48] The Army Corps of

Engineers constructed a ring dike (nine feet tall and 340 feet in diameter) around the springs. The springs could not escape above the dike. A constructed feeder stream diverted upstream waters around the dike and back to the main channel of the river. The dike stopped 240 tons of chlorides from entering the Red River each day and has done so since January 1964.

The ring dike, however, worked only for Estelline Springs. Authorities concluded that the same technique used at Estelline Springs (the ring dike) would not work on the other seeps and springs. Those proved more difficult to control. In 1966, Congress authorized design studies for the Big Wichita River Basin, funding participation by the US Army Corps of Engineers and the US Fish and Wildlife Service to find ways to remove other natural saltwater pollutants from entering the river.[49] Officials examined alternative techniques for each brine source. On the South Wichita Fork of the Big Wichita River Basin, the solutions came in the form of pumps and brine tanks. Engineers pumped brine waters through a pipeline to a storage and evaporation reservoir. Congress authorized construction of the pump, pipeline, and collection pool on the South Fork of the Wichita River under the Water Resources Development Act of 1974. The act funded construction of water-control structures that diverted low flows with high salinity from the South Wichita River to the Bateman pump station. The corps designed the so-called water-control structures as inflatable dams. The dam inflated when river flows were low and from there, diverted the salty waters to the Bateman pump station. The Bateman pumps transported the water through a pipeline to Truscott Brine Lake, where the water collected and eventually evaporated. Construction of Bateman pump station and Truscott Brine Lake began in 1976. The corps completed Truscott Brine Lake in 1982 and diversions of low flows began in May 1987.[50]

With some successes, the US government deemed continued desalinization "correct and in the national interest." Elimination of natural pollution improved water quality not only in Wichita County in the local Big Wichita watershed but also in the Red River basin, including parts of the downstream areas of four states: Texas, Oklahoma, Arkansas, and Louisiana.[51] Generally, all agreed with the federal government that the Big Wichita River's natural salinity problem had been particularly acute and deserved continued and immediate attention.[52] Consensus, however, broke down in the 1990s. In fact, work on the desalinization project abruptly halted in 1994 when the US Fish and Wildlife Service, the Oklahoma Department of Wildlife Conservation, and the Texas Parks and Wildlife Department expressed concerns regarding the environmental impacts of the desalinization project. These groups believed decreased salinity levels impacted downstream fish populations and habitat. The Army Corps of Engineers were forced by law to suspend construction and evaluate the concerns. The corps planned to resolve the complaints through a process known as an environmental issue resolution process (EIRP). According to the corps, it suspended construction because it wanted "to achieve sustainable solutions" in accordance with new concepts of sustainability emerging from wildlife agencies. In 1997, the Texas Parks and Wildlife Department relented somewhat and allowed the corps to complete construction of the remaining chloride control features within the Big Wichita River Basin. The corps continued to espouse that the Red River Chloride Project would result in greater crop yields in irrigated areas, which would in turn allow Lake Kemp to be used for drinking water. If Lake Kemp could be utilized for drinking water, a reverse osmosis plant would not be needed, nor would more water supply reservoirs. The corps believed that the Red River Chloride Project would reduce the risk of water shortages in Wichita Falls and other communities in Northwest Texas.[53]

The corps, however, failed to address recreational purposes and to consider the interests of downstream fishermen. In the post-industrial and agricultural economy that emerged in the 1990s, general interests in rivers and lakes shifted from industry and agriculture to recreation. By 2002 the corps' Wichita River Basin Reevaluation Chloride Control Project was forced to address the fishermen's concerns at a public meeting. The engineers assured sportsmen that downstream fish habitats would not be disturbed by the reduction of chlorides in the water.[54] The environmental concern the US Fish and Wildlife Service, the Oklahoma Department of Wildlife Conservation, and the Texas Parks and Wildlife Department expressed over desalinization was the project's impact on species of striped bass and hybrid striped bass in Lake Texoma.

The most intense grassroots opposition to the Big Wichita desalinization project came from conservationists, primarily sports fishermen on Lake Texoma. The fishermen considered themselves conservationists because they wished to conserve fish habitats so that fishing conditions would be optimal. The fishermen worried that less saline waters might affect striped bass fish populations in the Red River Basin, especially in Lake Texoma, Lake Diversion, and Lake Kemp. According to many area businessmen, striped bass fishing was "very good" for the area's leisure economy, and they believed the local sports fishing industry might be hurt by the desalinization project. Neither fishermen nor related recreational businessmen wanted the Red River Chloride Control Project to change fish habitats.

Striped bass fishing in the area was "put and take" fishing, meaning that striped bass populations depended on the aquaculture of the Texas Parks and Wildlife Department (TPWD) and the Oklahoma Department of Wildlife Conservation stocking programs. The Oklahoma Department of Wildlife Conservation stocked Lake Texoma with striped bass from 1965 until 1974. Striped bass, anadromous like sturgeon and salmon, lived in both fresh and saltwater habitats. The corps assured the fishermen that striped bass in their natural environment, the ocean, migrate to freshwater rivers to spawn and not saltier areas. Data clearly indicated striped bass sought out the freshest water available to begin reproduction cycles. In fact, state-owned hatcheries raised the striped bass in freshwater hatcheries.

Striped bass do not reproduce in Lake Kemp nor in Lake Diversion. High-salinity conditions on the Big Wichita and Red Rivers, especially above Lake Kemp, do not allow for successful spawning. All the striped bass (a foreign species) caught from Lakes Kemp, Diversion, and Texoma were put there by government hatcheries. The corps asserted that the chloride control project would not affect striped bass in Lakes Kemp, Diversion, or Texoma, nor in the Wichita or Red Rivers. Plus, the corps admitted that the proposed chloride control project could never remove all of the salt. It could only remove about 83 percent of the chlorides and 67 percent of the sulfates that entered the Big Wichita River. The corps argued that normal sedimentation in Lake Texoma would probably have a bigger impact on Lake Texoma fish habitats over time than less salt as sedimentation influenced water temperature patterns and affected fish distribution.[55]

Even with desalinization, the Big Wichita River Valley was not turned into an agricultural Eden with intensively cultivated five- and ten-acre tracts of land as once hoped, and the long-term effects of that failed vision were in many cases unforeseeable. They included the potential changing of fish habitats and a reorganization of the landscape that favored oil producers over farmers. An unshakable belief in progress and a naïve faith in technology could not solve all the problems. There were natural limitations to what man might achieve.[56] Stephen Bogener, when looking at the Pecos River, made a similar discovery that projects "never lived up to the expectations of promoters or reclamationists of the nineteenth centuries, its failure in many ways was the result of the very thing that promised to make the desert productive, the Pecos River itself." As with the Pecos, developers ignored local ecological knowledge of the Big Wichita River. Early promoters, like those of the Pecos River Valley, "did not acknowledge the river's drawbacks in an era when unbridled optimism and the investment of millions of dollars carried the day." Today only shadows remain of the Pecos and Wichita irrigation projects.[57]

Irrigation agriculture required fundamental knowledge of water, soils, drainage, and an understanding of the crop from the planting to the harvesting and marketing stages.[58] Inhabitants in the Big Wichita River Basin faced these problems head on through the early twentieth century and by the 1950s learned the problem was not quantity of water but, as one report noted, "the greatest problem facing all irrigated areas . . . [was] an ample supply of water of suitable quality."[59] In the Gilded Age and Progressive Era (1880–1917), city boosters ignored local environmental conditions. In the following years, water districts were forced to confront them. Yet both groups preferred to stay focused on business opportunities afforded by real estate and land development rather than submit to ecological limitations.[60]

In other words, Joseph Kemp's vision created the impoverished world of Sonny and Duane seen in Larry McMurtry's *The Last Picture Show*. The novel and the film showcased the problems of a dying way of life where town stores shuttered windows and roughnecks struggled to make a consistent income in the ups and downs of the oil field economy, a place where kids tried to make sense of it all and going-out-of-business movie theaters showed a last film. Unfortunately, not much changed from the 1950s to the 2000s. The problems depicted in *The Last Picture Show* echo in new films about the current Red Rolling Plains. For example, modern films like *Hell or High Water* depict similar and dire economic situations encouraging desperate moves by their human inhabitants. Many struggle and leave. Some struggle and stay. Those that stay experience the effects of the heat and poverty, either directly or indirectly. These experiences manifest in depression, violence, and gambling and other addictions. Thus, *The Last Picture Show* and *Hell or High Water* share more in common than the star Jeff Bridges—both depict harsh realities on the Red Rolling Plains' cultural landscape.

CHAPTER 5

HELL OR HIGH WATER

Here's to Charlie Goodnight and Mr. Loving too
Here's to Coronado, the Comanche, and the blues
Here's to the bootleggers and the oil field crews
Here's to the one and all of us Red River fools

—GUY CLARK, "RED RIVER," *Cold Dog Soup*, 1999.[1]

O
rganizers of the annual "Hotter'N Hell Hundred," which features a hundred-mile bicycle race through Wichita County during the hundred-degree days of August, held their first race in 1982. Bikers crowded the starting line in Wichita Falls, racing out onto the hard, hot roads of the city and the surrounding countryside. As the sun beat down on helmeted riders guzzling water bottles, they pedaled past a landscape of suburban sprawl passing fields filled with cattle and dotted by oil pumps.[2] By the 1980s, the Southern Plains had experienced one of the most rapid environmental transformations on the continent.[3] In particular on the Red Rolling Plains, railroads, irrigation networks,

reservoirs, airfields, suburbs, and oil extraction transformed the region in less than one hundred years into a zone of commercial production for a global economy. Local government, industry, and business downplayed concerns about the environment in order to make the most profits and as quickly as possible.

Environmental historian Samuel P. Hays wrote that for many the "environment" was a term hardly used. Instead, people in the early twentieth century used the term conservation, which "emphasized physical resources, their more efficient use and development."[4] After World War II, a transformation in human values occurred that set the stage for the 1980s and transformed people's perceptions of the land, changing their land ethic to include concerns about pollution of the environment, especially pollution of rivers and lakes.[5] From 1959 to 1960, Luna B. Leopold wrote circulars for the United States Geological Survey (USGS) that expressed this new outlook on water resources. Leopold made sophisticated new arguments in works like *Ecological Systems and the Water Resources* and *The Challenge of Water Management.* Interestingly enough, authorities in charge of West Texas water resources read and archived these circulars. Leopold explained that lands were "not only altered from their original state" but "constantly in the state of still further change." Furthermore, Leopold questioned whether man could be unraveled "from nature in the records."[6] Leopold called for a new land philosophy, one that extended into "the field of esthetic values as well as economic ones." Another publication, Rachel Carson's *Silent Spring* in 1962, also worked to change the perception in popular culture. By the 1960s, the growth of an environmental movement reflected an expanding concern about the earth and its water resources.[7]

In 1964, more than seven million acres were irrigated in the state of Texas: 65 percent on the High Plains, 17 percent on the Rio Grande Plain, 6 percent on the Coastal Prairie, 4 percent in the Trans-Pecos region, 4 percent on the Rolling Plains, and 4 percent in other regions. "Drip" and "spray" irrigation took off on the High Plains, while the "flood" irrigation of the Rolling Plains diminished in importance.[8]

Irrigating with saline waters and endeavoring to remove the salt proved expensive and costly and is still a long-term proposition. Due to these failures, some people started to realize that they were part of the environment and should learn to live by working within its limitations. Starting with the system or ideology first and attempting to mold it to the landscape had proven damaging and costly. The "City That Faith Built" (Wichita Falls) rests atop a very different landscape than what the city builders imagined. It is definitely not an agrarian paradise of intensively cultivated fields. The water of the Big Wichita still runs muddy, salty, and sluggishly through the city. The Scottish travel writer Duncan McLean in *Lone Star Swing: On the Trail of Bob Wills and His Texas Playboys* described the waters of the Big Wichita River in the 1990s as: "Exactly the colour of the caramel layer in Mars bars."[9] The chocolate brown waters flow through a landscape of pump horses that rock on small ranches at the rural edges where suburbia sprawls out onto cow pastures. Or as James McMurtry, the son of the Pulitzer Prize–winning Larry McMurtry, sings in his song "Out Here in the Middle": "Where the buffalo roam, we're putting up towers for your cell phones."[10]

In 2016, the film *Hell or High Water* revived the western bank heist genre. Set in the 2008 Great Recession, the Red Rolling Plains provided a stunning cinematic backdrop for the small-town bank robberies. Oil pumps, cattle, and Indian casinos filled the screen as two desperate men made an attempt to provide for their families by beating a system rigged by bankers and greedy capitalists.[11] The depiction of gun violence and economic hardship in a semi-arid environment was not too far from the mark; moreover, the inclusion of Indian casinos in the film highlights an important feature of the modern cultural landscape. In the film, the two bank robbers launder their stolen bills through the casino. Near where Theodore Roosevelt once hunted in the Big Pasture, the Kiowa and Comanche casinos—known as "Little Vegas"—light up the nighttime sky, casting a neon glow across the parking lots adjacent to pasturelands filled with cows. Patrons from across the Red River, including citizens from Wichita Falls and pilots from Sheppard Air Force Base, drive their automobiles across the bridge for gambling and entertainment, a "vice" not allowed in the state of Texas. The Kiowas and Comanches have done well with the arrangement and, interestingly enough, choose to share the wealth of the casino profits among what the Comanches call their "tribal members." They have resisted corporatizing their system so that the casino profits fund healthcare, education programs, museums, language preservation, and, most importantly, provide per capita or "per cap" payments each year to "tribal members" on the "tribal rolls."[12]

Anglo Texans, Mexican Americans, African Americans, Kiowas, Comanches, and airmen from all over Europe, among many others, live and work next to each other every day in Texoma (on the Red Rolling Plains). Yet, the Kiowas and Comanches have found a way to share their resources, much like they did in their ancient past with resources distributed equally among the members of the group. On the other hand, the Anglo Texans persist in an individualized pursuit of wealth that creates wealth disparities as highlighted by the films *The Last Picture Show* and *Hell or High Water*. These films critique capitalism and are a short- and long-term warning about such a system's effects on the environment. Other systems exist in plain sight and have existed for millennia. Proving this are the Comanches and Kiowas, who boosted healthcare, education, and basic services because of the shared wealth from the casinos. The Plains Indians continue to focus profits on "kinship and obligations of reciprocity" and "graft 'traditional' methods onto modern economics and politics to produce a uniquely 'Indian way' . . . to outflank government strictures."[13]

The "Indian casino" represents an important juxtaposition to the "cowboy myth" of rugged individualism as a central feature of the Red Rolling Plains cultural landscape. In *Hell or High Water*, the Texan bank robbers use the Indian casino to launder their stolen money. What many viewers might not realize or even think about is the real-life cashier at the Indian casino on the other end of that exchange of cash and chips. In 2005, Comanche Justin Munsee cashed chips and made change at the Comanche Red River Casino in Randlett, Oklahoma. Munsee grew up in a small community north of Randlett called Cache, Oklahoma. After graduating high school, he attended college at Midwestern State University in Wichita Falls, Texas. He married an Anglo-Texan woman and, in 2005, he was preparing to move his family—a son and a daughter—back to Cache. Justin Munsee added his Comanche-Anglo kids to the Comanche "tribal rolls." Since then, the Comanche Nation provides him and his children with healthcare, community enriching programs, and a per capita annuity that every Comanche on the tribal roll receives from casino profits and other Comanche ventures. Comanches use casino revenues—a political-economic resource from outside the community—and redistribute the wealth within the Comanche community. This is not European-style socialism. It is a system based on native local knowledge. Comanche identity is grounded in the idea of bringing "outsiders" into Comanche kinship networks. The ability to expand kinship networks and redistribute wealth among kinship groups has "deep historical roots" on the Red Rolling Plains.[14] By 2005, the Comanche Nation operated as an integral part of the economy of Southwest Oklahoma, bringing economic development and tourism to the area and employing 700 people, which made it the third largest employer in Cotton and Comanche Counties. The Comanche Nation's total payroll exceeded seven million dollars, of which three-fourths was spent on goods and services in Texoma. Between 1999 and 2005, the Comanche Nation spent $7,913,916 on roads and $1,801,860 on bridges.[15] The Comanche system produced wealth for not only Comanches but the entire area.

Similarly, capitalism and its vestiges have had an extensive influence on the Red Rolling Plains, from the diseases, livestock, and enslaved Africans brought by Spaniards and other colonizers to the oil booms that made a few men millionaires. Among those few men were John G. Hardin and Joseph A. Kemp. John G. Hardin, for example, born in Tennessee in 1854 to a poor farmer, moved to Texas in 1876 and settled in a dugout in Wichita County in 1879. Despite a rough start, including the death of his wife and two small children, by 1886, Hardin acquired more than 1,000 acres of land that lay atop a massive oil field. By the time the oil boom struck in 1918, Hardin had purchased 13,000 acres of oil-rich lands. By the end of his life, Hardin made a "colossal fortune." With that fortune, he set up foundations for Texas universities and colleges and donated $6 million to educational and humanitarian institutions, including Abilene Christian University, Baylor University, Hardin-Simmons University, Mary Hardin-Baylor University, Howard Payne University, and Hardin Junior College in Wichita Falls, which became Midwestern State University. Capitalism worked for John G. Hardin, but it failed many others. As Wichita County historian Kenneth Hendrickson points out, "unlike so many others, he [Hardin] did not allow his great wealth to alter or ruin his life."[16]

Many wildcatters came and went, but men like Hardin and Kemp stayed and invested. Like John G. Hardin, Joseph A. Kemp maintained his fortune throughout his lifetime. When Kemp died in 1930 at the age of 69, the *Dallas Morning News* characterized him as the "well-known financier and capitalist of Wichita Falls."[17] Despite the failure of the Big Wichita irrigation project, several newspaper obituaries called Kemp the banker, railroad builder, and oilman, and they continued to celebrate his successful smaller irrigation project on Lake Wichita. His tombstone epitaph on his grave in the Riverside Cemetery, located in the center of the city of Wichita Falls above the new man-made falls, reads, "If ye would seek my monument, look around ye."[18] In a sense, the epitaph rings true. The vestiges of a failed irrigation project hide in the shadows of oil derricks, suburbs, and a massive air force base. Lake Wichita, Lake Kemp, and Lake Diversion remain part of the cultural landscape, but if the cultural landscape is a monument to Kemp then the monument looks much different than his original agrarian vision for the valley.

Kemp's vision was more of a marketing ploy to be sold while trying to develop his own commercial potential, real estate, and business endeavors. Thus, the modern landscape reflects his successes and failures, but the historical narrative (up until this point) ignored the failures. The Texas Historical Commission's plaque for Joseph Alexander Kemp, for example, remembers Kemp as "a visionary and entrepreneur . . . vital to the development of Wichita Falls."[19] His contributions include working "to provide the community with an adequate water supply."[20] It argues he helped do this through the "creation of Lakes Kemp and Diversion, which provided water and flood control to Wichita Falls."[21] The plaque does not mention, however, that the Lake Kemp and Diversion irrigation project was a spectacular failure and that actually the "adequate water supply" would be built after Kemp's death from the 1940s through the 1960s with the aid of private-public partnerships (which included funding and expertise provided by state and federal governments) and that the "adequate water" came from an entirely different watershed because the water in the Big Wichita River proved unfit to drink. Although he is remembered for his Lake Kemp and Diversion vision, his vision failed. Yet, the THC reframed the failures and success as just overall successes. Indeed, he was a successful individual and capitalist, but should that erase his failures? The plaque also points out that he "worked to diversify the community's economy in the face of its early 20th century oil boom."[22] The boom and the economic diversification doomed his agrarian vision. Capitalism found profits in oil and gas, and the irrigation project, in fact, restricted (by blocking up the land in irrigated farms) the full potential of the development of oil and gas leases to the chagrin of many oil producers.

Although Joseph Kemp and his brother-in-law Frank Kell lived and died in Wichita Falls, their heirs do not. In fact, Wichita Falls journalist Bridget Knight of the *Times Record News* asked an interesting question in 2017 about the heirs of Kemp and Kell. She reported: "The names of Wichita Falls founders Frank Kell and Joseph A. Kemp are well represented in the city's streets, buildings and businesses, but one place you won't find them is the residential listings of the local phone book. This begs the question, what became of their families?" The answer revealed that most Kemp and Kell family members moved out of Wichita Falls and now live in Dallas and Houston.[23] Did their family give up on Kemp and Kell's dreams? Although their reasons for leaving Wichita

Falls are unknown, one of Larry McMurtry's characters in his novel *The Last Picture Show* explained wealth and its paradoxical relationship to the Red Rolling Plains landscape this way: "The land's got too much power over you. Being rich here is a good way to go insane. Everything is flat and empty and there's nothing to do but spend money."[24]

Some historians lauded Hardin for his fortitude and philanthropy, and they celebrated Kemp for his vision and entrepreneurship, but most historians remained blind to the contributions of the Comanches. While capitalism and native systems have coexisted side by side since the sixteenth century, in 2005, many people still misunderstood the Comanches, their casinos, and their systems. The silencing of capitalism's failures and the denigrating of other systems continues. Many Anglos remained outright hostile to Comanche economic development into the twenty-first century. For example, a non-profit (501c) One Nation United created by "Movement Conservatives" in Oklahoma City hired Toby Keith to make television and radio commercials to point out what some saw as unfair practices by the American Indians. Its impetus stemmed from the Indian casino competition, including Oklahoma City competitors and the Remington Park racehorse facility, which used the Oklahoma City newspaper *The Oklahoman* to campaign against the Indian casinos. In a press release One Nation United declared, "No one is blind to the fact tribes and their government-owned businesses provide many benefits . . . jobs, housing, health care, education, etc., raising living standards for Indian people. That is a good thing. We believe the tribes can do this without tax, regulatory, and other advantages that distort the free market."[25] In other words, One Nation United believed American Indians and their communal system threatened individualism and the "free market system" and posited the idea that "You cannot become thorough Americans if you think of yourselves in groups." The non-profit group argued, "America does not consist of groups." Using country music superstar Toby Keith and the myth of the individual ruggedness of the cowboy, they challenged the way American Indians organized themselves and their resources. It is an implicit bias that leads to ideological pitfalls and apparently blindness to local environmental knowledge and native know-how.[26]

A host of journalists, historians, filmmakers, songwriters, and other storytellers shrouded the complex history of the region in myth, which allows dated, destructive ideas and policies to remain popular. Some of those myths, however, are unraveling in the face of modern historical scholarship. Walter Prescott Webb in *The Great Plains* (1931), for example, argued that technological development in the form of the Colt revolver, barbed wire, and the windmill allowed "pioneers" to settle beyond the 98th meridian. Geoff Cunfer's *On the Great Plains* (2005), however, dismantled Webb's environmental determinism and showed the ecological limitations of "progress," especially in the face of the Dust Bowl. Webb's racialized mythmaking in *The Texas Rangers: A Century of Frontier Defense* (1935) falls apart in the face of the historical analysis offered by Doug J. Swanson's *Cult of Glory: The Bold and Brutal History of the Texas Rangers* (2020). Walter Prescott Webb's *The Great Frontier* (1952) postulated a "boom hypothesis" that European arrival on the wild frontiers of North America since the fifteenth century led to the rise of great wealth and new institutions, such as capitalism. *The Falls of Wichita Falls* is an attempt to help dismantle some of those myths and to encourage policymaking based on the historical realities of private-public partnerships and local ecological knowledge rather than the fallacies of the myths of individualism and the supposed human conquest over nature.[27] The tyranny of a place name—Wichita Falls— which vexed the citizens of the city provides a perfect example for this point. How could Wichita Falls *be* Wichita Falls without a falls? Their failed attempt to restore the falls perfectly illustrates the realities of the relationship between humans and nature.

In 1955, the City of Wichita Falls attempted to overcome nature again and built a falls in the Big Wichita River. Citizens donated more than $10,000 to place boulders in the Big Wichita River near downtown, creating a series of small waterfalls. *Life* magazine featured the "new" falls in a photograph spread, media personality Paul Harvey praised the community's efforts on his nationally syndicated radio broadcast, and the Texas Senate passed a resolution commending the effort. Accolades poured in from around the country. Wichita Falls was going to restore the falls in Wichita Falls. Slogans like "put the falls back in Wichita Falls" helped to raise the money for the effort. "Unfortunately," journalist Jody Cox wrote, "the Wichita River, as had so many times before reasserted its superiority in the matters concerning its course." A month after the opening ceremony heavy rains led to flooding, washing away the freshly planted grass in the new park, destroying the falls, and ruining the project. The floods had washed out the falls again.[28]

In 1986, a new campaign emerged to return the falls to Wichita Falls. This time, the falls were put next to the river—not in it—so that future floods would not wash out the falls. The community raised more than $250,000 to construct a 54-foot-tall waterfall (the original falls were seven feet tall, at most). After installing a 75-horsepower motor that pumped river water up to the top of the bluff, the water fell back into the river over the man-made falls.[29] The city planned a three-day dedication celebration hosted by the famed weathercaster Willard Scott. On Monday, June 1, 1987, floodwaters on the Big Wichita River submerged part of the falls, restricting the use of the pump. The floodwaters did not recede by the day of the national televised opening ceremony, so the city hooked up water hoses to fire hydrants and let the water from the hoses flow over the waterfalls.[30]

The history of the falls of Wichita Falls highlights the main theme in the environmental history of the Red Rolling Plains. The people never conquered the environment. Instead, they negotiated an existence based on local environmental realities. Humans pushed ecological limits, but nature pushed back. Neither environment nor man dominated because humans were not separate from the environment. Instead, they were a part of nature. If humans developed the landscape knowing that man was part of nature and with knowledge of the local environment, it is possible that it might lead to more sustainable development in the future.[31]

NOTES

INTRODUCTION

1. Around 1884, J. A. Foreman, president of the Water Power Company, started construction on a dam across the Big Wichita River above the waterfalls of Wichita Falls. The dam held less than two years when the flood and dam debris washed out the falls in 1886. "Wichita County," *Dallas Morning News*, October 20, 1886, P2; Registration Sheet of Aaron Dodson, Historical Survey of Wichita Falls, Texas, Center for American History (CAH), University of Texas at Austin, Austin, Texas; "Reminiscences of Mart Banta," Wichita Falls Reminiscences, Wichita Falls Public Library (WFPL), Wichita Falls, TX; "Visitor Can Remember Viewing Falls on River," *Wichita Daily Times*, May 4, 1952, Wichita Falls Scrapbook from 1950 to 1989, Vertical File, CAH; Registration Sheet of Fritz Hendrich, Historical Survey of Wichita Falls, Texas, CAH; Judy Cox, "Where Is the Falls," *Wichita Falls Times*, December 31, 1978, Wichita Falls, Texas, Vertical File, CAH; Harry Parks, "When Earthen Dam Broke in 1886 to Erase River Falls Recalled by Pioneer Now 74," *Wichita Daily Times*, February 27, 1949; "Wichita River Falls Being Rebuilt Here," *Wichita Falls Times*, April 22, 1955, Wichita County Archives (WCA), Wichita Falls, TX; Jody Cox, "Where is the Falls in Wichita Falls?" *Wichita Falls Times*, December 31, 1978, WCA; and "Place Names in Wichita County," Wichita County, Texas,

Vertical File, CAH.

2. Registration Sheet of Aaron Dodson, Historical Survey of Wichita Falls, Texas, CAH; Jonnie R. Morgan, *The History of Wichita Falls* (Wichita Falls, TX: Nortex Offset Publications Inc., 1931); "A Historical Sketch of Wichita Falls," Reminiscences of Mrs. A. H. Carrigan, Wichita Falls Reminiscences, WFPL.

3. Buckley B. Paddock, editor of the *Fort Worth Democrat* and an amateur historian, often wrote about northwest Texas and praised Joseph Kemp's development of Wichita Falls. Buckley B. Paddock, *A Twentieth Century History and Biographical Record of North and West Texas*, Volume II (New York: The Lewis Publishing Company, 1906), 444; Buckley B. Paddock, ed., *History of Texas: Fort Worth and the Texas Northwest Edition* (New York: The Lewis Publishing Company, 1922); Buckley B. Paddock, *Early Days in Fort Worth, Much of Which I Saw and Part of Which I Was* (s.l.: s.n., 19–?) in Special Collections, Texas Christian University, Fort Worth, TX; Patricia Lenora Duncan, "Enterprise: B. B. Paddock and Fort Worth: A Case Study of Late Nineteenth Century American Boosterism" (master's thesis, University of Texas at Arlington, 1982).

4. Progressive Era northwest Texans often used the term "upbuilding" to describe economic development in the Big Wichita River Valley. Wichita Falls Chamber of Commerce President R. E. Huff, for example, stated: "What we aim to do is to promote . . . upbuilding of any and all enterprise which make [a] progressive city." The quote is taken from the president's toast at the annual chamber of commerce banquet. January 11, 1910, Wichita Falls Chamber of Commerce Records 1901–1964 (WFCC), Southwest Collection (SWC), Texas Tech University, Lubbock, Texas. For a traditional interpretation of local history see Morgan, *History of Wichita Falls*.

5. Texas and federal official government documents define saline water "as water containing more than 1,000 parts per million of dissolved solids." Allen G. Winslow and L. R. Kister, *Saline-Water Resources of Texas*, Geological Survey water-supply paper, 1365 (Washington, DC: US Government Printing Office, 1956), 1; Jack T. Hughes, *Archeological*

Reconnaissance in the Wichita River Drainage of North-Central Texas (Canyon, TX: Archeological Research Laboratory, Killgore Research Center, West Texas State University, 1972), 2–33.

6. Frederick Jackson Turner, "The Significance of the Frontier in American History," in *The Turner Thesis: Concerning the Role of the Frontier in American History*, edited by George Rogers Taylor (Boston: D. C. Heath and Company, 1956); Frederick Jackson Turner, *The Frontier in America History* (New York: Henry Holt & Co., 1921), 134–36; Walter L. Buenger and Robert A. Calvert, "The Shelf Life of Truth in Texas," in *Texas Through Time: Evolving Interpretations*, edited by Walter L. Buenger and Robert A. Calvert (College Station, TX: Texas A&M University Press, 1991), xiv; Eugene C. Barker, *Life of Stephen F. Austin, Founder of Texas, 1793–1836: A Chapter in the Westward Movement of the Anglo-American People* (Nashville, TN: Cokesbury, 1925); Stephen Stagner, "Epics, Science, and the Lost Frontier: Texas Historical Writing, 1836–1936," *Western Historical Quarterly* 12 (April 1981): 165–81; George P. Garrison, *Texas: A Contest of Civilizations* (New York: Houghton Mifflin, 1903).

7. Terry G. Jordan, "Pioneer Evaluation of Vegetation in Frontier Texas," *Southwestern Historical Quarterly* 76 (January 1973): 232–54; Walter Prescott Webb, *The Great Plains* (Boston: Ginn and Company, 1931); Walter Prescott Webb, "The American West: Perpetual Mirage," *Harper's Magazine* (May 1957).

8. Environmental determinism studies how physical environments predispose societies (or states) towards particular development trajectories. Ellen C. Semple, "Influences of Geographic Environment," *Human Geography: An Essential Anthology*, edited by John Agnew, David N. Livingston, and Alisdair Rogers (Malden, MA: Blackwell Publishers, 1996), and Jordan, "Pioneer Evaluation of Vegetation in Frontier Texas," 232–54.

9. Jordan, "Pioneer Evaluation of Vegetation in Frontier Texas," 232–54; Webb, *The Great Plains*; Norris Hundley, "Water and the West in Historical Imagination," *The Western Historical Quarterly* 27, no. 1 (Spring 1996): 6–7.

10. Donald Worster, *Rivers of Empire: Water, Aridity, and the Growth of the*

American West (New York: Oxford University Press, 1985), 264; Webb, *The Great Plains*, 322; Jordan, "Pioneer Evaluation of Vegetation in Frontier Texas," 232–54.

11. Webb, "The American West"; Patricia Nelson Limerick, *Desert Passages: Encounters with the American Desert* (Albuquerque, NM: University of New Mexico Press, 1985), 77–90; William E. Smythe, *The Conquest of Arid America* (New York: The Macmillan Company, 1911); F. H. Newell, *Principles of Irrigation Engineering: Arid Lands, Water Supply, Storage Works, Dams, Canals, Water Rights and Products* (New York: McGraw-Hill Book Company, 1913); George Thomas, *The Development of Institutions Under Irrigation: With Special Reference to Early Utah Conditions* (New York: The Macmillan Company, 1920).

12. Carl N. Tyson, *The Red River in Southwestern History* (Norman, OK: University of Oklahoma Press, 1981); Harry Sinclair Drago, *Red River Valley: The Mainstream of Frontier History from the Louisiana Bayous to the Texas Panhandle* (New York: Clarkson N. Potter, 1962); Kenneth F. Neighbours, "The Marcy-Neighbours Exploration of the Headwaters of the Brazos and Wichita Rivers in 1854," *Panhandle-Plains Historical Review* 27 (1954): 24–46.

13. Benjamin Kline, *First Along the River: A Brief History of the US Environmental Movement* (San Francisco, CA: Acada Books, 1994), 32–35; Henry David Thoreau, "Walking," *Excursions, The Writings of Henry David Thoreau* (Boston: Riverside Edition, 1893); Henry David Thoreau, *Essay on the Duty of Civil Disobedience and Walden* (New York: Lancer Books, 1968); Ralph Waldo Emerson, *Nature* (Boston: J. Munroe and Company, 1836); George P. Marsh, *The Earth as Modified by Human Action: A New Edition of Man and Nature* (New York: Scribner, Armstrong, and Company, 1874).

14. Frederic L. Bender, "Historical and Theoretical Backgrounds of the *Communist Manifesto*," *The Communist Manifesto* (New York: W. W. Norton & Company, 1988), 26; Karl Marx and Friedrich Engels, "The German Ideology," *The Essential Writings*, edited by Frederic L. Bender (Boulder, CO: Westview, 1986), 165–81; and Friedrich Engels,

Dialectics of Nature, edited and translated by Clemens Dutt (New York: International Publishers, 1940).

15. Alan M. Klein, "Plains Economic Analysis: The Marxist Compliment," *Anthropology on the Great Plains*, edited by W. Raymond Wood and Margot Liberty (Lincoln, NE: University of Nebraska Press, 1980), 129–40; Donald Worster, *Nature's Economy: The Roots of Ecology* (New York: Doubleday, 1979); Worster, *Rivers of Empire*; Donald Worster, "The Dirty Thirties: A Study in Agricultural Capitalism," *Great Plains Quarterly* 6, no. 2 (1986): 107–16; and Donald Worster, *The Ends of the Earth: Perspectives on Modern Environmental History* (New York: Cambridge University Press, 1988). James C. Malin was "the first historian to understand and make constructive use of ecological theory." He analyzed the Dust Bowl and discovered that the newly settled plains farmers did not understand natural limitations. Allan G. Bogue, "James C. Malin: A Voice from the Grassland," *Writing Western History: Essays on Major Western Historians*, edited by Richard W. Etulain (Albuquerque, NM: University of New Mexico Press, 1991); James C. Malin, "The Adaptation of the Agricultural System to Sub-Humid Environment," *Agricultural History* 10 (1936): 339–72; James C. Malin, *History and Ecology: Studies of the Grassland*, edited by Robert P. Swierenga (Lincoln, NE: University of Nebraska Press, 1984).

16. Samuel P. Hays, *Conservation and the Gospel of Efficiency: The Progressive Conservation Movement, 1880–1920* (Pittsburgh, PA: University of Pittsburgh Press, 1959); Roderick Nash, *Wilderness and the American Mind*, Fifth Edition (New Haven, CT: Yale University Press, 2014); William Cronon, *Nature's Metropolis: Chicago and the Great West* (New York: W. W. Norton & Company, 1991); Patricia Nelson Limerick, *Something in the Soil: Legacies and Reckonings in the New West* (New York: W. W. Norton & Company, 2000); Richard White, *Land Use, Environment, and Social Change: The Shaping of Island County, Washington* (Seattle, WA: University of Washington Press, 1992); Mark Fiege, *Irrigated Eden: The Making of an Irrigated Landscape in the American West* (Seattle, WA: University of Washington Press, 1999); Marc Reisner,

Cadillac Desert: The American West and Its Disappearing Water (New York: Penguin Books, 1993).

17. Donald Worster, "Hydraulic Society in California," *Under Western Skies: Nature and History in the American West* (New York: Oxford University Press, 1992), 53; Donald Worster, *Dust Bowl: The Southern Plains in the 1930s* (New York: Oxford University Press, 1979); Worster, *Rivers of Empire*, 22–66; Karl Wittfogel, *Oriental Despotism* (New Haven, CT: Yale University Press, 1957); Donald Worster, "Doing Environmental History," *The Ends of the Earth: Perspectives on Modern Environmental History*, edited by Donald Worster (New York: Cambridge University Press, 1988), 289–307; Donald Worster, "Seeing beyond Culture," *Journal of American History* 76 (March 1990): 1132–36; and Dan Flores, "Nature's Children: Environmental History as Human Natural History," *The Natural West: Environmental History in the Great Plains and Rocky Mountains* (Norman, OK: University of Oklahoma Press, 2001), 9–28.

18. Geoff Cunfer, *On the Great Plains: Agriculture and Environment.* (College Station, TX: Texas A&M University Press, 2005), 10; Donald Worster, "New West, True West: Interpreting the Region's History," *The Western Historical Quarterly* 18, no. 2 (April 1987): 141–46; and Flores, "Nature's Children," 12–13.

19. For histories of the environment and water resources in Texas, see Char Miller, ed., *Fluid Arguments: Five Centuries of Western Water Conflict* (Tucson, AZ: University of Arizona Press, 2001); Char Miller, ed., *On the Border: An Environmental History of San Antonio* (Pittsburgh, PA: University of Pittsburgh Press, 2001); Char Miller, "Streetscape Environmentalism: Floods, Social Justice, and Political Power in San Antonio, 1921–1974," *Southwestern Historical Quarterly* 118, no. 2 (October 2014): 158–77; Dan L. Flores, *Journal of an Indian Trader: Anthony Glass and the Texas Trading Frontier, 1790–1810* (College Station, TX: Texas A&M University Press, 1985); Dan L. Flores, *Caprock Canyonlands: Journeys into the Heart of the Southern Plains* (Austin, TX: University of Texas Press, 1990); Dan L. Flores, *Horizontal Yellow: Nature and History in the Near Southwest* (Albuquerque, NM: University of New Mexico Press, 1999); Dan L.

Flores, *The Natural West: Environmental History in the Great Plains and Rocky Mountains* (Norman, OK: University of Oklahoma Press, 2001); John Opie, Char Miller, and Kenna Lang Archer, *Ogallala: Water for a Dry Land*, Third Edition (Lincoln, NE: University of Nebraska Press, 2018); John Miller Morris, *El Llano Estacado: Exploration and Imagination on the High Plains of Texas and New Mexico, 1536–1860* (Austin, TX: Texas State Historical Association, 1997). For histories of water resources on the Great Plains and in the American West, see Todd M. Kerstetter, *Flood on the Tracks: Living, Dying, and the Nature of Disaster in the Elkhorn River Basin* (Lubbock: Texas Tech University Press, 2018); Donald J. Pisani, *From Family Business to Agribusiness: The Irrigation Crusade in California and the West, 1850–1931* (Berkeley: University of California Press, 1984); Donald Pisani, *To Reclaim a Divided West: Water, Law, and Public Policy, 1848–1902* (Albuquerque: University of New Mexico Press, 1992); Donald Pisani, *Water, Land, and Law in the West: The Limits of Public Policy, 1850–1920* (Lawrence: University Press of Kansas, 1996); Donald Pisani, *Water and American Government: The Reclamation Bureau, National Water Policy, and the West, 1902–1935* (Berkeley: University of California Press, 2002); Norris Hundley, *Water and the West: The Colorado River Compact and the Politics of Water in the American West* (Berkeley: University of California Press, 1975); Norris Hundley Jr., "Water and the West in Historical Imagination: Part Two—A Decade Later," *The Historian* 66, no. 3 (Fall 2004): 455–90. For an environmental history of the Mississippi River, see Christopher Morris, *The Big Muddy: An Environmental History of the Mississippi and Its Peoples from Hernando de Soto to Hurricane Katrina* (New York: Oxford University Press, 2012).

20. Stephen Bogener, *Ditches Across the Desert: Irrigation in the Lower Pecos Valley* (Lubbock, TX: Texas Tech University Press, 2003), 6.

21. James Sherow, *Watering the Valley: Development along the High Plains Arkansas River, 1870–1950* (Lawrence, KS: University Press of Kansas, 1990).

22. James C. Scott, *Seeing Like a State: How Certain Schemes to Improve the Human Condition Have Failed* (New Haven, CT: Yale University

Press, 1998), 2–7, 201, 221, 304–6; James Murton, "Creating Order: The Liberals, the Landowners, and the Draining of Sumas Lake, British Columbia," *Environmental History* 13, no. 1 (January 2008): 95; Benedict Anderson, *Under Three Flags: Anarchism and the Anti-Colonial Imagination* (New York: Verso, 2005), 14–15; Samuel P. Hays, *Conservation and the Gospel of Efficiency: The Progressive Conservation Movement, 1880–1920* (Cambridge, MA: Harvard University Press, 1959), 271.

23. Several firsthand accounts of the hunt exist, including John R. Abernathy, *"Catch 'Em Alive Jack": The Life and Adventures of an American Pioneer* (New York: Association Press, 1936); Theodore Roosevelt's *Outdoor Pastime of an American Hunter* (New York: Charles Scribner's Sons, 1919). Roosevelt's *Scribner's Magazine* article "A Wolf Hunt in Oklahoma." Theodore Roosevelt, "A Wolf Hunt in Oklahoma," *Scribner's Magazine* 39, no. 5 (November 1905). Numerous magazine articles, newspaper stories, and popular history books address Roosevelt's exploits on the prairies, including J. W. Williams's *Big Ranch Country* (Wichita Falls, TX: Nortex, 1954). Only two major scholarly articles tangentially touch on the topic— Brian Lee Smith, "Theodore Roosevelt Visits Oklahoma" *The Chronicles of Oklahoma* (1973) and William T. Hagan, "Kiowas, Comanches, and Cattleman, 1867–1906: A Case Study of the US Reservation Policy," *Pacific Historical Review* 40 (1971): 333–55. This is the first academic treatment to focus on the land ethics of the men involved in the wolf hunt, as well as other environmental aspects of the event. I am using the term "land ethic" as defined by Aldo Leopold. Leopold authored the well-known environmental treatise *A Sand County Almanac*. Aldo Leopold, *A Sand County Almanac* (New York: Oxford University Press, 1972); Aldo Leopold, "The Land Ethic," *Human Geography: An Essential Anthology*, edited by John Agnew, David N. Livingston, and Alisdair Rogers (Malden, MA: Blackwell Publishers, 1996). For traditional views of Abernathy, see: Marilyn Waida, "Jack Abernathy—Oklahoma Legend," *Old West* 5, no. 4 (Summer 1969): 34–37; Wayne Gard, "Teddy Roosevelt's Wolf Hunt," *True West* 9, no. 6 (July–August 1962): 34–35, 52; Glenn Shelton, "The Abernathys Were Amazing," *Wichita Falls Times*

Record News, February 21, 1986; Gertrude Perkins, "Chief Executive's 1905 Visit Is Recalled: Cityan Loaned President Teddy a Gun for Hunt," *The Frederick Daily Leader*, October 22, 1967.

24. Margaret Lee Morgan, "The History and Economic Aspect of the Wichita Valley Irrigation Project" (master's thesis, Southern Methodist University, 1939).

25. For a detailed history of the oil industry, see Kenneth E. Hendrickson Jr., "Red River Uplift: The Emergence of the Oil Industry in North Central Texas, 1901–1921," *Tales of Texoma: Episodes in the History of the Red River Border*, edited by Michael Collins (Wichita Falls, TX: Midwestern State University Press, 2005), 351–81, and Marguerite Sandefer, "The Development of the Oil Industry in Wichita County" (master's thesis, University of Texas, 1938).

26. For excellent regional histories on environmental issues since the mid-twentieth century, see Whitney A. Snow, "A Great Dream for the Valley: Louis Bromfield and the Wichita Falls Malabar Farm, 1949–1954," *Southwestern Historical Quarterly* 119, no. 4 (April 2016): 378–405; Margaret A. Bickers, *Red Water, Black Gold: The Canadian River in Western Texas, 1920–1999* (Denton, TX: Texas State Historical Association, 2014), and Kenna Lang Archer, *Unruly Waters: A Social and Environmental History of the Brazos River* (Albuquerque, NM: University of New Mexico Press, 2015).

CHAPTER 1

1. Several celebratory histories of railroads, cities, and their boosters exist on the Red Rolling Plains. Many of these works were printed in centennial years and now sit on library shelves at local genealogical libraries. Works can be found for Wichita, Clay, Wilbarger, and other Northwest Texas and Southwest Oklahoma counties. For example, see Louise Kelly, *Wichita County Beginnings* (Burnett, TX: Eakin Press, 1982); Steve Wilson, *Wichita Falls: A Pictorial History* (Norfolk, VA: The Donning Co., 1982); Morgan, *The History of Wichita Falls*; Katherine Douthitt,

Romance and Dim Trails: A History of Clay County (Dallas, TX: William T. Tardy Publishers, 1938); Sylvia Jo Jones, *Wilbarger County* (Lubbock, TX: Wilbarger County Historical Commission, 1986); J. P. Earle, *History of Clay County and Northwest Texas* (Austin, TX: The Brick Row Book Shop, 1963); William Charles Taylor, *A History of Clay County* (Austin, TX: Jenkins Publishing Co., 1972); Minnie King Benton, *Boomtown: A Portrait of Burkburnett* (Quanah, TX: Nortex Offset Publications, 1972); Michael Duty, *Wichita Falls: A Century of Photographs* (Wichita Falls, TX: Midwestern State University Press, 1982); and Nancy Hansen, *Wichita Falls: Where Enterprise and Opportunity Meet* (Wichita Falls, TX: Anniversary 100, 1982).

2. Timothy Paul Bowman, *Blood Oranges: Colonialism and Agriculture in the South Texas Borderlands* (College Station, TX: Texas A&M University Press, 2016).

3. Fort Worth and Denver City Railway Company Papers, Manuscript Collection, Southwest Collection, Texas Tech University, Lubbock, TX.

4. Donovan Hofsommer, *Katy Northwest: The Story of a Branch Line Railroad* (Boulder, CO: Pruett Publishing Co., 1976); Morgan, *History of Wichita Falls*; Kelly, *Wichita County Beginnings*; and Missouri, Kansas and Texas Railway Company Records, 1871–1972, Southwest Collection, Texas Tech University, Lubbock, TX.

5. J. W. Williams, "Frank Kell," *West Texas Historical Association Yearbook* 17 (1941). The Frank Kell Collection, CAH; Llerena Friend, "The Frank Kell Collection" in "Frank Kell," Vertical File, CAH and Llerena Friend, "The Frank Kell Collection," *Library Chronicle of the University of Texas* 7 (Fall 1961): 3–6, 7; and Donovan Hofsommer, "Townsite Development on the Wichita Falls and Northwestern Railway," *Great Plains Journal* 16 (Spring 1977): 107–22.

6. "Roosevelt's Hunt," *Dallas Morning News*, April 4, 1905, 2.

7. Ibid.

8. Roosevelt's personal retinue included personnel security agent and Texas Ranger Capt. William J. McDonald, retired Lt. Gen. S. B. M. Young, Rough Rider Lt. B. L. Fortescue, personal physician Dr. Alexander

Lambert, Col. Cecil Lyons, and former Rough Riding sidekick Sloan Simpson. According to Oklahoman historian Brian Lee Smith many of Teddy's Rough Riders (First United States Volunteer Cavalry in Cuba) in the Spanish-American War hailed from Oklahoma and Indian Territories. Brian Lee Smith, "Theodore Roosevelt Visits Oklahoma," *The Chronicles of Oklahoma* LI, no. 3 (Fall 1973): 263–79. Also, see Teddy Roosevelt, *Outdoor Pastime of an American Hunter* (New York: Charles Scribner's Sons, 1919), 112–13 for listing of the wolf-hunt attendees. Sloan Simpson was from Fort Worth. According to the *Handbook of Texas Online* Captain McDonald "moved to Wichita County [1883], where he occupied himself first with cattle, then with lumber. After reinvesting in cattle about two years later, he filed on school land in Hardeman County, where he soon became deputy sheriff, special ranger, and United States deputy marshal of the Northern District of Texas and the Southern District of Kansas [and Texas] ranger captain from 1891 to 1907." According to Albert Bigelow Paine, a biographer of Capt. Bill McDonald, McDonald was unhappy with the governor's assignment to protect President Theodore Roosevelt, telling the Texas governor he was a "hell-roarin' democrat, and don't care much for republican presidents in general and this one in particular. I'd rather you picked another man for the job." The governor ordered McDonald to join the president's party at the Fort Worth railway stop despite his objections. Albert Bigelow Paine, *Captain Bill McDonald: Texas Ranger* (New York: J.J. Little and Ives Co., 1909), 273–74; Harold J. Weiss Jr. and Rie Jaratt, "McDonald, William Jesse," *Handbook of Texas Online*, accessed November 14, 2022, https://www.tshaonline.org/handbook/entries/mcdonald-william-jesse. Also, see Virgil E. Baugh, *A Pair of Texas Rangers: Bill McDonald and John Hughes* (Washington, DC: Potomac Corral, the Westerners, 1970) and Tyler Madeleine Mason, *Riding for Texas: The True Adventures of Captain Bill McDonald of the Texas Rangers* (New York: Reynal and Hitchcock, 1936); *Frederick Enterprise*, April 14, 1905, in microfiche box Frederick Weekly Enterprise, June 17, 1904 thru June 25, 1908 (3292-17) at Frederick Public Library, Frederick, OK (hereafter cited as FPL).

9. Maj. H. L. Ripley led the contingent from Fort Sill. *Frederick Enterprise*, April 7, 1905; *The Davidson Post*, April 7, 1905; *Frederick Enterprise*, April 14, 1905; and Brian Lee Smith, "Theodore Roosevelt Visits Oklahoma," *The Chronicles of Oklahoma* LI, no. 3 (Fall 1973): 271–72.

10. *Frederick Enterprise*, April 14, 1905, and Smith, "Theodore Roosevelt Visits Oklahoma," 274–75. Despite the president's request to go unmolested and the soldiers from Fort Sill guarding the perimeter of the hunt, several onlookers bypassed the pickets. Texas Ranger Capt. Bill McDonald intercepted these interlopers and "sent them packing." Paine, *Captain Bill McDonald*, 287.

11. Paine, *Captain Bill McDonald*, 276.

12. Ibid., 276–77.

13. Paine, *Captain Bill McDonald*, 273–77; "President Enters Texas: Big Crowds Cheer Him," *New York Tribune*, April 6, 1905; "President Ready to Begin Hunt. Week's Tour of Southwest at an End and He is Now on Ranch in Territory," *Fort Worth Telegram*, April 9, 1905; "President Roosevelt," *Fort Worth Telegram*, April 8, 1905; "The Daddy of 'Em All," *Fort Worth Telegram*, April 9, 1905; "Fort Worth Gives Roosevelt Record-Breaking Reception," *Fort Worth Telegram*, April 8, 1905, Fort Worth Star-Telegram Collection, University of Texas at Arlington (UTA) Libraries; "President Theodore Roosevelt's visit to Fort Worth near City Hall, 1905," Fort Worth Star-Telegram Collection, UTA Libraries Digital Gallery, 1905, https://library.uta.edu/digitalgallery/img/10021048; "President Theodore Roosevelt in Fort Worth, Texas, 1905," Fort Worth Star-Telegram Collection, UTA Libraries Digital Gallery, 1905, https://library.uta.edu/digitalgallery/img/10009760; "President Theodore Roosevelt's visit to Fort Worth, 1905," Fort Worth Star-Telegram Collection, UTA Libraries Digital Gallery, 1905, https://library.uta.edu/digitalgallery/img/10021050

14. "Pres. Roosevelt Arrived in Frederick last Sunday afternoon and Welcomed by about 6,000 Oklahomans: IS IN FAVOR OF IMMEDIATE STATEHOOD," *Frederick Enterprise*, April 14, 1905.

15. Smith, "Theodore Roosevelt Visits Oklahoma," 264.

16. Roosevelt, *Outdoor Pastime of an American Hunter*, 113. John R. Abernathy, born on January 28, 1876, worked in his youth on the ranch of Charles Goodnight where he discovered his wolf-catching ability. Abernathy, not only a wolf hunter, was also a talented lawman. After establishing his own ranch in Greer County, he worked as a deputy marshal in Southwestern Oklahoma, Roosevelt-appointed Marshal of Oklahoma, Secret Service agent, and even as an agent for the Mexican secret service during the Francesco Madero presidency. He later became a wildcat oil driller, lost his fortune during the Depression, and retired to California. He died on January 11, 1941. It would be an understatement to say that Abernathy was an interesting character.

17. Abernathy, *"Catch 'Em Alive Jack": The Life and Adventures of an American Pioneer*; Roosevelt, *Outdoor Pastime of an American Hunter*; Roosevelt, "A Wolf Hunt in Oklahoma"; Smith, "Theodore Roosevelt Visits Oklahoma"; and Hagan, "Kiowas, Comanches, and Cattleman, 1867–1906."

18. "Echoes from the Wolf Chase," *Frederick Enterprise*, Friday, April 21, 1905. The subheading to the newspaper article read, "John R. Abernathy, by his Phenomenal Prowess as a Wolf Catcher, During his Recent Hunt With President Roosevelt and Party in the Big Pasture East of Frederick, is now the recognized World's Champion."

19. "Echoes from the Wolf Chase," *Frederick Enterprise*, Friday, April 21, 1905; Abernathy, *"Catch 'Em Alive Jack."* "To Hunt in Texas," *Dallas Morning News*, January 30, 1904, 1. Lyons served as the chairman of the Texas State Republican Executive Committee.

20. "Echoes from the Wolf Chase," *Frederick Enterprise*, April 21, 1905.

21. Ibid.

22. Robert G. Bailey, ed., *Description of the Ecoregions of the United States*, Forest Service, US Department of Agriculture (October 1980), prepared in cooperation with US Fish and Wildlife Service, Government Documents Division, Mary Couts Burnett Library, Texas Christian University, Fort Worth, TX.

23. Roosevelt, "A Wolf Hunt in Oklahoma," 514.

24. Teddy Roosevelt, *Outdoor Pastime of an American Hunter*, 113.

25. Dan Flores, "Wolf Song Redux," *Horizontal Yellow: Nature and History in the Near Southwest* (Albuquerque, NM: University of New Mexico Press, 1999), 257.

26. See Robert Darnton, *The Great Cat Massacre* and Flores, "Wolf Song Redux," 250–79.

27. Flores, "Wolf Song Redux," 257.

28. Flores, "Wolf Song Redux," 264.

29. Roosevelt, "A Wolf Hunt in Oklahoma," 528.

30. John Terbough, and J. A. Estes, *Trophic Cascades: Predators, Prey, and the Changing Dynamics of Nature* (Washington, DC: Island Press, 2010), 1–7.

31. George Monbiot, *Feral: Rewilding the Land, the Sea, and Human Life* (Chicago, IL: University of Chicago Press, 2017), and Dave Foreman, *Rewilding North America: A Vision for Conservation in the 21st Century* (Washington, DC: Island Press, 2004). For a discussion of rewilding the Great Plains, see Dan Flores, *American Serengeti: The Last Big Animals of the Great Plains* (Lawrence, KS: University Press of Kansas, 2016).

32. Dan Flores, *Coyote America: A Natural and Supernatural History* (New York: Basic Books, 2016); Flores, "Wolf Song Redux," 258; Andrew Isenberg, *The Destruction of the Bison: An Environmental History, 1750–1920* (New York: Cambridge University Press, 2000); and George Caitlin, *Letters and Notes of the Manners, Customs, and Conditions of the North American Indians*, Vol. 2 (London, 1841).

33. "Black Wolf Captured," *Dallas Morning News*, March 16, 1905, 9.

34. Ibid.

35. Ibid.

36. Cristina Eisenberg, *The Carnivore Way: Coexisting with and Conserving North America's Predators* (Washington, DC: Island Press, 2014), 120 and Flores, *Coyote America*, 34.

37. Flores, *Coyote America*, 34.

38. "Fate of Abernathy's Wolf," *Dallas Morning News*, July 29, 1905, 7.

39. Ibid. Stephanie Rutherford, "The Anthropocene's Animal? Coywolves as Feral Cotravelers," *Environment & Planning E: Nature & Space* 1, no.

1/2 (March 2018): 206–23.

40. "Black Wolf Captured," *Dallas Morning News,* March 16, 1905, 9, and Rutherford, "The Anthropocene's Animal?," 206–23.

41. Roosevelt, *Outdoor Pastime of an American Hunter,* 113.

42. Paine, *Captain Bill McDonald,* 278.

43. Smith, "Theodore Roosevelt Visits Oklahoma," 273–74. Quote from "Sam Bass" painting Photo #4 in John R. Abernathy Photographic Collection, Museum of the Great Plains, Lawton, OK. The teams of hounds photographed include "trail hounds" and "greyhounds." See Photograph #1, Photograph #3, Photograph #4, Photograph #5, Photograph #6, Photograph #8, Photograph #12, *Scribner's Magazine* Collection, Museum of the Great Plains, Lawton, OK.

44. Roosevelt, "A Wolf Hunt in Oklahoma," 524.

45. Ibid.

46. Photo #6 in John R. Abernathy Photographic Collection, Museum of the Great Plains.

47. Abernathy, *"Catch 'Em Alive Jack"*; Smith, "Theodore Roosevelt Visits Oklahoma," 273–74; Photo #8 in John R. Abernathy Photographic Collection, Museum of the Great Plains. Other accounts describe a similar scene of amazement at Abernathy's hunting abilities and Roosevelt's riding abilities, for example, Albert Bigelow Paine described Captain McDonald's account of Abernathy this way: "Abernathy by a quick movement of his hand caught the wolf by the lower jaw and held him fast. . . . Well, of course, President Roosevelt admired that beyond any feature of the expedition. He had Abernathy do it again and again." Paine also wrote that "As the Ranger Captain saw the Chief Executive of the nation go careering over ditches and washouts and through prairie dogs cities, his admiration grew literally by leaps and hounds." Paine, *Captain Bill McDonald,* 278–80; W. Sloan Simpson, "President Theodore Roosevelt and Group of Noted West Texans on Famous Wolf Hunt, May 1906," Doris A. and Lawrence H. Budner, Theodore Roosevelt Collection, DeGolyer Library, Southern Methodist University, Dallas, TX.

48. Smith, "Theodore Roosevelt Visits Oklahoma," 263–79.

49. Frederick Jackson Turner, "The Significance of the Frontier in American History," *The Turner Thesis: Concerning the Role of the Frontier in American History*, edited by George Rogers Taylor (Boston, MA: D. C. Heath and Company, 1956).

50. Theodore Roosevelt, *The Winning of the West* (New York: The Current Literature Publishing Company, 1905).

51. Smith, "Theodore Roosevelt Visits Oklahoma," 266.

52. Remarks from the President, *Frederick Enterprise*, April 14, 1905, found online at https://www.presidency.ucsb.edu/documents/remarks-frederick-oklahoma.

53. Ibid.

54. Denevan, "The Pristine Myth"; Thomas W. Kavanagh, *Comanche Political History: An Ethnohistorical Perspective, 1705–1875* (Lincoln, NE: University of Nebraska Press, 1996); Hagan, "Kiowas, Comanches, and Cattleman, 1867–1906: A Case Study of the US Reservation Policy," 333–55; William T. Hagan, *United States-Comanche Relations: The Reservation Years* (New Haven, CT: Yale University Press, 1976); William T. Hagan, *Quanah Parker, Comanche Chief* (Norman, OK: University of Oklahoma Press, 1993); Morris W. Foster, *Being Comanche: A Social History of an American Indian Community* (Tucson, AZ: The University of Arizona Press, 1991); and Blue Clark, Lone Wolf v. Hitchcock: *Treaty Rights and Indian Law at the End of the Nineteenth Century* (Lincoln, NE: University of Nebraska Press, 1994).

55. Roosevelt, "A Wolf Hunt in Oklahoma," 524.

56. Samuel Hays, *Conservation and the Gospel of Efficiency* (Cambridge, MA: Harvard University Press, 1959).

57. "Echoes from the Wolf Chase," *Frederick Enterprise*, April 21, 1905.

58. Flores, "Wolf Song Redux," 259–60.

59. "Echoes from the Wolf Chase," *Frederick Enterprise*, April 21, 1905.

60. Roosevelt, "A Wolf Hunt in Oklahoma," 530.

61. Abernathy, *"Catch 'Em Alive Jack,"* 5.

62. Smith, "Theodore Roosevelt Visits Oklahoma," 271, and Photographs and Newspapers Collection, Pioneer Heritage Townsite Center, Tillman

County, Historical and Educational Society, Frederick, OK.

63. "Echoes from the Wolf Chase," *Frederick Enterprise*, April 21, 1905.

64. Hagan, "Kiowas, Comanches, and Cattleman, 1867–1906," 355.

65. B. W. Allred, "Distribution and Control of Several Woody Plants in Texas and Oklahoma," *Journal of Range Management* 2, no. 1 (January 1949): 17–29.

66. Allred, "Distribution and Control of Several Woody Plants in Texas and Oklahoma," 17–29, and B. G. Freeman, et al., *An Economic Analysis of Mesquite Spraying in the Rolling Plains of Texas* (Lubbock, TX: Texas Tech University, College of Agricultural Sciences, 1978).

67. Kelly, *Wichita County Beginnings*, 8.

68. Kelly, *Wichita County Beginnings*, 8, and Electra, Texas Photograph Collection, Southwest Collection, Texas Tech University, Lubbock, TX.

69. Memoirs of John Hirshi As Told to Ms. Edith Slaten, February 27, 1957, Diamond Jubilee 1882–1957: Early History Wichita County and North Texas, Wichita County, Texas, Historical Series, February 1957, Moffett Library, Special Collections, Midwestern State University, Wichita Falls, TX.

70. Roosevelt, *Outdoor Pastime of an American Hunter*, 113. The buggy with its occupants was photographed and can be seen in Photograph #3 in *Scribner's Magazine* Collection, Museum of the Great Plains.

71. C. L. Douglas, *Cattle Kings of Texas* (Fort Worth, TX: Branch-Smith, 1939, 1968), 351; Samuel Burk Burnett, Wichita County Folder, Recorded Texas Historic Landmarks, Texas Historical Commission (THC), Austin, TX; and Kelly, *Wichita County Beginnings*, 8–9.

72. Samuel Burk Burnett, Wichita County Folder, Recorded Texas Historic Landmarks, THC, Austin, TX; Kelly, *Wichita County Beginnings*, 8–9; Douglas, *Cattle Kings of Texas*, 353.

73. Samuel Burk Burnett, Wichita County Folder, THC; and *Wichita Daily Times*, May 14, 1907.

74. Roosevelt, *Outdoor Pastime of an American Hunter*, 113.

75. Williams, *Big Ranch Country*, 144.

76. Martin, "Samuel Burk Burnett: Old 6666," 28.

77. Hagan, *United States-Comanche Relations*, 279–80. Photograph #13 *Scribner's Magazine* Collection, Museum of the Great Plains.
78. *Frederick Enterprise*, April 14, 1905.
79. Hagan, *United States-Comanche Relations*, 280.
80. "Echoes from the Wolf Chase," *Frederick Enterprise*, April 21, 1905.
81. "Pres Roosevelt Ended his Big Hunt and Left Last Night for Colorado—Makes a Characteristic Talk," *Frederick Enterprise*, April 14, 1905.
82. Hagan, *United States-Comanche Relations*, 284–85.
83. Roosevelt, "A Wolf Hunt in Oklahoma," 514.
84. Paine, *Captain Bill McDonald*, 281–82 and "Sweet Wolfhowl," *Dallas Morning News*, April 12, 1905, 2.
85. *Frederick Enterprise* had United States Congressman John Hall Stephens's name wrong. Roosevelt, "A Wolf Hunt in Oklahoma," 528 and "Pres Roosevelt Ended his Big Hunt," *Frederick Enterprise*, April 14, 1905.
86. "Pres Roosevelt Ended his Big Hunt," *Frederick Enterprise*, April 14, 1905.
87. *Frederick Enterprise*, April 14, 1905, and Smith, "Theodore Roosevelt Visits Oklahoma," 274–75. After the wolf hunt, Roosevelt carried on to Colorado for a bear hunt. Paine, *Captain Bill McDonald*, 288.
88. "Stockmen May Come," *Dallas Morning News*, March 19, 1905, 11.
89. September 26, 1892, Jerome Commission Council Minutes Comanche, Kiowa, and Apache at Fort Sill, Indian Territory, File 061, Central Files, Record Group 75 Bureau of Indian Affairs, Kiowa Agency, National Archives and Records Administration (NARA), Fort Worth, Texas.
90. Alta Abernathy and Temple Abernathy, *Bud & Me: The True Adventures of the Abernathy Boys* (Irving, TX: Dove Creek Press, 1998).

CHAPTER 2

1. Registration Sheet of A. E. Gwinn for Golden Jubilee, Wichita Falls, Texas, September 26, 27, and 28, 1932, Historical Survey, Wichita Falls, TX, CAH.
2. Registration Sheet of Noland Howard for Golden Jubilee, Wichita

Falls, Texas, September 26, 27, and 28, 1932, Historical Survey, Wichita Falls, TX, CAH.

3. Mary Basham Loggie, "Joseph Sterling Bridwell" (master's thesis, Midwestern State University, 1967), 28.

4. August 27, 1918, Meeting Minutes, WFCC.

5. Randolph B. Marcy, *Exploration of the Red River of Louisiana in the Year 1852* (Washington, DC, 1854), 6; Katricia Cochran, "Early Area Explorer Reported 'Land Not Fit For Habitation,'" *Wichita Falls Times*, October 7, 1962, Expeditions and Trails Section, Book 16, WCA; Williams and Neighbours, *Old Texas Trails*, 254; Randolph B. Marcy, *Exploration of the Big Wichita, Etc.* (Wichita Falls, TX: Terry Brothers, 1962), 3–5 and 7; W. Eugene Hollon, *Beyond the Cross Timbers: The Travels of Randolph B. Marcy, 1812–1887* (Norman, OK: University of Oklahoma Press, 1955), 163–81; Reminiscences of Mrs. A. H. Carrigan, Wichita Falls Reminiscences, WFPL; C. H. Gordon, *Geology and Underground Waters of the Wichita Region, North-Central Texas* (Washington, DC: Government Printing Office, 1913). After his initial exploration in 1852, from July 15, 1854, to August 21, 1854, Marcy and his bluecoats explored and surveyed Northwest and North Central Texas in detail in search of reservation lands for Texas Indians. Marcy observed in his journal of the Big Wichita River Basin environment, "a barren and parsimonious soil . . . of scarcity of wood or good water" rendering "it probable that this section was not designed by the Creator for occupation." Marcy questioned if the next century would see it populated at all. The lack of woodland, "and the very great scarcity of good water," rendered the Big Wichita River "unsuited to . . . agriculture." Marcy, *Exploration of the Big Wichita, Etc.*

6. Winslow and Kister, *Saline-Water Resources of Texas*. The Wichita Rivers are tributaries in the Red River Basin, and thus the greater Mississippi River drainage basin. According to ecologists and biologists, the Upper Red River Basin lies on the "Great Plains" province in the "Osage Plains" section. This portion of the Great Plains, often called the "Rolling Red Plains," creates an undulating topography. The Big and Little Wichita River Valleys run through the gently rolling mesquite plains, with

elevations near 1,000 feet.

7.   J. O. Joerns, *Investigations of Sources of Natural Pollution, Wichita River Basin Above Lake Kemp, Texas, 1951–1957* (Austin, TX: Surface Water Branch, 1961), and Gene R. Wilde and Bailey Gaines, *Identification of Refugia Habitat, Faunal Survey of Collection Areas, and Monitoring of Riparian and Stream Habitat and Biotic Communities in the Wichita River Basin, Texas* (Tulsa, OK: Weston Solutions, Inc. and US Army Corps of Engineers, Tulsa District, October 26, 2006), Department of Range, Wildlife, and Fisheries Management, Texas Tech University, Lubbock, TX. Wilde and Gaines's study is an unprocessed document at the Southwest Collection, Texas Tech University, Lubbock, TX.

8.   Hughes, *Archeological Reconnaissance in the Wichita River Drainage of North-Central Texas*, 2–34.

9.   Wilde and Gaines, *Identification of Refugia Habitat*; Joerns, *Investigations of Sources of Natural Pollution*; Leo D. Lewis and Walter Woelber Dalquest, *A Fisheries Survey of the Big Wichita River System and Its Impoundments* (Austin, TX: Texas Game and Fish Commission, 1957); Winslow and Kister, *Saline-Water Resources of Texas*, 18–19. Texas A&M University System, *Agricultural Resources Related to Water Development in Texas* (College Station, TX: Texas A&M University, Water Resources Institute, 1968); Morris E. Bloodworth, *Some Principles and Practices in the Irrigation of Texas Soils* (College Station, TX: Texas Agricultural Experiment Station, 1959), 27; Wichita Falls, Texas, 1963, Local Climatological Data with Comparative Data, Weather Bureau, US Department of Commerce, Wichita Falls, Texas, Vertical File, CAH.

10.   Annual average rainfall in Wichita, Baylor, Archer, and Wilbarger was 24 inches in the Wichita County irrigation districts. Of the thirty-one rainfall station locations on the High Plains and Rolling Plains the lowest annual precipitation ever recorded was about twelve or thirteen inches, and in most cases, it occurred in 1917. The highest annual precipitation was in the range of forty-nine to fifty-nine inches and at most locations occurred in 1941. The normal annual rainfall in Wichita Falls was around 26.2 inches per year. John T. Carr, *The Climate and Physiography*

of Texas (Austin, TX: Texas Water Development Board, 1967); Wichita Falls, Texas, 1963, Local Climatological Data with Comparative Data; Bloodworth, *Some Principles and Practices in the Irrigation of Texas Soils*, 6; Texas Technological College, Abstracts of Publications on West Texas Water Resources, 1967; and R. J. Hildreth and Gerald W. Thomas, *Farming and Ranching Risk As Influenced by Rainfall 1: High and Rolling Plains of Texas* (College Station, TX: Texas Agricultural Experiment Station, 1956), 1–39.

11. Charles J. Bicak, "The Rigors of Existence on the Great Plains: The Role of Water," *Water on the Great Plains: Issues and Policies*, edited by Peter J. Longo and David W. Yoskowitz (Lubbock, TX: Texas Tech University Press, 2002), 3–15. Geologic history and climatologic data indicate the region ill-suited for human habitation. Water resources certainly did not determine but limited sizes of groups residing in or traveling across the Rolling Red Plains. Gerald Meek Etchieson, Roberta D. Speer, and Jack T. Hughes, *Archeological Investigations in the Crowell Reservoir Area, Cottle, Foard, King, and Knox Counties, Texas* (Canyon, TX: West Texas State University Killgore Research Center, August 1979), 21.

12. Baldys, Bush, and Kidwell, *Effects of Low-Flow Diversions*, 1–32; J. Keller, J. Rawson, H. Grubb, J. Kramer, G. Sullivan, *Report on the Evaluation of the Effectiveness of Operation Area VIII Red River Chloride Control Project: Red River Chloride Control Project Report* (Washington, DC: Government Printing Office, 1988), 35; Bloodworth, *Some Principles and Practices in the Irrigation of Texas Soils*, 6, and Hildreth and Thomas, *Farming and Ranching Risk As Influenced by Rainfall*, 1–39. According to the Texas Agricultural Experiment Station, for example, eighteen to twenty-four inches of annual rainfall resulted in relatively high yields for most crops. But farmers in the upper Red River Basin found they could not depend on average annual rainfall.

13. Samuel P. Hays, *Conservation and the Gospel of Efficiency: The Progressive Conservation Movement, 1880–1920* (Cambridge: Harvard University Press, 1959).

14. The *Dallas Morning News* and its agricultural editor V. H. Scoeffelmayer

often referred to Kemp as the "Father of Texas Irrigation." Furthermore, Kemp was billed as the Father of Texas Irrigation at several meetings across the state in the late 1890s and early 1900s. *Wichita Falls Record News*, November 17, 1930, 1; "Irrigation Meeting Called for Oct. 3–4," *Dallas Morning News*, Section 1, p. 4; *The Better City* 1, no. 6 (June 1, 1920), WFCC, SWC; Paddock, *A Twentieth Century History and Biographical Record of North and West Texas*; Buckley B. Paddock, *The History of Texas: Fort Worth and the Texas Northwest Edition*, Vol. III (Chicago, IL: Lewis Publishing, 1922), 8–11; Buckley B. Paddock, *Early Days in Fort Worth* (Fort Worth, n.d.); Patricia L. Duncan, "Enterprise: B. B. Paddock and Fort Worth—A Case Study of Late Nineteenth Century American Boosterism" (master's thesis, University of Texas at Arlington, 1982); Worth Robert Miller, "Building a Progressive Coalition in Texas: The Populist-Reform Democrat Rapprochement, 1900–1907," *The Journal of Southern History* 102, no. 2 (May 1986): 164; and Alwyn Barr, *Reconstruction to Reform: Texas Politics, 1876–1906* (Austin, 1971), 125; June 15, 1909, Reel 1, 1901–1918 Minutes, WFCC, SWC; James Aubrey Tinsley, "The Progressive Movement in Texas" (PhD diss., University of Wisconsin, 1953); Norman D. Brown, *Hood, Bonnet, and Little Brown Bag: Texas Politics, 1921–1928* (College Station, TX: Texas A&M University Press, 1984); George B. Tindall, *The Emergence of the New South, 1913–1945* (Baton Rouge, LA: Louisiana State Press, 1967); Larry D. Hill, "Texas Progressivism: A Search for Definition," *Texas Through Time: Evolving Interpretations*, edited by Walter L. Buenger and Robert A. Calvert (College Station, TX: Texas A&M University Press, 1991), 246; "Irrigation in Texas," *Dallas Morning News*, May 17, 1903, 18.

15. Henry Sayles Jr. Papers, Manuscript Collection, SWC; Hays, *Conservation and the Gospel of Efficiency*; Samuel P. Hays, "The Politics of Reform in Municipal Government in the Progressive Era," *Pacific Northwest Quarterly* 55 (October 1964), 157–69; John T. Cumbler, "Conflict, Accommodation, and Compromise: Connecticut's Attempt to Control Industrial Wastes in the Progressive Era," *Environmental History* 5 (July 2000): 315, 328; Robert E. Bonner, "Buffalo Bill Cody and Wyoming

Water Politics," *Western Historical Quarterly* 33, no. 4 (Winter 2002): 433–52; Brian Balough, "Scientific Forestry and the Roots of the Modern American State: Gifford Pinchot's Path to Progressive Reform," *Environmental History* 7 (April 2002): 198–225; Luna B. Leopold, *Conservation and Water Management—Part C—the Conservation Attitude*, circular 414, US Geological Survey, 1960.

16. "Prominent Financier and Texas Railroad Builder Passes Away," *Dallas Morning News*, November 17, 1930; "Joseph Alexander Kemp," Vertical File, CAH; Registration Sheet of Mary McKissack, Historical Survey of Wichita Falls, CAH; and Memoirs of Mrs. J. A. Kemp in *Diamond Jubilee 1882–1957: Early History Wichita County and North Texas*, Wichita County, Texas, Historical Series (February 1957), Recorded by Edith Slaten, January 10, 1957, Moffett Library, Midwestern State University, Wichita Falls, TX.

17. The United States Census indicates the Wichita County population in 1880 at 433 and 4,831 in 1890. In 1883 Texas opened some western school lands, drawing thousands of immigrant farmers to the area. And one of the worst droughts in Texas history occurred from 1884 to 1886, causing most of the farmers to fail and to return to the East. *Dallas Morning News*, October 4, 1924, 1; J. W. Williams, "A Statistical Study of the Drought of 1886," *West Texas Historical Association Yearbook* 21 (1945); and "Droughts," *Handbook of Texas Online*, Texas State Historical Association, http://www.tshaonline.org/handbook/online/articles/DD/ybd1.html; US Department of Commerce, Bureau of the Census Records, 1860–1930.

18. "Subject of Irrigation," *Dallas Morning News*, February 27, 1897, 7.

19. *Dallas Morning News*, October 4, 1924, 1, and John S. Spratt, *The Road the Spindletop* (Austin, TX: University of Texas Press, 1970).

20. Morgan, "The History and Economic Aspect of the Wichita Valley Irrigation Project," 123–24; Condor Petroleum Company, Folder, Henry Sayles Jr. Papers, Manuscript Collection, SWC; Morgan Jones, Hutton Sam Bellah, Gus Newby, Jack Jones, Alex Albright, George Fleming, and Will Rayburn claimed to have all served on some of these early surveying

trips. The engineer mentioned here was Hutton Sam Bellah of Decatur. "Joseph Alexander Kemp," Vertical File, CAH; "Subject of Irrigation," *Dallas Morning News*, February 27, 1897, 7; Registration Sheet of George Fleming, Historical Survey of Wichita Falls, CAH; Registration Sheet of Alex Albright, Historical Survey of Wichita Falls, CAH; and "Wichita Falls Irrigation Project," *Wichita Daily Times*, April 24, 1924.

21. Morgan, "The History and Economic Aspect of the Wichita Valley Irrigation Project," 124, and *Wichita Daily Times*, June 14, 1922.

22. "Constitution of 1876," *Handbook of Texas Online*, Texas State Historical Association, http://www.tshaonline.org/handbook/online/articles/CC/mhc7.html.

23. John Opie, "John Wesley Powell Was Right: Resizing the Ogallala High Plains," *Fluid Arguments: Five Centuries of Western Water Conflict*, edited by Char Miller (Tucson, AZ: University of Arizona Press, 2001), 223–47.

24. The Frank Kell Collection, CAH; Llerena Friend, "The Frank Kell Collection" in "Frank Kell," Vertical File, CAH; and Llerena Friend, "The Frank Kell Collection," *Library Chronicle of the University of Texas* 7 (Fall 1961): 3–6, 7.

25. Judge Henry Sayles Sr., born in Washington County, Texas, studied law and became a lawyer. He practiced law in Galveston from 1873 to 1886 and moved to Abilene in 1886. "Subject of Irrigation," *Dallas Morning News*, February 27, 1897, 7, and Henry Sayles Jr. Papers, Manuscript Collection, SWC.

26. Morgan, "The History and Economic Aspect of the Wichita Valley Irrigation Project," 124.

27. "From Congressman Stephens," *Dallas Morning News*, June 27, 1897, 8.

28. *Dallas Morning News*, October 4, 1924, 1; "Holliday Creek," *Handbook of Texas Online*, Texas State Historical Association, http://www.tshaonline.org/handbook/online/articles/HH/rbh92.html; Taylor, *Irrigation Systems of Texas*.

29. Highland Irrigated Farms, Highland Irrigation and Land Company, Wichita Falls, Texas, 1910, CAH, Austin, TX; T. U. Taylor, *Irrigation Systems of Texas* (Washington, DC: Government Printing Office, 1902),

79; *Holliday and McGrath Creeks, Wichita Falls, Texas, Flood Plain Information*, Prepared for the City of Wichita Falls by the Department of the Army, Tulsa District, Corps of Engineers, Tulsa, OK, May 1976; "Big Profit in Irrigation," *Dallas Morning News*, November 5, 1900, 1; Henry Sayles Jr. Papers, Manuscript Collection, SWC, Texas Tech University, Lubbock, TX; "Round About Town," *Dallas Morning News*, June 24, 1901, 5.

30. Highland Irrigated Farms, Highland Irrigation and Land Company, Wichita Falls, Texas, 1910, CAH, Austin, TX.

31. "Farming by Irrigation," *Dallas Morning News*, September 23, 1903, 7; "Joseph Alexander Kemp," Vertical File, CAH.

32. Morgan, "The History and Economic Aspect of the Wichita Valley Irrigation Project," 126.

33. "Urge Amendment to State Constitution," *Dallas Morning News*, March 16, 1917, 18.

34. George McQuaid, "Conservation Plans Follow the Streams," *Dallas Morning News*, February 16, 1918, 5; "Urge Amendment to State Constitution," *Dallas Morning News*, March 16, 1917, 18.

35. March 4, 1913, WFCC, SWC; October 28, 1913, WFCC, SWC; and Registration Sheet of J. L. Jackson Sr., Historical Survey of Wichita Falls, CAH; *Flood Plain Information: Holiday and McGrath Creeks*, 2; Agriculture, Thirteenth Census of the United States, Vol. VII (Washington, DC: 1910); "Joseph Alexander Kemp," *Handbook of Texas Online*, Texas State Historical Association, http://www.tshaonline.org/handbook/online/articles/KK/fke14.html; Jimmy E. Banks, article, Iowa Park Centennial, published by the Iowa Park Leader, October 1988, Personal Papers of Jimmy E. Banks; John Gunther, *Taken at the Flood: The Story of Albert D. Lasker* (New York: Harper, 1960); Natalie Ornish, *Pioneer Jewish Texans* (Dallas, TX: Texas Heritage, 1989); Isaac H. Kempner, *H. Kempner: The First One Hundred Years* (Houston: Texas Gulf Coast Historical Association Publication, 1958); Katharyn Duff, "The Story of a Prairie Newspaper," *Abilene Remembered: Our Centennial Treasury Book* (Abilene, TX: Abilene Reporter, 1981); Henry J. Sayles

Papers, SWC; Paddock, *History and Biographical Record of North and West Texas*, Vol. II, 444–45; and Memoirs of Mrs. J. A. Kemp, Recorded by Edith Slaten, January 10, 1957, WFPL.

36. "Texas Irrigation Laws and Their Application," *Dallas Morning News*, June 24, 1910, 7.

37. March 18, 1918, Board of Directors' Meeting Minutes, WFCC, SWC.

38. Kemp, Scurry, and Vernon Sullivan lobbied on behalf of Wichita Falls and Pecos, Texas. "Texans Urge Passage of Irrigation Bond Measure," March 23, 1918, *Dallas Morning News*; "Pecos Valley Farmers Ask Aid in Building Dam," February 27, 1918, *Dallas Morning News*; September 3, 1918, Board of Directors' Meeting Minutes, WFCC, SWC.

39. Morgan, "The History and Economic Aspect of the Wichita Valley Irrigation Project," 129.

40. Ibid.

41. Morgan, "The History and Economic Aspect of the Wichita Valley Irrigation Project," 129; "Joseph Alexander Kemp," Vertical File, CAH; July 8, 1919, WFCC, SWC.

42. "Wichita Falls: Where Today's Dream is Tomorrow's Achievement," October 1919, WFCC, SWC.

43. Ibid.

44. December 16, 1919, WFCC, SWC; "Wichita Falls: Where Today's Dream is Tomorrow's Achievement," October 1919, WFCC, SWC.

45. Swing musicians such as Harry James toured through Texas, stopping off to perform at the Lake Wichita pavilion. Lana Thomas, "Lake Wichita: Early Resort," Irrigation Highland Subsection, Irrigation District Section, Book 19, WCA; "To Play for Lake Wichita Dance," *Wichita Daily Times*, September 29, 1946, Lake Wichita Section, Book 19, WCA. For an excellent discussion of city boosters in mass-developing cities, as well as commodification during the Gilded Age and Progressive Era, see William Cronon, *Nature's Metropolis: Chicago and the Great West* (New York: W. W. Norton & Company, 1991); "Prominent Financier and Texas Railroad Builder Passes Away," *Dallas Morning News*, November 17, 1930; and "Joseph Alexander Kemp," Vertical File, CAH.

46. The state complied with the provisions of Chapter 25, Acts of the 4th called session of the Thirty-fifth Legislature. Morgan, "The History and Economic Aspect of the Wichita Valley Irrigation Project," 130–35.

47. For many the irrigation project moved excruciatingly slowly. *The Better City*, a newsletter printed by the Wichita Falls Chamber of Commerce, for example, related, "The big irrigation and water project is working slowly, but steadily forward. There isn't much being said about it, but it keeps right on moving." Book 1, 1919–1922, Wichita County Water Improvement District (WCWID) #1, SWC; Jimmy E. Banks, article, October 1988; and *The Better City* 1, no. 2 (March 30, 1920); *Wichita Daily Times*, December 21, 1919, Wichita County Water District Number One Subsection, Irrigation District Section, Book 19, WCA; Harvey, "Irrigation District History;" Wichita County Water Improvement District Number One Records, 1919–1961, Wichita County Water Improvement District Number One, SWC; "Joseph Alexander Kemp," Vertical File, CAH; July 24, 1920, Director's Meeting, WCWID #1, SWC; *Wichita Daily Times*, December 21, 1919, Wichita County Water District Number One Subsection, Irrigation District Section, Book 19, WCA; Ralph Harvey, "Irrigation District History," Wichita County Water District Number One Subsection, Irrigation District Section, Book 19, WCA; "Irrigation System Was Voted in 1921," *Wichita Falls Times*, May 12, 1957, Wichita County Water District Number One Subsection, Irrigation District Section, Book 19, WCA.

48. Agricultural Editor V. H. Scoeffelmayer of the *Dallas Morning News* wrote many pro-irrigation pieces for Kemp. The first directors were President J. A. Kemp, Vice President T. B. Noble, Treasurer N. H. Martin, and members G. C. Wood and J. S. Bridwell. V. H. Scoeffelmayer, "Dream of J. A. Kemp, Banker, Realized Through Issue of Bonds Totaling $4,500,000," *Dallas Morning News*, August 2, 1925, Section 6, 1; Jimmy E. Banks, article, October 1988; Meeting Minutes, Book 1, 1919–1922, WCWID #1, SWC; Records indicate in 1923 $1 per $100 of taxable value, 1928 70 cents of taxable value, 1931 80 cents of taxable value; and in 1939 80 cents of taxable value. Meeting Minutes, Book 1, 1919–1922,

WCWID #1, SWC.

49. Book 1, 1919–1922, WCWID #1, SWC, and "Wichita Falls to Have New Resort," *Dallas Morning News*, April 19, 1922, Section 2, 9. Scoeffelmayer, "Dream of J. A. Kemp"; Cleo LaFoy Dowell and Seth Darnaby Breeding, *Dams and Reservoirs in Texas Historical and Descriptive Information, December 31, 1966* (Austin, TX: Texas Water Development Board, 1967); Book 2, 1923–1925, WCWID #1, SWC; Director's Meeting, May 3, 1923, Book 2, 1923–1925, WCWID #1, SWC; Director's Meeting November 16, 1921, Book 1, 1919–1922, WCWID #1, SWC; Director's Meeting, November 5, 1921, Book 1, 1919–1922, WCWID #1, SWC.

50. Jimmy E. Banks, article, October 1988.

51. Irrigation water from the Big Wichita River was released from Diversion in 1925. By 1925 there were 19,825 acres irrigated and in 1931, 30,195 acres were under irrigation. The maximum rate charged for irrigation water from 1925 to 1934 was $3.50 an acre-foot. It was dropped in 1934 (at the depth of the Depression) to $1.75 an acre-foot. "Irrigation System of Valley Opened," *Dallas Morning News*, May 25, 1924, Section 1, 8; Jimmy E. Banks, article, October 1988; "Irrigation System Was Voted in 1921," *Wichita Falls Times*, May 12, 1957, Irrigation Section, Book 19, WCA; and Harvey, "Irrigation District History"; *Community Builder* [newsletter] 2, no. 5, February 1924, WFCC, SWC.

52. *Community Builder* 2, no. 10, September 1924, WFCC, SWC.

53. *Dallas Morning News*, January 18, 1921, 1. Kemp claimed that if the state would pay for engineers in the districts their scientific expertise would alone enable the district to sell bonds without difficulty. People found comfort and economic security in the scientific expertise engineers offered.

54. "Irrigation Meeting Called for Oct. 3–4," *Dallas Morning News*, Section 1, 4. The association invited businessmen, promoters, and bureaucrats to their meetings and argued for cooperation from Progressive Era Texas citizens. The association urged members to solicit county judges, mayors, legislators, state officials, engineers, chambers of commerce, and other

civic leaders and to convince them of the benefits of reclamation and conservation for development of the state. In 1925 Texas "Irrigationists" reelected Joe Kemp president of the Texas Conservation Association. Members praised Kemp for "conquering" the semi-arid environment but Kemp declared his greatest obstacle to be "legislative" rather than natural.

55. "Conservation Group Again Names Kemp," *Dallas Morning News*, September 27, 1925, Section 1, 1; "J. A. Kemp Speaks to Brownwood Rotarians," *Dallas Morning News*, April 18, 1926, Section 1, 11; *Dallas Morning News*, October 4, 1924, 1.

56. *Dallas Morning News*, September 28, 1927, Section 2, 14; *Dallas Morning News*, October 4, 1924, Section 1, 1.

57. The second district encompassed 76,784 acres for possible irrigation and organized on "an assessment of benefit basis of taxation," meaning owners of all lands within the district paid the same rate per acre per year, the only distinction in rates being based on the classification of the land as irrigable or non-irrigable. From 1925 to 1932 the rate per acre on irrigable lands was three dollars and fifty cents, and on non-irrigable lands, seventy cents per acre." 1932–1934 $2 on irrigable & 3 cents non-irrigable; 1935 & 1936 75 cents on irrigable; 1937–1938 $2 on irrigable. Morgan, "The History and Economic Aspect of the Wichita Valley Irrigation Project," 142–50; "Irrigation System Was Voted in 1921," *Wichita Falls Times*, May 12, 1957, Irrigation Section, Book 19, WCA; Harvey, "Irrigation District History"; Jimmy E. Banks, article, October 1988; Wichita County Water Improvement District Number Two (WCWID #2) Records, 1898–1983, Water Commissioner of Wichita County Water Improvement District Number Two, Wichita Falls, TX, SWC.

58. The maximum rate charged for irrigation water from 1925 to 1934 was $3.50 an acre-foot. It was dropped in 1934 (at the depth of the Depression) to $1.75 an acre-foot. Minutes of Board of Equalization, September 16, 1927, Book 1, 1919–1922, Wichita County Water Improvement District No.1 Minutes, 1919–1961, File Box 1 of 1, Minutes, 1919–1922, Minutes, 1959–1961, WCWID #1, SWC. An acre-foot equals one acre of flat land with water covering it one foot

deep. "Irrigation System Was Voted in 1921," *Wichita Falls Times*, May 12, 1957, Irrigation Section, Book 19, WCA; and Harvey, "Irrigation District History."

59. *Community Builder* 2, no. 2, October 1923, WFCC, SWC.

60. *Community Builder* 1, no. 5, January 1923, WFCC, SWC.

61. Ibid.

62. January 5, 1927, Meeting Minutes, WFCC, SWC; October 8, 1924, Meeting Minutes, WFCC, SWC; December 27, 1926, Minute Book No. 3, WCWID #1, SWC; April 7, 1925, Meeting Minutes, WFCC, SWC.

63. December 29, 1927, Meeting Minutes, WFCC, SWC; December 10, 1926, Meeting Minutes, WFCC, SWC; October 8, 1924, Meeting Minutes, WFCC, SWC; July 7, 1927, Meeting Minutes, WFCC, SWC.

64. *Community Builder* 2, no. 10, September 1924, WFCC, SWC. Local real estate agent G. B. Anderson and irrigation engineer Dillard Anderson, for example, after they returned from irrigated farms in Colorado, Utah, Wyoming, Montana, and Idaho, reported bumper crops being grown under severe climatic conditions. Market conditions, however, were poor and irrigation farmers were no longer getting rich.

65. July 1, 1926, Meeting Minutes, WFCC, SWC.

66. December 8, 1929, Meeting Minutes, WFCC, SWC.

67. "Joseph Alexander Kemp," Vertical File, CAH; July 21, 1931, Meeting Minutes, WFCC, SWC; September 15, 1931, Meeting Minutes, WFCC, SWC; January 16, 1933, Meeting Minutes, WFCC, SWC.

68. "The Value of Irrigation," March 29, 1897, *Dallas Morning News*.

69. Margaret Lee Morgan, "The History and Economic Aspect of the Wichita Valley Irrigation Project" (master's thesis, Southern Methodist University, 1939), 159–69.

70. John Gould, "Furthermore and However," *Wichita Falls Daily Times*, November 12, 1951, in Wichita Falls File and Scrapbook, Vertical File, CAH.

71. Stanley Baldys, Peter W. Bush, and Charles C. Kidwell, *Effects of Low-Flow Diversions from the South Wichita River on Downstream Salinity of the South Wichita River, Lake Kemp, and the Wichita River,*

North Texas, October 1982–September 1992, Water-resources investigations report, 95-4288 (Austin, TX: US Department of the Interior, US Geological Survey, 1996), 1–32; Morgan, "The History and Economic Aspect of the Wichita Valley Irrigation Project," 63.

72. United States, *Wichita River Basin Reevaluation Red River Chloride Control Project* (Tulsa, OK: Department of Defense, Department of the Army, Corps of Engineers, Tulsa District, 2002).

73. United States, *Wichita River Basin Reevaluation Red River Chloride Control Project* (Tulsa, OK: Department of Defense, Department of the Army, Corps of Engineers, Tulsa District, 2002); Winslow and Kister, *Saline-Water Resources of Texas*, 1; Hughes, *Archeological Reconnaissance in the Wichita River Drainage of North-Central Texas*; Subchapter F: Drinking Water Standards Governing Drinking Water Quality and Reporting Requirements for Public Water Systems, Chapter 290 Public Drinking Water, Texas Commission on Environmental Quality; Water Analysis, Lake Kemp, Lake Diversion, and Bradford Canal, Wichita County Water Improvement District No. 2, City of Wichita Falls, 2002, in author's possession; Morgan, "The History and Economic Aspect of the Wichita Valley Irrigation Project," 70.

74. Morgan, "The History and Economic Aspect of the Wichita Valley Irrigation Project," 171; June 18, 1926, Meeting Minutes, WFCC, SWC.

75. "Irrigation System of Valley Opened," *Dallas Morning News*, May 25, 1924, Section 1, 8; February 5, 1924, Meeting Minutes, WFCC, SWC; April 3, 1923, Meeting Minutes, WFCC, SWC; "Joseph Alexander Kemp," *Handbook of Texas Online*, Texas State Historical Association, http://www.tshaonline.org/handbook/online/articles/KK/fke14.html; V. H. Scoeffelmayer, "Texans Will Study Farms in California," *Dallas Morning News*, July 17, 1927, Section 1, 1. The cattleman and oilman Samuel Burk Burnett ran up against the interests of the Wichita County irrigation district. Burnett's ranching estate complained about the district's taxing methods. When the irrigation districts first organized, the water commissioners proposed boundary lines that did not include any of Burnett's ranchlands, specifically excluding some 1,200 or 1,500 acres

southwest of Iowa Park. But before the commissioners voted, the district changed the boundary line so that it included some of Burnett's land. The district determined two hundred acres of Burnett's land were within the district's new boundaries. Burnett made an agreement with the irrigation board to change the classification of the land from irrigable to non-irrigable, and S. B. Burnett paid the small tax on non-irrigable land year to year. Later Burnett bought the Ellison farm, an irrigated farm. The farm contained about 120 acres of land within the bounds of the irrigation district. Burnett refused to pay the taxes on the irrigable land, insisting all the time that it should not have been included in the irrigation district and that the land was not subject to an irrigable tax rate. Burnett's attorneys met several times with district officials in an attempt to make a settlement on the unpaid taxes, but the stubborn cattle rancher never let his attorneys make any settlement. After Burnett's death the district continued to press the Burnett estate on the question of the unpaid taxes on irrigable land. The estate attorney found it impossible to get the land excluded from the district and talks between the board and Burnett estate continued through the 1940s and 1950s. Ranchers, such as S. B. Burnett and their attorneys, complained about land classifications, even bringing their arguments to the attorney general of Texas in an attempt to get tax reductions. But the attorney general argued in favor of the irrigation district that lands could not be reclassified. Letter from John C. Murphee, Attorney at Law, Iowa Park, Texas, to Mrs. Anne Burnett Hall, Fort Worth, Texas, May 8, 1939. Box 49 of 64 Financial Material Taxes, King County, 1936–1951 and undated, Electra ISD, Wichita County, #2, 1923-1960, File #8 Financial Materials, Taxes, Wichita County Water District #2, 1938–1962, S. B. Burnett Estate Records, 1874–1981; Letter from John C. Murphee, Attorney at Law, Iowa Park, Texas, to George T. Halsell, Fort Worth, Texas, February 21, 1957, Box 49 of 64 Financial Material Taxes, King County, 1936–1951 and undated, Electra ISD, Wichita County, #2, 1923-1960, File #8 Financial Materials, Taxes, Wichita County Water District #2, 1938–1962, S. B. Burnett Estate Records, 1874–1981.

CHAPTER 3

1. Houston Marchman and the Contraband, "Wichita Falls," *Tryin' for Home* (Blind Nello Records, 2000).

2. James Ward Lee, *Adventures with a Texas Humanist* (Fort Worth, TX: Texas Christian University Press, 2004), 141.

3. James Edward Grant, "The Lady Comes to Burkburnett," *Cosmopolitan* (August 1939); *Boom Town*, directed by Jack Conway (Beverly Hills, CA: Metro-Golden-Mayer, 1940); and Lee, *Adventures with a Texas Humanist*, 140–50.

4. Kenneth E. Hendrickson Jr., "Red River Uplift: The Emergence of the Oil Industry in North Central Texas, 1901–1921," *Tales of Texoma: Episodes in the History of the Red River Border*, edited by Michael L. Collins (Wichita Falls, TX: Midwestern State University Press, 2005), 351.

5. Hendrickson Jr., "Red River Uplift"; Marguerite Sandefer, "The Development of the Oil Industry in Wichita County" (master's thesis, University of Texas, 1938); and *The Electra Oil Field: A Proven Field* (Dallas, TX: The Electra Oil Field Co. (General Offices Slaughter Bldg, n.d.), SWC, Texas Tech University, Lubbock, TX.

6. Brian Hart, "Burkburnett, TX," *Handbook of Texas Online*, Texas State Historical Association, http://www.tshaonline.org/handbook/online/articles/heb14.

7. May 28, 1918, Meeting Minutes, WFCC.

8. August 27, 1918, Meeting Minutes, WFCC.

9. May 25, 1926, Meeting Minutes, WFCC.

10. Donald Worster, *Dust Bowl: The Southern Plains in the 1930s* (New York: Oxford University Press, 1979); Donald Worster, *Rivers of Empire: Water, Aridity, and the Growth of the American West* (New York: Oxford University Press, 1985), 182, 230, 243, 245, 250, 253–54, 262, 278; Donald Worster, "The Dirty Thirties: A Study in Agricultural Capitalism," *Great Plains Quarterly* 6, no. 2 (1986), 107–16; Kline, *First Along the River*, 31; Marc Reisner, *Cadillac Desert: The American West and Its Disappearing Water* (New York: Penguin Books, 1993), 43–48. Texas did not have many

federally owned public lands since the State of Texas maintained ownership of the bulk of its public lands, thus, the acts coming from the federal
government in the nineteenth century excluded most of Texas.

11. May 6, 1924, Directors' Meeting, Book 2, 1923–1925, WCWID No.
1, SWC; August 2, 1926, Minute Book No. 3, WCWID No. 1, SWC;
October 19, 1926, Minute Book No. 3, WCWID No. 1, SWC; May
25, 1926, Meeting Minutes, WFCC. By 1924 the county water board
decided to allow Big Wichita waters to be used on acreage once irrigated
by the better-quality Holliday Creek waters. WCWID decided water be
delivered immediately to irrigators located on the Lake Wichita system.
Shortly thereafter in 1926, J. Solon Downing appeared before the water
district board regarding the seepage condition on his property located
below the city aqueduct that ran from Lake Wichita to the city pumping
plant. He complained that seepage developing on his land was making it
impossible for him to mature crops. For the most part, the water district
ignored the early drainage and seepage complaints. The board informed
Downing and other irrigators near the old project "that the District did
not assume any responsibility for the seepage condition in the vicinity."
Ultimately the Wichita Falls Chamber of Commerce decided not to
back the municipal bond election that Taylor proposed to fix the drainage
problems. Taylor's drainage recommendations went unheeded, because
people wanted more time for further investigations. The water district
and chamber of commerce stalled in the decision-making process to
improve the drainage situation.

12. September 21, 1928, Minute Book No. 3, WCWID No. 1, Box 1
of 1, SWC.

13. Morgan, "The History and Economic Aspect of the Wichita Valley
Irrigation Project," 155–57. Morgan interviewed A. H. Britain in her
study of the Wichita County irrigation project. June 25, 1930, Meeting
Minutes, WCWID No. 1, SWC.

14. Rhea Howard, "Irrigation and Irrigation System One of City's
Great Achievements: Low Water Charges, Fertile Land and Steady
Development Point to Future Wichita Valley Prosperity," *Wichita Falls*

Daily Times, October 11, 1936, Irrigation Section, Book 19, WCA, Wichita Falls, TX.

15. "Much Irrigation in Wichita County," *Dallas Morning News*, June 1, 1925, Section 4, 11.

16. Wichita Falls Chamber of Commerce, Report 1930, WFCC, SWC. The only person benefiting from the irrigation project in the 1930s seemed to be A. H. Britain, attorney for the irrigation districts, who made a tremendous amount of money from litigation. Wichita County Drainage District No. 1., WCWID No. 1, SWC.

17. September 20, 1928, Minute Book No. 3, WCWID No. 1, SWC. The meeting was called for the purpose of discussing a proposal made by E. W. Napier, attorney for Mrs. J. M. McGrath, in the seepage case "now pending against the District."

18. October 21, 1931, Minute Book No. 3, WCWID No. 1, SWC.

19. See Wichita County Drainage District No. 1 Records, WCWID No. 1, SWC.

20. February 5, 1929, Minute Book No. 3, WCWID No.1, SWC; June 28, 1929, Minute Book No. 3, WCWID No. 1, SWC. The board accepted F. P. Brown, drainage engineer from El Paso, Texas. Once hired Brown proceeded with an investigation of lands with seepage problems. The district employed Brown to take charge of all seepage investigations, seepage losses from the canal system, and the necessary construction work to drain the waterlogged lands and prevent any seepage losses that might be found, at a salary of $400.00 per month.

21. April 20, 1929, Minute Book No. 3, WCWID No. 1, SWC. This was a joint meeting of WCWID's No. 1 and No. 2.

22. October 30, 1929, and May 5, 1930, Minute Book No. 3, WCWID No. 1, SWC. The district adopted "the following resolution regarding drainage of the area between Wichita Falls and Lake Wichita included within the boundaries of proposed Wichita County Drainage District No. 2. . . ." Wichita County Drainage District No. 2 was set up as a result. Indeed, developers found the cost of drainage quite expensive. When C. M. Crowell, president of the Board of Directors of Wichita County

Drainage District No. 2, appeared before the Water District Board, regarding the matter of beginning drainage construction, he estimated the cost of the work to be $58,816.00 for just a small portion of the irrigated acreage lying between the city and Lake Wichita. Wichita County Water Improvement District No. 1 and Drainage District No. 2 were going to have to bear an equal share in paying for the drainage improvements. March 28, 1931, Minute Book No. 3, WCWID No. 1, SWC.

23. February 18, 1930, Minute Book No. 3, WCWID No. 1, SWC. Financing drainage operations worried the board. Many believed the only solution to the matter was to pass on the burden to the taxpayers. Water board members argued the cost should "be borne by the lands directly benefited," March 7, 1930, and March 12, 1930, Minute Book No. 3, WCWID No. 1, SWC. After the drainage report had been submitted, the districts called a mass meeting to discuss the waterlogged condition of the district lands and the drainage of the lands. The gathered farmers, bureaucrats, and scientists established drainage improvement as necessary and to be made immediately. They found to make such improvements would cost $430,000, on the basis of $10.00 per acre for 43,000 acres of irrigable land within the district. The water district, however, did not have the funds necessary to make the drainage improvements. They planned to raise the funds by the issuance of $430,000 in new bonds. Taxes would be levied upon the uniform assessment of benefits of $10.00 per acre upon all irrigable lands and thirty cents upon each acre of non-irrigable land within the district. January 9, 1931, Minute Book 2, WCWID No. 2, SWC; March 14, 1931, Minute Book 2, WCWID No. 2, SWC; March 14, 1931, Minute Book 2, WCWID No. 2, SWC. Many agreed at the meeting that the bond election was necessary to relieve the land, the high-water table, seepage, and the waterlogged condition, and to keep unaffected lands in the water district from being affected, injured, or damaged by saline waters. Overall, the water district deemed the improvements necessary and to be made immediately so that certain lands might be saved.

24. May 28, 1931, Minute Book 2, WCWID No. 2, SWC. Voters declared

the bonds to be unfavorable. Only forty-five voted yes to authorize the bonds, while fifty-five voted no.

25. February 22, 1932, Meeting Book No. 4, WCWID No. 1, SWC. The district would need drag lines and other machinery to make the changes. May 12, 1932, Meeting Book No. 4, WCWID No. 1, SWC. At the same time, farmers and landowners presented petitions to the water district that asked the districts to construct some type of deep drainage to relieve the waterlogged condition without any additional tax levy. Water commissioners voted that the petition not be considered because of the lack of necessary funds.

26. See September 2–19, 1932, Meeting Book No. 4, WCWID No. 1, SWC.

27. February 19, 1926, Minute Book No. 3, WCWID No. 1, SWC.

28. March 27, 1926, Minute Book No. 3, WCWID No. 1, SWC. The district sent complaints about taxation to the general manager or the water district attorney. Depending on the person and their legal representation the matter would be referred to the district manager, G. A. Remington, for adjustment or to the attorney for the district, A. H. Britain, for litigation.

29. March 8, 1935, Business Council Meeting, WFCC, SWC. Only a relative few continued to stress a local solution. At a business council meeting of the Chamber of Commerce some argued "permanent progress depended on settling . . . problems by community efforts, rather than out of Washington."

30. July 31, 1935, WFCC, SWC; and see October 22, 1935, Minute Book No. 2, WCWID No. 2, SWC. The water districts applied to the Texas Rehabilitation and Relief Commission for labor to be used in cleaning ditches. September 27, 1933, Minute Book No. 2, WCWID No. 2, SWC. Plus, the Glen Smith Bill offered relief to water improvement districts in times of financial distress. The Wichita County Water Improvement Districts, the Wichita Falls Chamber of Commerce, the Valley Development Association, and local congressmen all lobbied for the passing of the measure. December 31, 1931, Minute Book No. 2, WCWID No. 2, SWC. This was a joint Meeting of Districts No. 1 and No. 2.

31. December 12, 1933, Minute Book No. 2, WCWID No. 2, SWC; and August 25, 1934, Minute Book No. 2, WCWID No. 2, SWC.
32. February 26, 1934, and May 9, 1934, Minute Book No. 2, WCWID No. 2, SWC; and Morgan, "The History and Economic Aspect of the Wichita Valley Irrigation Project," 181–82.
33. June 14, 1935, Minute Book No. 2, WCWID No. 2, SWC. The Board applied again in March 9, 1936, Report of Special Committee on City Water Plant Improvements, PWA Application No. 1501, Filed by the City of Wichita Falls; October 21, 1935, Minute Book No. 2, WCWID No. 2, SWC.
34. May 9, 1934, Minute Book No. 2, WCWID No. 2, SWC.
35. See Minute Book No. 2, WCWID No. 2, SWC.
36. February 2, 1937, Minute Book No. 4, WCWID District No. 1, SWC. The growing groups of officials built the needed drainage ditches and finally with the New Deal aid a well-funded effort relieved "the bad situation that has arisen on these lands in the way of seepage." December 17, 1938, Minute Book No. 2, WCWID No. 2, SWC.
37. May 18, 1939, Minute Book No. 3, WCWID No. 2, SWC.
38. Kenneth E. Hendrickson, "The Texas River Authorities and the Water Question: A Case Study in Conservation," *Agricultural History* 59, no. 2 (April 1985): 272; Kenneth E. Hendrickson, *The Waters of the Brazos: A History of the Brazos River Authority, 1929–1979* (Waco, TX: The Texian Press, 1981), 18–49; and *Annual Report*, Lower Colorado River Authority (1983), 2.
39. February 16, 1938, Minute Book No. 2, WCWID No. 2, SWC; and Winslow and Kister, *Saline-Water Resources of Texas*, 5. The naturally occurring brines in the Big Wichita's water were sodium chloride with high sulfate concentrations that reflected Permian geology and oceanic origins. Wilde and Gaines, *Identification of Refugia Habitat*, 1–25. Structurally, Lake Kemp Dam was built by "force-account or the cost-plus method," which kept the cost as low as possible. As a result, construction crews mixed together local sand, gravel, and river water for concrete. Later when the University of Texas tested the use of alkali water in

making concrete, the tests indicated saline water as "very unsatisfactory.

40. Baldys, Bush, and Kidwell, *Effects of Low-Flow Diversions from the South Wichita River*, 1–32; and Keller, Rawson, Grubb, Kramer, and Sullivan, *Report on the Evaluation of the Effectiveness of Operation Area VIII Red River Chloride Control Project.*

41. Winslow and Kister, *Saline-Water Resources of Texas*, 6.

42. Winslow and Kister, *Saline-Water Resources of Texas*, 2. John P. Ruhman, director for the City of Wichita Falls Utilities, illustrated this point in a letter to the water district in the 1950s. He wrote that from time to time the city of Wichita Falls required water from the Lake Diversion water supply. Ruhman requested efforts be made not to increase the total solids and chlorides of Lake Diversion by adding Lake Kemp water unless Lake Diversion evaporated to such a point where further control was worthless. He argued that the Lake Diversion supply was considerably better than Lake Kemp "because the watershed of Lake Diversion does not contain the alkalinity and salinity beds that the Lake Kemp watershed does." May 3, 1955, Minute Book No. 4, WCWID No. 2, SWC.

43. Morgan, "History and Economic Aspect of the Wichita Valley Irrigation Project"; Huser, *Rivers of Texas*, 43; Baldys, *Effects of Low-Flow Diversions from the South Wichita River*, 1–32; Keller, Rawson, Grubb, Kramer, and Sullivan, *Report on the Evaluation of the Effectiveness of Operation Area VIII Red River Chloride Control Project*, 1–6.

44. Morgan, "History and Economic Aspect of the Wichita Valley Irrigation Project," 160–61. These facts come from interviews with "well-known" Wichita florist Edwin Babb and owner of one of the region's largest laundries, Ralph Pond.

45. Bromfield was an American author and conservationist. He gained international recognition when he won the Pulitzer Prize. Bromfield innovated scientific farming concepts. After spending a decade in France, Bromfield returned to Central Ohio in 1938. He put into place the principles of grass-based, sustainable farming at Malabar Farm. Bromfield's writings turned from fiction to nonfiction and his reputation and influence as a conservationist and farmer continued expanding.

46. United States, Arkansas-Red River Basins Water Quality Conservation Summary Report on a Basic Study of Water Quality, Sources of Natural and Manmade Salt Pollution, and Suggested Corrective Measures (Dallas, TX: US Department of Health, Education, and Welfare, Public Health Service, Region VII, 1964).

47. United States and Ezra Taft Benson, "Water: The Yearbook of Agriculture" (Washington, DC: US Government Printing Office, 1955), 436; and Louis L. McDaniels, *Consumptive Use of Water by Major Crops in Texas*, Bulletin 6019 (Austin, TX: Texas Board of Water Engineers, November 1960, rpt. July 1962); April 18, 1949, Minute Book No. 2, WCWID No. 2, SWC.

48. "Wichita Falls, Texas Chamber of Commerce," Vertical File, CAH; Joe Brown, "When Nature Fails, Irrigation Makes Farmers 'Drought-Resistant,'" *Wichita Falls Record News*, April 30, 1971, Irrigation Section, Book 19, WCA; Morgan, "History and Economic Aspect of the Wichita Valley Irrigation Project," 165; W. L. Underwood, "Irrigation Districts Winning Drainage Battle," *Wichita Falls Record News*, April 12, 1947, Irrigation Section, Book 19, WCA. The salt-tolerant Bermuda required thirty-six inches of saline water every year. The water districts shipped Bermuda grass into Wichita County from Tifton, Georgia. The invasive immigrant grass species affected regional lawns as it spread beyond the irrigation farms.

49. Winslow and Kister, *Saline-Water Resources of Texas*, 6.

50. See the years 1951–1952 in Minute Book No. 3, WCWID District No. 2, SWC.

51. Baldys, *Effects of Low-Flow Diversions from the South Wichita River.*

52. Brown, "When Nature Fails," WCA; and Morgan, "History and Economic Aspect of the Wichita Valley Irrigation Project," 165.

53. United States, *Wichita River Basin Reevaluation Red River Chloride Control Project* (Tulsa, OK: Department of Defense, Department of the Army, Corps of Engineers, Tulsa District, 2002). Over time, the salts accumulated and caused a number of problems for regular crops. To accommodate the salt-tolerant crops, the farmers still needed to practice

irrigation leaching to avoid buildup of salts in the soil. Leaching meant irrigation farmers applied more water than otherwise necessary. The excess water kept salts in solution and drained them below the root zone. The excess amount of water became known as the "leaching fraction." Rainfall contributed to leaching and farmers considered rainfall when estimating the leaching fraction of water.

54. December 9, 1941, Minute Book No. 3, WCWID District No. 2, SWC. World War II momentarily shifted focus from financial and environmental problems to issues of security. At the onset of World War II new concerns arose for the district, including the placement of armed guards at both Lake Kemp and Lake Diversion dams to forestall attempts at sabotage. Plus, the water district took out an insurance policy in 1942 to further safeguard against sabotage. See Minute Book No. 3, WCWID District No. 2, SWC. Work with the Reconstruction Finance Corporation (RFC) temporarily slowed and then sputtered out when the war began. US Congressman Ed Gossett arranged meetings just to keep in touch with RFC directors. January 6, 1942, Minute Book No. 3, WCWID District No. 2, SWC. W. L. Underwood, "Irrigation Districts Winning Drainage Battle," *Wichita Falls Record News*, April 12, 1947, Irrigation Section, Book 19, WCA. Water on the irrigated farms still did not drain and escape satisfactorily. In many locations, the water table rose rapidly, bringing excessive concentrations of minerals to or near the surface. Texas Water Development Board, *A Summary of the Preliminary Plan for Proposed Water Resources Development in the Red River Basin* (Austin, TX: Texas Water Development Board, 1966), 23.

55. Call Field, Kell Field, and Staley Field all precluded Sheppard Air Force Base. Norman Bayne Cranford, "The History of Sheppard Air Force Base" (master's thesis, Midwestern State University, January 1965), 1–8. The topography had attracted training airmen since the First World War.

56. Kelly, *Wichita County Beginnings*; *Sheppard Senator*, September 8, 1981, Vertical Files, CAH; *Wichita Falls Times*, May 15, 1957; Cranford, "The History of Sheppard Air Force Base," 6–7.

57. William T. Chambers, "Shopping Areas of the Near Southwest," *Economic*

Geography 17, no. 2 (April 1941): 126.

58. Cranford, "The History of Sheppard Air Force Base," 96.
59. Kelly, *Wichita County Beginnings*; *Sheppard Senator*, September 8, 1981, Vertical Files, CAH; and *Wichita Falls Times*, May 15, 1957.
60. Minute Book No. 2, WCWID No. 1, SWC; and Cranford, "The History of Sheppard Air Force Base," 96, 121.
61. Memoirs of Elmer Figo, As Told to Edith Slaten, February 12, 1957, Manuscript in Kemp Public Library, Wichita Falls, Texas, North Texas Genealogy and Historical Association, Wichita Falls, North Texas Pioneer 4, no. 1, Texas State Library Genealogy Collection, Austin, TX, 45.
62. "Farmers Win Irrigation Writ," *Wichita Falls Daily Times*, January 30, 1942, Irrigation Section, Book 19, WCA.
63. December 29, 1927, Meeting Minutes, WFCC, SWC.
64. November 18, 1930, Meeting Minutes, WFCC, SWC; House Document No. 308, 69th Congress, First Session; United States, *Estimate of Cost of Examinations, Etc., of Streams Where Power Development Appears Feasible Letter from the Secretary of War Transmitting a Letter from the Chief of Engineers, US Army, and the Secretary of the Federal Power Commission, Showing All Navigable Streams Upon Which Power Development Appears to Be Feasible and the Estimate of Cost of Examinations of the Same Submitted in Accordance with the Requirements of Section 3 of the River and Harbor Act of March 3, 1925* (Washington, DC: Government Printing Office, 1926); and United States, *Potential Water Power Sites As Summarized from Reports by the Corps of Engineers to the Congress* (Washington, DC: Engineer Reproduction Plant, 1935).
65. Wichita Falls, Texas, Report on the Development of Hydro-Electric Power at Storage and Diversion Dams of Wichita County District No.1 on Wichita River, CAH; September 21, 1928, Minute Book No. 3, WCWID No. 1, SWC. In 1928 engineers prepared reports on the development of hydroelectric power. Interestingly engineers ignored unfavorable water samples, pointing out instead favorable water samples taken during high water stages. Despite salinity issues, engineers at first

recommended the building of hydroelectric power plants. The power plant issue even perplexed county historian Louise Kelly, who wrote Kemp and local leaders "had surveyors and engineers to consult [and] mysteriously, none of them recognize the gypsum and salt from the watershed." Kelly, *Wichita Beginnings*, 36.

66. April 20, 1944, Minute Book No. 3, WCWID District No. 2, SWC.

67. June 26, 1945, Minute Book No. 3, WCWID District No. 2, SWC.

68. June 26, 1945, Minute Book No. 3, WCWID District No. 2, SWC .

69. "Irrigation in Texas," *Dallas Morning News*, May 17, 1903, 18.

70. Randolph B. Marcy, "Marcy's Exploration to Locate the Texas Indian Reservations in 1854," edited by J. W. Williams and Ernest Lee, *West Texas Historical Association Yearbook* 23 (October 1947): 107–32; Del Weniger, *The Explorers' Texas: The Lands and Waters* (Austin, TX: Eakin Press, 1984), 111–16; "William Benjamin Hamilton House," Wichita County, National Register Records, Texas Historical Commission, Austin, TX; Texas Water Development Board, "A Summary of the Preliminary Plan for Proposed Water Resources Development in the Red River Basin" (Austin, TX: The Board, 1966), 6–7.

71. Guy Earl Harbeck, Robert O. R. Martin, Ronald L. Hanson, and N. O. Thomas, *Reservoirs in the United States* (Washington, DC: US Government Printing Office, 1966).

72. Cleo LaFoy Dowell and Seth Darnaby Breeding, *Dams and Reservoirs in Texas Historical and Descriptive Information, December 31, 1966* (Austin, TX: Texas Water Development Board, 1967); and Etchieson, Speer, and Hughes, *Archeological Investigations in the Crowell Reservoir Area, Cottle, Foard, King, and Knox Counties, Texas*.

73. Donald E. Morris, *Occurrence and Quality of Ground Water in Archer County, Texas*, Texas Water Development Board Report (Austin, TX: Texas Water Development Board, 1967), 52; and Dowell and Breeding, *Dams and Reservoirs in Texas Historical and Descriptive Information*.

74. "Lake Kickapoo," *Handbook of Texas Online*, Texas State Historical Association, https://www.tshaonline.org/handbook/entries/lake-kickapoo.

75. Jimmy E. Banks, article, October 1988.

CHAPTER 4

1. Guy Clark, "Desperados Waiting for a Train," *Old No. 1* (RCA, 1975).
2. Larry McMurtry, *The Last Picture Show* (1966; rpt. New York: Penguin Books, 1979); *The Last Picture Show*, directed by Peter Bogdanovich (Culver City, CA: Columbia Pictures, 1971); Grayson Holmes, Leo Zonn, and Altha J. Cravey, "Placing Man in the New West: Masculinities of *The Last Picture Show*," *GeoJournal* 59 (2004): 277–88.
3. Brian Hart, "Texhoma City, TX," *Handbook of Texas Online*, Texas State Historical Association, https://www.tshaonline.org/handbook/entries/texhoma-city-tx; David Minor, "Clara, TX (Wichita County)," *Handbook of Texas Online*, Texas State Historical Association, https://www.tshaonline.org/handbook/entries/clara-tx-wichita-county; David Minor, "Newtown, TX [#1] (Wichita County)," *Handbook of Texas Online*, Texas State Historical Association, https://www.tshaonline.org/handbook/entries/newtown-tx-1-wichita-county; Louise Kelly, *Wichita County Beginnings* (Burnet, TX: Eakin Press, 1982); and *Wichita Falls Times*, May 15, 1957.
4. In the novel, the town was named Thalia. In the film, the town was named Anarene. Larry McMurtry, *The Last Picture Show* (1966); *The Last Picture Show*, directed by Peter Bogdanovich (Columbia, 1971); *Boom Town*, directed by Jack Conway (Metro-Golden-Mayer, 1940); *There Will Be Blood* (Hollywood, CA: Paramount Pictures, 2007); and Upton Sinclair, *Oil!* (New York: Albert and Charles Boni, 1926).
5. Brief written by Jesse B. Roote, Attorney for the Burke-Divide Oil Company Consolidated, December 5, 1923, Newton Crane Collection, 1919–1962 and undated. The Newton Crane collection consists of legal material that reveals how the northern boundary of Texas was established. The United States Supreme Court declared the southern boundary of Oklahoma to be mid-point in the Red River and the northern boundary

of Texas to be the south bank of the Red River. When oil was discovered in the river the federal government claimed ownership.

6. After the Great War, in 1920, an oil boom struck outside Okemah, Oklahoma. Across the southwest in the Roaring Twenties oil booms brought prosperity. But along with wealth came the men and women who preyed on the euphoric success. As a kid Woody watched as men became wealthy overnight in a carnival-like atmosphere, and he saw the hustlers, drifters, grafters, fraudsters, pickpockets, gamblers, and conmen sweep through his town. It certainly left Woody Guthrie from an early age with a wry and unique way of looking at the world. Unfortunately, the hard times hit Woody Guthrie's father Charles Guthrie especially hard. Then the Great Depression hit in 1929 and the ruination of the national economy sunk the family into deeper despair. Woody Guthrie, *Pastures of Plenty: A Self Portrait*, edited by Dave Marsh and Harold Leventhal (New York: Harper Perennial, 1992).

7. Guthrie, *Pastures of Plenty*.

8. Woody Guthrie, "I Ain't Got No Home in This World Anymore," *Dust Bowl Ballads* (Victor, 1940); Woody Guthrie, "Dust Bowl Refugee," *Dust Bowl Ballads* (Victor, 1940); and Woody Guthrie, "So Long, It's Been Good To Know Yuh," *Dust Bowl Ballads* (Victor, 1940).

9. Karl Butzer, "Collapse, Environment, and Society," *Proceedings of the National Academy of Sciences* 109, no. 10 (March 2012): 3632–39.

10. "Subject of Irrigation," *Dallas Morning News*, February 27, 1897, 7.

11. Donald Worster, "Hydraulic Society in California: An Ecological Interpretation," *Agricultural History* 56, no. 3 (July 1982): 503–15.

12. Karl Wittfogel, *Oriental Despotism: A Comparative Study of Total Power* (New Haven, CT: Yale University Press, 1957); Thorkild Jacobsen and Robert Adams, "Salt and Silt in Ancient Mesopotamian Agriculture," *Science* 128 (November 21, 1958): 1254–58; Donald Worster, "Hydraulic Society in California: An Ecological Interpretation," *Agricultural History* 56, no. 3 (July 1982), 503–15; G. S. Morozova, "A Review of Holocene Avulsions of the Tigris and Euphrates Rivers and Possible Effects on the Evolution of Civilizations in Lower Mesopotamia," *Geoarchaeology* 20

(2005): 401–23; Butzer, "Collapse, Environment, and Society," 3632–39.

13. "Local Climatological Data with Comparative Data, 1963, Wichita Falls, Texas, Weather Bureau, US Department of Commerce," Vertical File, Wichita Falls, Texas, CAH, University of Texas at Austin, Austin, Texas. For an environmental history of natural disasters, see Ted Steinberg, *Acts of God: The Unnatural History of Natural Disaster in America* (Oxford: Oxford University Press, 2006).

14. Lawrence E. Estaville and Richard A. Earl, *Texas Water Atlas* (Texas A&M University Consortium Press, 2008); John W. Nielsen-Gammon, "The 2011 Texas Drought: A Briefing Packet for the Texas Legislature," October 31, 2011; Neil Wilkins, "Texas Drought: Now and Then," *TXH2O: A Publication of the Texas Water Resource Institute* 7, no. 1 (Fall 2011): 1–29.

15. Roger I. Glass, Robert B. Craven, Dennis J. Bergman, Barbara J. Stoll, Neil Horowitz, Peter Kerndt, and Joe Winkle, "Injuries from the Wichita Falls Tornado: Implications for Prevention," *Science* 207, Issue no. 4432 (February 15, 1980): 734–38; Chapter 1 of the NOAA Natural Disaster Report 80-1, "The Red River Valley Tornadoes of April 10, 1979," National Weather Service (Rockville, MD: U.S. Department of Commerce, January 1980); T. P. Grazulis, *Significant Tornadoes, 1680–1991* (np: Environmental Films, 1990); Tillman County Historical Society and Carolyn Maxwell, *A Diamond Jubilee History of Tillman County, 1901–1976* (Frederick, OK: The Society, 1976); Johnie Harris, Kay Jackson, Jim Webre, and Chuck Hurt, "Final Report of April 12, 1979, to October 30, 1981, of Interfaith Disasters Services (IDS)" (Wichita Falls, TX: IDS, 1981).

16. Chapter 1 of the NOAA Natural Disaster Report 80-1, "The Red River Valley Tornadoes of April 10, 1979," 2.

17. Roger I. Glass, Robert B. Craven, Dennis J. Bergman, Barbara J. Stoll, Neil Horowitz, Peter Kerndt, and Joe Winkle, "Injuries from the Wichita Falls Tornado: Implications for Prevention," *Science* 207, Issue 4432 (February 15, 1980): 734–38; Chapter 1 of the NOAA Natural Disaster Report 80-1, "The Red River Valley Tornadoes of April 10,

1979"; Grazulis, *Significant Tornadoes, 1680–1991*; Tillman County Historical Society and Carolyn Maxwell, *A Diamond Jubilee History of Tillman County, 1901–1976* (Frederick, OK: The Society, 1976); Johnie Harris, Kay Jackson, Jim Webre, and Chuck Hurt, "Final Report of April 12, 1979, to October 30, 1981, of Interfaith Disasters Services (IDS)" (Wichita Falls, TX: IDS, 1981).

18. Whitney A. Snow, "A Great Dream for the Valley: Louis Bromfield and the Wichita Falls Malabar Farm, 1949–1954," *Southwestern Historical Quarterly* 119, no. 4 (April 2016): 379.

19. July 17, 1959, Minute Book No. 4, WCWID No. 2, SWC. Still wanting to improve the water in the Big Wichita River Valley, city leaders followed the Watershed Protection and Flood Prevention Act through Congress in the 1950s. The act established a permanent legislative machinery under which the federal government could cooperate with local organizations, including the states, in planning and carrying out works of improvement for flood prevention and agricultural phases of conservation development. The US Congress also amended the Water Facilities Act enabling long-term loans (that could be made in all of the states) for water and soil conservation practices, irrigation, and drainage. With lobbyists on the water district's payroll for the past three years, the Wichita Falls Chamber of Commerce and Wichita County water districts finally made headway on federal projects in the valley, capitalizing on the new acts of Congress. In 1951 water district attorney Jack Connell presented a plan to the assembly of the National Rivers and Harbors Congress for flood control of Lakes Kemp and Diversion. Planning occurred all year through 1950. See Minute Book No. 3, WCWID No. 2, SWC; and April 3, 1953, Minute Book No. 6, WCWID No. 1, SWC. Many landowners in the irrigation districts called on Dr. W. O. Trogdon, the soil scientist, to analyze soil and water samples for legal proceedings in saltwater damage claims. When Trogdon reported the numerous requests back to the water district, the board ordered Trogdon not to make soil or water analyses for legal proceedings in damage suits.

20. February 27, 1953, and April 3, 1953, Minute Book No. 4, WCWID

No. 2, SWC. WCWID "employed as water policeman" E. B. Crocker for sixty days. The water was very low at this time and the water district board was worried about water storage.

21. January 9, 1953, Minute Book No. 4, WCWID No. 2, SWC. In the past the water district filled Lake Wichita with water from Lake Kemp and Lake Diversion. But in the early 1950s, the water district feared getting saline water to the farmers on the Lake Wichita irrigation system southeast of Wichita Falls, especially after losing the lawsuit to the irrigation farmers with damaged crops. Since the farmers had a prior water right from Lake Wichita the district believed farmers should be furnished water "as long as it would gravity flow from Lake Wichita." The state did not require the district to furnish Lake Kemp water to the Lake Wichita farmers for irrigation. May 14, 1953, Minute Book No. 4, WCWID No. 2, SWC.

22. February 26, 1957, Minute Book No. 7, WCWID No. 1, SWC; July 27, 1954, Minute Book No. 6, WCWID No. 1, SWC. According to the record: "It is the understanding of the Bankers that the water supply of the City is inadequate and that the composition of the bonded indebtness [sic] of the City is such that it cannot itself finance additional reservoir and raw water transmission facilities at optimum terms. It is understood, however, that the District, which entirely overlaps the City, is in such position as to permit financing the water supply facilities required by the City and that it is willing to do so provided an arrangement can be devised whereby principal and interest maturities on any bonds to be issued will be paid by the City in the form of water purchases through the facilities provided."

23. July 23, 1954, Minute Book No. 6, WCWID No. 1, SWC. The district negotiated with investment bankers, "namely: M. E. Allison and Company, Inc., Rauscher, Pierce and Company, Inc., and Warren and Company for the execution to enable the engineering firm Freese and Nichols to commence preliminary study of the feasibility of the construction of a reservoir at the site proposed."

24. See the years 1954–1955 in Minute Book No. 6, WCWID No. 1, SWC.

25. November 16, 1956, Minute Book No. 7, WCWID No. 1, SWC.

26. November 28, 1956, Minute Book No. 7, WCWID No. 1, SWC.

27. Dowell and Breeding, *Dams and Reservoirs in Texas Historical and Descriptive Information.*

28. Box 15, Water Issues: Floods & Supply Contracts, Mayor J. C. Boyd Papers, Moffett Library, Special Collections, Midwestern State University, Wichita Falls, TX.

29. Ibid.

30. Dowell and Breeding, *Dams and Reservoirs in Texas Historical and Descriptive Information.*

31. Ibid.

32. Letter to Mayor Jack Mueller of Archer City, From City Manager Gerald G. Fox, July 21, 1976, Box 15, Water Issues: Floods & Supply Contracts, Mayor J. C. Boyd Papers, Moffett Library, Special Collections, Midwestern State University, Wichita Falls, TX.

33. See Minute Book No. 2, WCWID No. 1, SWC. General increases in statewide industrial and urban growth caused the state to pass some minor environmental legislation in the 1920s. In 1924 local officials first considered pollution of Wichita County streams because the district had to comply with newly enacted state laws. Other than to identify some sources of the pollution in the river, however, local officials mostly ignored pollution in the 1920s.

34. Bruce E. Fink, *Investigation of Ground- and Surface-Water Contamination Near Harrold, Wilbarger County, Texas* (Austin, TX: Texas Water Commission, 1965), 6.

35. November 10, 1952, Minute Book No. 4, WCWID No. 2, SWC. According to the record: "The purpose of this meeting was to take up the salt pits situation in the district with the following farmers: Claud & Lee Beisch, Munger Farm Company; J. D. Chastain; Wiley Bishop; Carroll Anderson; and J. L. Gage." Appointed to the committee to deal with the problem were soil scientist W. O. Trogdon, biologist Leo Lewis of the Texas Game and Fish Commission, US geologist John Joerns, and general manager of WCWID No. 1 and No. 2 Fred Parkey, among

others, including irrigation farmers Carroll Anderson, Claud Beisch, and Wiley Bishop.

36. "Waterflooding" is an enhanced oil recovery (EOR) "method used to recover more oil than would be produced by primary recovery. In primary production, oil is displaced to the production well by natural reservoir energy," which includes rock expansion, solution gas drive, gravity drainage, and the influx of water from aquifers. EOR processes involve injection of a fluid into the reservoir. "Water injection" in the oil fields expanded rapidly after 1921 and waterflooding and water-injection operations were reported in Texas by 1936. G. Paul Willhite, *Waterflooding* (Richardson: Society of Petroleum Engineers, 1985), 1.

37. December 2, 1952, Minute Book No. 4, WCWID No. 2, SWC.

38. December 18, 1952, Minute Book No. 4, WCWID No. 2, SWC.

39. September 4, 1956, Minute Book No. 4, WCWID No. 2, SWC.

40. United States, *Public Works for Water, Pollution Control, and Power Development, and Atomic Energy Commission Appropriations for Fiscal Year 1970, Hearings Before the Subcommittee of the Committee on Appropriations, US Senate, Ninety-First Congress, First Session* (Washington, DC: Government Printing Office, 1969); US Department of the Interior, *Federal Water Pollution Control Act* (Washington, DC: Government Printing Office, 1967).

41. United States, *Wichita River Basin Reevaluation Red River Chloride Control Project* (Tulsa, OK: Department of Defense, Department of the Army, Corps of Engineers, Tulsa District, 2002) and Baldys, Bush, and Kidwell, *Effects of Low-Flow Diversions*, 2. In 1960 irrigation manager Fred Parkey testified at a House committee hearing for appropriations on behalf of the Wichita County water district in favor of the Corps' proposed desalinization program. Parkey's testimony ensured continued funding for the Army Corps of Engineers' study of pollution problems on the Red River and its tributaries. The State of Texas also held hearings in Austin on the North Texas pollution problems and considered efforts to aid North Texans. March 29, 1960, Minute Book No. 8, WCWID District No. 1, SWC. Despite solutions to the drinking water issue, in

1958 citizens wanted to do "everything possible" to secure a brackish water de-mineralization plant. October 29, 1958, and November 14, 1958, Minute Book No. 7, WCWID No. 1, SWC. Fred Parkey, general manager of the water district, discussed with directors the application presented to the government for a brackish water de-mineralization plant to be located in the area of Lake Kemp and the Diversion Reservoir. Technology could still surely solve the problems of the irrigation district. Wichita County offered the United States Office of Saline Waters land for the site, free water use from Lakes Kemp and Diversion, and access to the Midwestern State University (MSU) soils and water laboratory. July 21, 1959, and August 4, 1959, Minute Book No. 8, WCWID District No. 1, SWC.

42. November 25, 1959, Minute Book No. 8, WCWID District No. 1, SWC. The corps started by collecting data from the local water districts and the US Public Health Department.

43. Dowell and Breeding, *Dams and Reservoirs in Texas Historical and Descriptive Information*, 32.

44. United States, *Wichita River Basin Reevaluation Red River Chloride Control Project*; and Baldys, Bush, and Kidwell, *Effects of Low-Flow Diversions*, 2.

45. June 7, 1960, Minute Book No. 8, WCWID District No. 1, SWC.

46. July 5, 1960, Minute Book No. 8, WCWID District No. 1, SWC.

47. United States, *Wichita River Basin Reevaluation Red River Chloride Control Project*; and Sergio Garza, "Projected Effects of Proposed Chloride-Control Projects on Shallow Ground Water Preliminary Results for the Wichita River Basin, Texas" (Austin, TX: US Department of the Interior, Geological Survey, 1983).

48. Ralph M. Parsons Company, *Preliminary Feasibility and Economics of Desalting Brackish Waters in Candidate Areas of West Texas* (Los Angeles, CA: Ralph M. Parsons Company, Engineers-Constructors, 1968).

49. United States, *Wichita River Basin Reevaluation Red River Chloride Control Project*; Baldys, Bush, and Kidwell, *Effects of Low-Flow Diversions*, 2; and Keller, Rawson, Grubb, Kramer, and Sullivan, *Report on the*

Evaluation of the Effectiveness of Operation Area VIII Red River Chloride Control Project.

50. United States, *Wichita River Basin Reevaluation Red River Chloride Control Project*; Baldys, Bush, and Kidwell, *Effects of Low-Flow Diversions*, 2; Keller, Rawson, Grubb, Kramer, and Sullivan, *Report on the Evaluation of the Effectiveness of Operation Area VIII Red River Chloride Control Project*; and Royal D. Suttkus and Clyde Jones, "Atlas of Fishes of the Upper Red River System in Texas and Oklahoma," Occasional Papers, Museum of Texas Tech University, Number 246, October 12, 2005.

51. United States, *Arkansas-Red River Basins Water Quality Conservation Summary Report on a Basic Study of Water Quality, Sources of Natural and Manmade Salt Pollution, and Suggested Corrective Measures* (Dallas, TX: US Department of Health, Education, and Welfare, Public Health Service, Region VII, 1964); and A. A. Echelle, W. L. Fisher, and A. F. Echelle. "Assessment of Fish Communities in Relation to Chloride Control in the Wichita River and the Distribution of Pupfish in the Red River Drainage," Completion Report (Tulsa, OK: US Army Corps of Engineers, Tulsa District, 1995).

52. Ibid.

53. Ibid.

54. United States, *Wichita River Basin Reevaluation Red River Chloride Control Project*; and F. P. Gelwick, N. J. Dictson, and M. D. Zinn, "Analysis of Fish Distribution in the Wichita River System and Red River Tributaries from the Wichita River Confluence to Lake Texoma as Related to Environmental Variables in Summer 1998 with Stochastic Models for Distribution of Two Salt-Tolerant Species under Conditions of Estimated Land Use and Concentration of Total Dissolved Solids for Five Alternative Plans by US Army Corps of Engineers for Control of Saltwater Inflows to the Wichita River," Report submitted to US Army Corps of Engineers, Tulsa District (College Station, TX: Texas A&M University, 2001).

55. United States, *Wichita River Basin Reevaluation Red River Chloride Control Project.*

56. In this regard, Texas fits into the broader narrative of the Progressive "gospel of efficiency." John T. Cumbler, "Conflict, Accommodation, and Compromise: Connecticut's Attempt to Control Industrial Wastes in the Progressive Era," *Environmental History* 5, no. 3 (July 2000): 315, 328. For examples of this faith in technology in Wichita Falls, see *The Better City* 1, no. 2, October 1, 1920, "The City That Faith Built," WFCC; "Rapid Progress on Irrigation Project," *Wichita Falls Today*, June 1922, WFCC; April 24, 1926, Minute Meetings, WFCC; October 21, 1925, Meeting Minutes, WFCC, SWC; April 28, 1925, Meeting Minutes, WFCC, SWC; September 15, 1922, Meeting Minutes, WFCC, SWC.
57. Stephen Bogener, *Ditches Across the Desert: Irrigation in the Lower Pecos Valley* (Lubbock, TX: Texas Tech University Press, 2003), 9.
58. Bloodworth, *Some Principles and Practices in the Irrigation of Texas Soils*, 5.
59. Ibid.
60. See Wichita Falls Wichita County Drainage District No. 1, WCWID No. 1, SWC, and Minute Book No. 1, WCWID No. 2, SWC. Many men of the Wichita Falls Chamber of Commerce and WCWID directors owned tracts of land in the irrigated valley including J. A. Kemp, N. H. Martin, and John O'Donohue. Kemp bought much of the land to be irrigated and sold the 160-acre tracts to farmers or speculators attempting to colonize the valley. V. H. Scoeffelmayer, "Dream of J. A. Kemp, Banker, Realized Through Issue of Bonds Totaling $4,500,000," *Dallas Morning News*, August 2, 1925, Section 6, 1. September 27, 1933, Meeting Book No. 2, WCWID No. 2, SWC. After Kemp's death his estate still maintained 2,843 acres of irrigable lands.

CHAPTER 5

1. Guy Clark, "Red River," *Cold Dog Soup* (Sugar Hill, 1999).
2. Robie Christie organized the first event, which became an annual event. "What's Happening," *Dallas Morning News*, August 15, 1982, 11; Joe Simnacher, "TEMPERATURE WILL BE RISING FOR HOTTER

'N HELL BIKE RACE," *Dallas Morning News*, August 26, 1988, 3B; Joe Simnacher, "12,000 RIDERS EXPECTED FOR HOTTER 'N HELL 100," *Dallas Morning News*, August 20, 1987, 15b.

3. Dan Flores, "A Long Love Affair," *The Natural West: Environmental History in the Great Plains and Rocky Mountains* (Norman, OK: University of Oklahoma Press, 2001), 167.

4. Samuel P. Hays, "From Conservation to Environment: Environmental Politics in the United States Since World War II," edited by Char Miller and Hal Rothman, *Out of the Woods: Essays in Environmental History* (Pittsburgh, PA: University of Pittsburgh Press, 1997), 102.

5. Ibid., 107.

6. Luna B. Leopold, *Ecological Systems and the Water Resources* (Washington, DC: US Department of the Interior, Geological Survey, 1960).

7. Rachel Carson, *Silent Spring* (Boston, MA: Houghton Mifflin, 1962), and Samuel P. Hays, "From Conservation to Environment," 114.

8. Texas A&M University System, *Agricultural Resources Related to Water Development in Texas* (College Station, TX: Texas A&M University, Water Resources Institute, 1968); and Paul T. Gillett, and I. G. Janca, Inventory of Texas Irrigation, 1958 and 1964, Bulletin (Texas Water Commission) 6515 (Austin, TX: Texas Water Commission, 1965).

9. Duncan McLean, *Lone Star Swing: On the Trail of Bob Wills and His Texas* (New York: W. W. Norton, 1998).

10. James McMurtry, "Out Here in the Middle," *Saint Mary of the Woods* (Signal Hill Records, 2002). Born in Fort Worth, Texas, James McMurtry (1962) has been steeped from birth in the Texas plains culture by his author-father novelist Larry McMurtry of *Lonesome Dove* fame. Not to be outdone in the prose department, James McMurtry has written numerous songs that depict place and politics. He often criticizes the crass commercialism of twenty-first century lives. Larry McMurtry, *Lonesome Dove* (New York: Simon & Schuster, 1985).

11. *Hell or High Water*, directed by David Mackenzie (Santa Monica, CA: Lionsgate, 2016).

12. Stacy Horany, "Coming Up Aces: Tribal Casinos at the Center of

Development Plan to Bring a Little Bit of Vegas to Southwestern Oklahoma," *Wichita Falls Times Record News*, October 9, 2005. Journalist Stacy Horany with the *Wichita Falls Times Record News* ran a series of stories on Comanche casino gaming called "Little Vegas."

13. The history of casino gaming on the Red Rolling Plains has its origins in Plains Indian business associations and committees established throughout the twentieth century. Specifically, the Kiowa-Comanche-Apache (KCA) Business Committee focused on "kinship and obligations of reciprocity." Eventually, the Comanche Nation Business Committee was formed in 1970 after breaking with the Kiowas and Apaches. For early development of these groups, see David LaVere, "Minding Their Own Business: The Kiowa-Comanche-Apache Business Committee of the Early 1900s," *Native Pathways: American Indian Culture and Economic Development in the Twentieth Century*, edited by Brian Hosmer and Colleen L. Fixico (Boulder, CO: University Press of Colorado, 2004), 52–65. For the mid to latter parts of the twentieth century, see Foster, *Being Comanche*, 131–65. There have been some studies of American Indian casino gaming, including in *Native Pathways: American Indian Culture and Economic Development in the Twentieth Century*, but no specific studies on the Comanche gaming industry. To understand the development of Indian gaming on the Red Rolling Plains, see the Oklahoma Tribal-State Gaming Compact, Procedures Manual, State Compliance Agency, The Oklahoma Office of State Finance, January 26, 2005, Oklahoma City, OK. For a history of Indian casino gaming in general, see Manley A. Begay Jr., Stephen Cornell, and Joseph P. Kalt, "Making Research Count in Indian Country: The Harvard Project on American Indian Economic Development," The Harvard Project on American Indian Development, John F. Kennedy School of Government, Harvard University, October 1997; Katherine A. Spilde, Jonathan B. Taylor, and Kenneth W. Grant II, "Social and Economic Analysis of Tribal Government Gaming in Oklahoma," The Harvard Project on American Indian Development, John F. Kennedy School of Government, Harvard University, July 2002; Katherine A. Spilde, Statement of Katherine A.

Spilde, PhD, Research Fellow, Harvard Project on American Indian Development, Kennedy School of Government, Harvard University, Testimony Before the Select Committee on Indian Affairs United States Senate, Hearing on S.519, The Native American Capital Formation and Economic Development Act of 2003, July 21, 2004.

14. Justin Ely Munsee, Interview by author, October 20, 2005, Randlett, Oklahoma, Tape Recording, Department of History, Texas Christian University, Fort Worth, TX; Kavanagh, *Comanche Political History*, xi; Clifford Geertz, "The Native Perspective," *Local Knowledge: Further Essays in Interpretive Anthropology* (New York: Basic Books, 1983); Gerald Betty, *Comanche Society: Before the Reservation* (College Station, TX: Texas A&M University Press, 2002). Forney Beaver, Operations Manager, Interview by author, October 19, 2005, Randlett, Oklahoma, Tape Recording, Department of History, Texas Christian University, Fort Worth, TX; Louis Eschiti, Interview by author, October 19, 2005, Randlett, Oklahoma, Tape Recording, Department of History, Texas Christian University, Fort Worth, TX; Clifford Keith Red Elk, Floor Manager, Interview by author, October 19, 2005, Randlett, Oklahoma, Notes, Department of History, Texas Christian University, Fort Worth, TX.

15. "What you may not know about the Comanche Nation," Pamphlet, Comanche Nation Tourism and Information Center, Lawton, OK; and Louis Eschiti, Interview by author, October 19, 2005, Randlett, Oklahoma, Tape Recording, Department of History, Texas Christian University, Fort Worth, TX.

16. Kenneth E. Hendrickson Jr., "Red River Uplift: The Emergence of the Oil Industry in North Central Texas, 1901–1921," *Tales of Texoma: Episodes in the History of the Red River Border*, edited by Michael L. Collins (Wichita Falls, TX: Midwestern State University Press, 2005), 351.

17. "Prominent Financier and Texas Railroad Builder Passes Away," *Dallas Morning News*, November 17, 1930.

18. Brian Hart, "Kemp, Joseph Alexander," *Handbook of Texas Online*, Texas State Historical Association, https://www.tshaonline.org/handbook/

entries/kemp-joseph-alexander.

19. "Kemp, Joseph Alexander," Atlas Number 5507015184, Marker Number 15184, Wichita Falls, Wichita County, Texas Historical Commission, 2008. The marker is located in the Riverside Cemetery in Wichita Falls, Texas.

20. Ibid.

21. Ibid.

22. Ibid.

23. Bridget Knight, "Back in the Day: The Kemp Family Disperses," *Wichita Falls Times Record News*, April 5, 2017.

24. Larry McMurtry, *The Last Picture Show* (1966).

25. One Nation United, website, www.onenationunited.org.

26. Martina Minthorn, Interview by author, October 18, 2005, Lawton, Oklahoma, Notes, Department of History, Texas Christian University, Fort Worth, TX; One Nation United, www.onenationunited.org; and Heather Cox Richardson, *How the South Won the Civil War: Oligarchy, Democracy, and the Continuing Fight for the Soul of America* (Oxford: Oxford University Press, 2020).

27. Webb, *The Great Plains*; Cunfer, *On the Great Plains*; Walter Prescott Webb, *The Texas Rangers: A Century of Frontier Defense* (Boston, MA: Houghton Mifflin Company, 1935); Doug J. Swanson, *Cult of Glory: The Bold and Brutal History of the Texas Rangers* (New York: Viking, 2020); Walter Prescott Webb, *Divided We Stand: The Crisis of Frontierless Democracy* (New York: Farrar & Rinehart, 1937); Walter Prescott Webb, *The Great Frontier* (Boston, MA: Houghton Mifflin Company, 1952); *Stagecoach*, directed by John Ford (Beverly Hills, CA: United Artists, 1939); *Red River Valley*, directed by B. Reeves Eason (Los Angeles, CA: Republic Pictures, 1936); *Red River Valley*, directed by Joseph Kane (Los Angeles, CA: Republic Pictures, 1941); and *Red River*, directed by Howard Hawkes (Beverly Hills, CA: United Artists, 1948).

28. Jody Cox, "Where Is the Falls," *Wichita Falls Times*, Sunday Morning, December 3, 1978, 1B, in "Wichita Falls, Texas" Vertical File, CAH, Austin, Texas.

29. John Pronk, "After Nature's Blow, City Built New Falls," Travel Section, Second Edition, 4I, *Dallas Morning News*, Sunday, November 27, 2005; and Kent Biffle, "NEW LIFE PUMPED INTO WICHITA FALLS— City to Make Reality Fit the Name Again," Texas & Southwest Section, 41A, *Dallas Morning News*, Sunday, May 25, 1986.

30. "FLOODING WON'T HALT DEBUT OF WICHITA FALLS WATERFALL," 12D, *Dallas Morning News*, Wednesday, June 3, 1987; Pronk, "After Nature's Blow," November 27, 2005.

31. Donald Worster, "Watershed Democracy: Recovering the Lost Vision of John Wesley Powell," edited by Marnie Leybourne and Andrea Gaynor, *Water: Histories, Cultures, Ecologies* (Crawley, Australia: University of Western Australia Press, 2006), 7–10; John Wesley Powell, *Report on the Lands of the Arid Region of the United States, With a More Detailed Account of the Lands of Utah*, The John Harvard Library (Cambridge, MA: Belknap Press of Harvard University Press, 1962); Jeremy D. Popkin, *From Herodotus to H-Net: The Story of Historiography*, Second Edition (New York: Oxford University Press, 2021), 194–95; and Andrew Shyrock and Daniel Lord Smail, eds., *Deep History: The Architecture of Past and Present* (Berkeley, CA: University of California Press, 2011), xiii, 8, 13, and 14.

BIBLIOGRAPHY

PRIMARY SOURCES

Archeological Reports

Etchieson, Gerald Meeks, Roberta D. Speer, and Jack T. Hughes.
  *Archeological Investigations in the Crowell Reservoir Area, Cottle, Foard,
  King, and Knox Counties, Texas.* Canyon, TX: Archeological Research
  Laboratory, Killgore Research Center, West Texas State University, 1979.
Hughes, Jack T. *Archeological Reconnaissance in the Upper Red River Drainage
  of Oklahoma and Texas.* Canyon, TX: Archeological Research Laboratory,
  Killgore Research Center, West Texas State University, 1973.
———. *Archeological Reconnaissance in the Wichita River Drainage of
  North-Central Texas.* Canyon, TX: Archeological Research Laboratory,
  Killgore Research Center, West Texas State University, 1972.

Archives

Burkburnett, Texas Photograph Collection. Southwest Collection. Texas
  Tech University, Lubbock, Texas.
Electra, Texas Photograph Collection. Southwest Collection. Texas Tech
  University, Lubbock, Texas.
Fort Worth and Denver City Railway Company Papers. Manuscript
  Collection. Southwest Collection. Texas Tech University,

Lubbock, Texas.

Henry Sayles Jr. Papers. Southwest Collection. Texas Tech University, Lubbock, TX.

Highland Irrigated Farms, Highland Irrigation and Land Company. Wichita Falls, TX. 1910. Center for American History. Austin, TX.

Historical Survey of Wichita Falls, Texas. Dolph Briscoe Center for American History. University of Texas at Austin. Austin, TX.

Kiowa Agency Records. Record Group 75. Bureau of Indian Affairs. National Archives, Southwest Region. Fort Worth, TX.

Memoirs. Moffett Library. Special Collections. Midwestern State University. Wichita Falls, TX.

Missouri, Kansas and Texas Railway Company Records, 1871–1972. Southwest Collection. Texas Tech University. Lubbock, TX.

National Register Records. Texas Historical Commission. Austin, TX.

Newspapers Collection. Frederick Public Library. Frederick, OK.

Newton Crane Collection, 1919–1962 and undated. Southwest Collection. Texas Tech University. Lubbock, TX.

Photographs and Newspapers Collection. Pioneer Heritage Townsite Center. Tillman County Historical and Educational Society. Frederick, OK.

Recorded Texas Historic Landmarks. Texas Historical Commission. Austin, TX.

S. B. Burnett Estate Records, 1874–1981 and undated. Southwest Collection/Special Collections Library. Texas Tech University. Lubbock, TX.

Special Collections. Moffett Library. Midwestern State University. Wichita Falls, TX.

Texas Archeological Research Laboratory. University of Texas at Austin. Austin, TX.

United States Census Bureau Records. Texas State University–San Marcos. San Marcos, TX.

Wichita County Archives. Wichita County Historical Commission. Wichita Falls, TX.

Wichita County Folder. Recorded Texas Historic Landmarks. Texas Historical Commission. Austin, TX.

Wichita County Folder. Texas Archeological Research Laboratory. University of Texas at Austin. Austin, TX.

Wichita County Tax Rolls, 1865–1910. Archives and Genealogy. State Library. Austin, TX.

Wichita County Water Improvement District No. 1 Meeting Minutes. Southwest Collection. Texas Tech University. Lubbock, TX.

Wichita County Water Improvement District No. 2 Meeting Minutes. Southwest Collection. Texas Tech University. Lubbock, TX.

Wichita County Water Improvement District. Photograph Collection, 1920–1950. Southwest Collection. Texas Tech University. Lubbock, TX.

Wichita Falls Cemetery Index. Wichita County Burial Records. Wichita Falls Public Library. Wichita Falls, TX.

Wichita Falls Chamber of Commerce Records. Southwest Collection. Texas Tech University. Lubbock, TX.

Wichita Falls Reminiscences. Prothro Genealogy Research Center. Wichita Falls Public Library. Wichita Falls, TX.

Wichita Falls, Texas. Photographic Collection. Southwest Collection. Texas Tech University. Lubbock, TX.

Wichita Falls, Texas. Vertical File. Center for American History. University of Texas at Austin. Austin, TX.

Wilbarger County Historical Society Collection, 1959. Southwest Collection. Texas Tech University. Lubbock, TX.

Published Books and Documents

Abernathy, Alta, and Temple Abernathy. *Bud & Me: The True Adventures of the Abernathy Boys.* Irving, TX: Dove Creek Press, 1998.

Abernathy, John R. *"Catch 'Em Alive Jack": The Life and Adventures of an American Pioneer.* New York: Association Press, 1936.

Carson, Rachel. *Silent Spring.* Boston: Houghton Mifflin, 1962.

The Electra Oil Field: A Proven Field. Dallas, TX: The Electra Oil Field Co. (General Offices Slaughter Bldg.). n.d. Southwest Collection. Texas

Tech University. Lubbock, TX.

Emerson, Ralph Waldo. *Nature*. Boston: J. Munroe and Company, 1836.

Engels, Friedrich. *Dialectics of Nature*. Edited and translated by Clemens Dutt. New York: International Publishers, 1940.

Hardin, John Gerham. *The Life Story of John Gerham Hardin: By His Own Pen*. Dallas, TX: Baptist Foundation of Texas, 1939.

Leopold, Aldo. *A Sand County Almanac*. New York: Oxford University Press, 1972.

Marcy, Randolph B. *The Earth As Modified by Human Action: A New Edition of Man and Nature*. New York: Scribner, Armstrong, and Company, 1874.

———. *Explorations of the Big Wichita, etc.: Report of an Expedition to Survey the Brazos and Big Wichita Rivers, during the Summer of 1854*. Wichita Falls, TX: Terry Brothers, 1962.

Marsh, George P. *Exploration of the Red River of Louisiana*. Washington, DC: US War Dept., 1854.

———. *Man and Nature*. New York: Charles Scribner, 1864.

Newell, Frederick H. *Principles of Irrigation Engineering: Arid Lands, Water Supply, Storage Works, Dams, Canals, Water Rights and Products*. New York: McGraw-Hill, 1913.

Paddock, Buckley B., ed. *Early Days in Fort Worth, Much of Which I Saw and Part of Which I Was*. Special Collections, Texas Christian University. Fort Worth, TX, (s.l.: s.n., 19–?).

———., ed. *History of Texas: Fort Worth and the Texas Northwest Edition*. New York: The Lewis Publishing Company, 1922.

———. *A Twentieth Century History and Biographical Record of North and West Texas*. New York: The Lewis Publishing Company, 1906.

Roosevelt, Theodore. *Outdoor Pastime of an American Hunter*. New York: Charles Scribner's Sons, 1919.

———. *The Winning of the West*. New York: The Current Literature Publishing Company, 1905.

Smythe, William E. *The Conquest of Arid America*. New York: Macmillan, 1905.

Suttkus, Royal D., and Clyde Jones. Atlas of Fishes of the Upper Red River System in Texas and Oklahoma. Occasional Papers, Museum of Texas Tech University, Number 246, October 12, 2005. Southwest Collection, Texas Tech University, Lubbock, Texas.

Thomas, George. *The Development of Institutions Under Irrigation: With Special Reference to Early Utah Conditions.* New York: The Macmillan Company, 1920.

Thoreau, Henry David. *Essay on the Duty of Civil Disobedience and Walden.* New York: Lancer Books, 1968.

———. "Walking." *Excursions: The Writings of Henry David Thoreau.* Boston: Riverside Edition, 1893.

Government Reports and Documents

"An Analysis of Texas Waterways." Austin: Texas Parks and Wildlife Department, 1974.

Bailey, Robert. "Description of the Ecoregions of the United States." Forest Service, United States Department of Agriculture (October 1980), prepared in cooperation with US Fish and Wildlife Service. Government Documents Division. Mary Couts Burnett Library. Texas Christian University. Fort Worth, TX.

Baldys, Stanley, Peter W. Bush, and Charles C. Kidwell. "Effects of Low-Flow Diversions from the South Wichita River on Downstream Salinity of the South Wichita River, Lake Kemp, and the Wichita River, North Texas, October 1982–September 1992." Water-resources investigations report, 95-4288. Austin, TX: US Department of the Interior, US Geological Survey, 1996.

Baldys, Stanley, and Grant Phillips. "Stream Monitoring and Educational Program in the Red River Basin, Texas, 1996–1997." Fort Worth, TX: United States Geological Survey, 1998.

Bloodworth, Morris E. "Some Principles and Practices in the Irrigation of Texas Soils." College Station: Texas Agricultural Experiment Station, 1959. Found in the Water Inc. Collection, Southwest Collection, Texas Tech University, Lubbock, Texas.

Carr, John T. "The Climate and Physiography of Texas." Austin: Texas Water Development Board, 1967.

Dowell, Cleo LaFoy, and Seth Darnaby Breeding. "Dams and Reservoirs in Texas: Historical and Descriptive Information, December 31, 1966." Austin, TX: Water Development Board, 1967.

Echelle, A. A., W. L. Fisher, and A. F. Echelle. 1995. "Assessment of Fish Communities in Relation to Chloride Control in the Wichita River and the Distribution of Pupfish in the Red River Drainage." Completion Report. Tulsa District. Tulsa, OK. US Army Corps of Engineers.

Fink, Bruce E. "Investigation of Ground- and Surface-Water Contamination Near Harrold, Wilbarger County, Texas." Austin, TX: Texas Water Commission, 1965.

Freeman, B. G., et al. *An Economic Analysis of Mesquite Spraying in the Rolling Plains of Texas*. Lubbock, TX: Texas Tech University, College of Agricultural Sciences, 1978.

Garza, Sergio. "Projected Effects of Proposed Chloride-Control Projects on Shallow Ground Water Preliminary Results for the Wichita River Basin, Texas." Austin, TX: US Department of the Interior, Geological Survey, 1983.

Gelwick, F. P., N. J. Dictson, and M. D. Zinn. "Analysis of Fish Distribution in the Wichita River System and Red River Tributaries from the Wichita River Confluence to Lake Texoma as Related to Environmental Variables in Summer 1998 with Stochastic Models for Distribution of Two Salt-Tolerant Species under Conditions of Estimated Land Use and Concentration of Total Dissolved Solids for Five Alternative Plans by US Army Corps of Engineers for Control of Saltwater Inflows to the Wichita River." Report submitted to US Army Corps of Engineers, Tulsa District. College Station, TX: Texas A&M University, 2001.

Geological Survey (US), and Luna Bergere Leopold. "Conservation and Water Management–Part C–the Conservation Attitude." Geological Survey circular, 414. 1960. Water Inc.

Gillett, Paul T., and I. G. Janca. "Inventory of Texas Irrigation, 1958 and 1964." Bulletin. Texas Water Commission, 6515. Austin: Texas Water

Commission, 1965.

Gordon, C. H. *Geology and Underground Waters of the Wichita Region, North-Central Texas*. Washington, DC: US Government Printing Office, 1913.

Harbeck, Guy Earl, Robert O. R. Martin, Ronald L. Hanson, and N. O. Thomas. *Reservoirs in the United States*. Washington, DC: US Government Printing Office, 1966.

Harris, Johnie, Kay Jackson, Jim Webre, and Chuck Hurt. "Final Report of April 12, 1979 to October 30, 1981 of Interfaith Disasters Services (IDS)." Wichita Falls, TX: IDS, 1981.

Hildreth, R. J., and Gerald W. Thomas. "Farming and Ranching Risk As Influenced by Rainfall 1, High and Rolling Plains of Texas." College Station: Texas Agricultural Experiment Station, 1956.

Irrigation, Agricultural Lands. 1930. Fifteenth Census of the United States. Bureau of the Census.

Joerns, J. O. "Investigation of Sources of Natural Pollution: Wichita River Basin above Lake Kemp, Texas, 1951–1957." US Geological Survey, Water Resources Division. Open File Release No. 62. Austin, TX, 1961.

Keller, J., J. Rawson, H. Grubb, J. Kramer, and G. Sullivan. "Report on the Evaluation of the Effectiveness of Operation Area VIII Red River Chloride Control Project." Red River Chloride Control Project Report, 1988.

Leopold, Luna B. "Ecological Systems and the Water Resource." Washington, DC: US Department of the Interior, Geological Survey, 1960. Found in the Water Inc. Collection, Southwest Collection, Texas Tech University, Lubbock, Texas.

Lewis, Leo D., and Walter Woelber Dalquest. *A Fisheries Survey of the Big Wichita River System and Its Impoundments*. Austin, TX: Texas Game and Fish Commission, 1957.

"Master Plan for Water Resource Development in the Texas Portion of the Red River Basin." Prepared for the Red River Authority of Texas. Fort Worth, TX: Endress, 1961.

McDaniels, Louis L. "Consumptive Use of Water by Major Crops in

Texas." Texas Board Water Engineers, 1960.

Morris, Donald E. "Occurrence and Quality of Ground Water in Archer County, Texas." Report. Texas Water Development Board, 52. Austin: Texas Water Development Board, 1967.

"Natural Resources Study for the North Texas Planning Region." Prepared by Nortex Regional Planning Commission. Wichita Falls, TX. March 1973.

Parkey, Fred. "A Study of Salt Water Contamination to the Underground Water in the Big Wichita River Valley." Wichita Falls, TX: Wichita County Water Improvement Districts, 1952.

Ralph M. Parsons Company. *Preliminary Feasibility and Economics of Desalting Brackish Waters in Candidate Areas of West Texas.* Los Angeles, CA: Ralph M. Parsons Company, Engineers-Constructors, 1968.

Richardson, Wayne E., Auline R. Goerdel, and K.T. Lofton. "Soil Survey of Wichita County, Texas, US Department of Agriculture, Soil Conservation Service, in Cooperation with Texas Agricultural Experiment Station." Washington, DC: US Government Printing Office, 1977.

The State of Oklahoma (Complainant) v. The State of Texas (Defendant). US Supreme Court. October Term, 1921. Part 1 Statement of Case and Arguments, 5–8.

Taylor, T. U. "Irrigation Systems of Texas." Washington, DC: Government Printing Office, 1902.

Texas. State of Texas Laws, Policies, and Programs Pertaining to Water & Related Land Resources. 1968.

Texas A&M University System. "Agricultural Resources Related to Water Development in Texas." College Station, TX: Texas A&M University, Water Resources Institute, 1968.

Texas Technological College. "Abstracts of Publications on West Texas Water Resources," 1967.

Texas Water Development Board. *A Summary of the Preliminary Plan for Proposed Water Resources Development in the Red River Basin.* Austin, TX: Texas Water Development Board, 1966.

Thomas, Gerald W. "Farming and Ranching Risk As Influenced by Rainfall Edwards Plateau and Trans-Pecos." College Station, TX: Texas Agricultural Experiment Station, 1957.

United States. "Arkansas-Red River Basins Water Quality Conservation Summary Report on a Basic Study of Water Quality, Sources of Natural and Manmade Salt Pollution, and Suggested Corrective Measures." Dallas, TX: US Department of Health, Education, and Welfare, Public Health Service, Region VII, 1964.

United States. "Red River, Okla., Oil-Land Royalties. Part 2 Hearings Before the United States House Committee on Public Lands, Sixty-Eighth Congress, Second Session, on Jan. 6, 1925." Washington, DC: US Government Printing Office, 1925.

US Army Corps of Engineers. "Arkansas-Red River Basins, Water Quality Control Study, Texas, Oklahoma and Kansas. Letter from the Secretary of the Army Transmitting a Letter from the Chief of Engineers, Department of the Army, Dated April 18, 1966, Submitting a Report, Together with Accompanying Papers and Illustrations on a Review of the Report of the Arkansas-Red River Basins Water Quality Control Study, Texas, Oklahoma and Kansas, Requested by a Resolution of the Committee on Public Works, United States Senate, Adopted December 16, 1959." Washington, DC: Office of the Chief of Engineers, Department of the Army, 1966. Midwestern State University, Moffett Library, Wichita Falls, Texas.

US Army Corps of Engineers. "Chloride-control. Part I, Arkansas-Red River Basins, Oklahoma, Kansas, and Texas." Tulsa District, US Army Corps of Engineers. Tulsa, OK, 1972.

US Army Corps of Engineers. "Flood Plain Information: Wichita River and Tributaries, Wichita Falls, Texas." United States Army Corps of Engineers, Tulsa District, 1976.

US Army Corps of Engineers. "Supplement to Final Environmental Statement for the Authorized Red River Chloride Control Project Wichita River Only Portion." Tulsa District, US Army Corps of Engineers. Tulsa, OK, 2002.

US Congress. *American State Papers, Military Affairs*, Vol. V. Washington, DC: Gales and Seaton, 1860.

US Congress. House. Document no. 308, 69th Cong., 1st Session.

US Department of the Interior. *Federal Water Pollution Control Act.* Washington, DC: Government Printing Office, 1967.

United States. *Statutes at Large*, Vol. IV. Washington: Government Printing Office, 1848 to present.

United States. *Estimate of Cost of Examinations, Etc., of Streams Where Power Development Appears Feasible Letter from the Secretary of War Transmitting a Letter from the Chief of Engineers, US Army, and the Secretary of the Federal Power Commission, Showing All Navigable Streams Upon Which Power Development Appears to Be Feasible and the Estimate of Cost of Examinations of the Same Submitted in Accordance with the Requirements of Section 3 of the River and Harbor Act of March 3, 1925.* Washington, DC: US Government Printing Office, 1926.

United States. *Potential Water Power Sites As Summarized from Reports by the Corps of Engineers to the Congress.* Washington, DC: Engineer Reproduction Plant, 1935.

United States. *Public Works for Water, Pollution Control, and Power Development, and Atomic Energy Commission Appropriations for Fiscal Year 1970. Hearings Before the Subcommittee of the Committee on Appropriations, US Senate, Ninety-First Congress, First Session.* Washington, DC: US Government Printing Office, 1969.

United States. 1964 United States Census of Agriculture. Farms, Farm Characteristics, Livestock and Products, Crops, Fruits, Values, Vol. 1, Part 37, Texas. Washington, DC: US Government Printing Office, 1967.

United States, and Ezra Taft Benson. "Water: The Yearbook of Agriculture." Washington, DC: US Government Printing Office, 1955.

United States. *Wichita River Basin Reevaluation Red River Chloride Control Project.* Tulsa, OK: Department of Defense, Department of the Army, Corps of Engineers, Tulsa District, 2002.

Wilde, Gene R., and Bailey Gaines. "Identification of Refugia Habitat, Faunal Survey of Collection Areas, and Monitoring of Riparian and

Stream Habitat and Biotic Communities in the Wichita River Basin, Texas." Weston Solutions, Inc. and US Army Corps of Engineers, Tulsa District. Department of Range, Wildlife, and Fisheries Management. Texas Tech University. Lubbock, TX. October 26, 2006.

Wilde, G. R., R. R. Weller, C. D. Smith, and R. Jimenez Jr. "Review and Synthesis of Existing Fish Collection Records for the Upper Red River Basin Upstream from Lake Texoma." Report submitted to US Army Corps of Engineers, Tulsa District. Texas Tech University. Lubbock, TX. 1996.

Winslow, Allen G., and L. R. Kister. "Saline-Water Resources of Texas." Geological Survey water-supply paper, 1365. Washington, DC: US Government Printing Office, 1956. Water Inc. Collection, Southwest Collection, Texas Tech University, Lubbock, Texas.

Yarbrough, Donald B. "Laws and Programs Pertaining to Water and Related Land Resources." Austin: Texas Water Development Board, 1968.

Magazines

Gard, Wayne. "Teddy Roosevelt's Wolf Hunt." *True West* 9, no. 6 (July–August 1962).

Grant, James Edward. "A Lady Comes to Burkburnett." *Cosmopolitan* (August 1939).

Roosevelt, Theodore. "A Wolf Hunt in Oklahoma," *Scribner's Magazine* 39, no. 5 (November 1905).

Waida, Marilyn. "Jack Abernathy–Oklahoma Legend." *Old West* 5, no. 4 (Summer 1969): 34–37.

Webb, Walter Prescott. "The American West: Perpetual Mirage." *Harper's Magazine* (May 1957).

Newspapers

Daily Oklahoman (Oklahoma City, OK)
Dallas Morning News (Dallas, TX)
Fort Worth Gazette (Fort Worth, TX)

Frederick Daily Leader (Frederick, OK)

Frederick Enterprise (Frederick, OK)

Iowa Park Centennial (Iowa Park, TX)

Iowa Park Leader (Iowa Park, TX)

Lawton News-Republican (Lawton, OK)

Wichita Daily Times (Wichita Falls, TX), May 14, 1907 to November 1955. Texas State Library, Austin, TX

Wichita Falls Record News (Wichita Falls, TX)

Wichita Falls Times (Wichita Falls, TX)

Wichita Falls Times Record News (Wichita Falls, TX)

Wichita Weekly Times (Wichita Falls, TX), June 1907 to September 1918. Texas State Library, Austin, TX.

Photographs

Burkburnett, TX (Wichita County) Photograph Collection. Southwest Collection. Texas Tech University. Lubbock, TX.

Electra, Texas Photograph Collection. SWCPC 47. Southwest Collection. Texas Tech University. Lubbock, TX.

John R. Abernathy Photographic Collection. Museum of the Great Plains. Lawton, OK.

Scribner's Magazine Collection. Museum of the Great Plains. Lawton, OK.

Wichita Falls, TX (Wichita County) Photograph Collection. SWPC 112. Southwest Collection. Texas Tech University. Lubbock, TX.

Unpublished Papers and Interviews

Banks, Jimmy E. Personal Papers of Jimmy E. Banks.

Beaver, Forney. Operations Manager. Interview by author. October 19, 2005. Randlett, OK. Tape Recording. Department of History. Texas Christian University. Fort Worth, TX.

Eschiti, Louis. Interview by author. October 19, 2005. Randlett, OK. Tape Recording. Department of History. Texas Christian University. Fort Worth, TX.

Minthorn, Martina. Interview by author. October 18, 2005. Lawton,

OK. Notes. Department of History. Texas Christian University. Fort Worth, TX.

Munsee, Justin Ely. Interview by author. October 20, 2005. Randlett, OK. Tape Recording. Department of History. Texas Christian University. Fort Worth, TX.

Red Elk, Clifford Keith. Floor Manager. Interview by author. October 19, 2005. Randlett, OK. Notes. Department of History. Texas Christian University. Fort Worth, TX.

SECONDARY SOURCES

Articles

Allred, B. W. "Distribution and Control of Several Woody Plants in Texas and Oklahoma." *Journal of Range Management* 2, no. 1 (January 1949): 17–29.

Anderson, A. A., C. Hubbs, K. O. Winemiller, and R. J. Edwards. "Texas Freshwater Fish Assemblages Following Three Decades of Environmental Change." *Southwestern Naturalist* 40 (1995): 314–21.

Anderson, Jahue. "The Wichita Valley Irrigation Project: Joseph Kemp, Boosterism, and Conservation in Northwest Texas, 1886–1939." *Agricultural History* 85, no. 4 (2011): 493–519.

Balough, Brian. "Scientific Forestry and the Roots of the Modern American State: Gifford Pinchot's Path to Progressive Reform." *Environmental History* 7 (April 2002): 198–225.

Bender, Frederic L. "Historical and Theoretical Backgrounds of the *Communist Manifesto*." *The Communist Manifesto*. New York: W. W. Norton & Company, 1988.

Bogue, Allan G. "James C. Malin: A Voice from the Grassland." *Writing Western History: Essays on Major Western Historians*. Edited by Richard W. Etulain. Albuquerque, NM: University of New Mexico Press, 1991.

Buenger, Walter L., and Robert A. Calvert. "The Shelf Life of Truth in

Texas." *Texas Through Time: Evolving Interpretations.* Edited by Walter
L. Buenger and Robert A. Calvert. College Station: Texas A&M
University Press, 1991.

Butzer, Karl W. "Collapse, Environment, and Society." *Proceedings of the
National Academy of Sciences* 109, no. 10 (March 2012): 3632–39.

Chambers, William T. "Shopping Areas of the Near Southwest." *Economic
Geography* 17, no. 2 (April 1941): 121–29.

Cumbler, John T. "Conflict, Accommodation, and Compromise:
Connecticut's Attempt to Control Industrial Wastes in the Progressive
Era." *Environmental History* 5, no. 3 (July 2000): 314–35.

Denevan, William M. "The Pristine Myth: The Landscape of the Americas
in 1492." *Annals of the Association of American Geographers* 82, no. 3
(1992): 369–85.

Ground, T. A., and A. W. Groeger. "Chemical Classification and Trophic
Characteristics of Texas Reservoirs." *Hydrobiologia* 549 (1994): 197–203.

Hagan, William T. "Kiowas, Comanches, and Cattleman, 1867–1906: A
Case Study of the US Reservation Policy." *Pacific Historical Review* 40
(1971): 333–55.

Hendrickson, Kenneth E. "Replenishing the Soil: The Civilian
Conservation Corps in the Lone Star State as an Example of
State-Federal Work Relief During the Great Depression." *The
Historian* (2003).

———. "The Texas River Authorities and the Water Question: A Study
in Conservation." *Agricultural History* 59, no. 2. The History of Soil and
Water Conservation: A Symposium. (April 1985): 269–79.

Higgins, C. L., and G. R. Wilde. "The Role of Salinity in Structuring
Fish Assemblages in a Prairie Stream System." *Hydrobiologia* 549
(2005):197–203.

Hoagland, Bruce. "The Vegetation of Oklahoma: A Classification for
Landscape Mapping and Conservation Planning." *The Southwestern
Naturalist* 45, no. 4 (December 2000): 385–420.

Hofsommer, Donovan. "Townsite Development on the Wichita Falls and
Northwestern Railway," *Great Plains Journal* 16 (Spring 1977): 107–22.

Holmes, Grayson, Leo Zonn, and Altha J. Cravey. "Placing Man in the New West: Masculinities of *The Last Picture Show.*" *GeoJournal* 59 (2004): 277–88.

Hoogland, J. L. "Sexual Dimorphism of Prairie Dogs." *Journal of Mammalogy* 84, no. 4 (2002): 1254–66.

Hundley, Norris, Jr. "Water and the West in Historical Imagination." *The Western Historical Quarterly* 27, no. 1 (Spring 1996).

———. "Water and the West in Historical Imagination: Part Two—A Decade Later." *The Historian* 66, no. 3 (Fall 2004): 455–90.

Jacobsen, Thorkild, and Robert Adams. "Salt and Silt in Ancient Mesopotamian Agriculture." *Science* 128 (November 21, 1958).

Jordan, Terry G. "Pioneer Evaluation of Vegetation in Frontier Texas." *Southwestern Historical Quarterly* 76 (January 1973): 232–54.

Kinnard, Knox. "A History of the Waggoner Ranch." *Panhandle Plains Historical Review* 16 (1943): 11–49.

Klein, Alan M. "Plains Economic Analysis: The Marxist Compliment." Edited by W. Raymond Wood and Margot Liberty. *Anthropology on the Great Plains.* Lincoln, NE: University of Nebraska Press, 1980.

Langford, R. A. "Uses of Mesquite." Edited by J. L. Schuster. *Literature on the Mesquite of North America.* Lubbock, TX: Texas Tech University, 1969.

LaVere, David. "Minding Their Own Business: The Kiowa-Comanche-Apache Business Committee of the Early 1900s." *Native Pathways: American Indian Culture and Economic Development in the Twentieth Century.* Edited by Brian Hosmer and Colleen L. Fixico. Boulder, CO: University Press of Colorado, 2004, 52–65.

Leopold, Aldo. "The Land Ethic." *Human Geography: An Essential Anthology.* Edited by John Agnew, David N. Livingston, and Alisdair Rogers. Malden, MA: Blackwell Publishers, 1996.

Malin, James C. "The Adaptation of the Agricultural System to Sub-Humid Environment." *Agricultural History* 10 (1936): 339–72.

Marx, Karl, and Friedrich Engels. "The German Ideology." Edited by Frederic L. Bender. *The Essential Writings.* Boulder, CO: Westview, 1986.

Miller, Char. "Streetscape Environmentalism: Floods, Social Justice, and Political Power in San Antonio, 1921–1974." *Southwestern Historical Quarterly* 118, no. 2 (October 2014): 158–77.

Morozova, G. S. "A Review of Holocene Avulsions of the Tigris and Euphrates Rivers and Possible Effects on the Evolution of Civilizations in Lower Mesopotamia." *Geoarchaeology* 20 (2005): 401–23.

Murton, James. "Creating Order: The Liberals, the Landowners, and the Draining of Sumas Lake, British Columbia." *Environmental History* 13, no. 1 (January 2008).

Paradiso, John, and Ronald Nowak. "Wolves: *Canis lupus* and Allies." *Wild Mammals of North America: Biology, Management, Economics*. Edited by Joseph Chapman and George Feldhammer. Baltimore: Johns Hopkins Press, 1982, 460–74.

Phillips, Edward Hake. "Teddy Roosevelt in Texas." *West Texas Historical Association Yearbook* 56 (1980): 58–67.

Riggs, C. D., and E. W. Bonn. "An Annotated List of the Fishes of Lake Texoma, Oklahoma and Texas." *Southwestern Naturalist* 4 (1959): 157–68.

Rutherford, Stephanie. "The Anthropocene's Animal? Coywolves as Feral Cotravelers." *Environment & Planning E: Nature & Space* 1, no. 1/2 (March 2018): 206–23.

Sauer, Carl O. "The Morphology of Landscape." *Human Geography: An Essential Anthology*. Edited by John Agnew, David N. Livingston, and Alisdair Rogers. Malden, MA: Blackwell Publishers, 1996.

Semple, Ellen C. "Influences of Geographic Environment." *Human Geography: An Essential Anthology*. Edited by John Agnew, David N. Livingston, and Alisdair Rogers. Malden, MA: Blackwell Publishers, 1996.

Sherow, James. "The Chimerical Vision: Michael Creed Hinderlider and Progressive Engineering in Colorado." *Essays and Monographs in Colorado History*, no. 9 (1989): 37–59.

Smith, Brian Lee. "Theodore Roosevelt Visits Oklahoma." *The Chronicles of Oklahoma* (1973).

Snow, Whitney A. "A Great Dream for the Valley: Louis Bromfield and the Wichita Falls Malabar Farm, 1949–1954." *Southwestern Historical Quarterly* 119, no. 4 (April 2016): 378–405.

Stagner, Stephen. "Epics, Science, and the Lost Frontier: Texas Historical Writing, 1836–1936." *Western Historical Quarterly* 12 (April 1981): 165–81.

Stahle, David, and Malcolm K. Cleveland. "Texas Drought History Reconstructed and Analyzed from 1698 to 1980." *Journal of Climate* 1 (January 1988): 64.

Taylor, C. M., M. R. Winston, and W. J. Matthews. "Fish Species-Environment and Abundance Relationships in a Great Plains River System." *Ecography* 16 (1993): 16–23.

Thomas, G. W., and R. E. Sosebee. "Water Relations of Honey Mesquite." *Proceedings of the First International Rangeland Congress.* Edited by D. N. Hyder. Denver, CO: Society for Range Management, 1978.

Turner, Frederick Jackson. "The Significance of the Frontier in American History." Edited by George Rogers Taylor. *The Turner Thesis: Concerning the Role of the Frontier in American History.* Boston: D. C. Heath and Company, 1956.

Ware, James. "Soldiers, Disasters and Dams: The Army Corps of Engineers and Flood Control in the Red River Valley, 1936–1946." *Chronicles of Oklahoma* 57 (Spring 1979): 26–33.

Williams, J. W. "Frank Kell." *West Texas Historical Association Yearbook* 17 (1941).

Williams, J. W., and Ernest Lee. "Marcy's Exploration to Locate the Texas Indian." *West Texas Historical Association Yearbook* 23 (October 1947): 107–32.

Worster, Donald. "The Dirty Thirties: A Study in Agricultural Capitalism." *Great Plains Quarterly* 6, no. 2 (1986): 107–16.

———. "Doing Environmental History." *The Ends of the Earth: Perspective on Modern Environmental History.* Edited by Donald Worster. New York: Cambridge University Press, 1988.

———. "Hydraulic Society in California: An Ecological Interpretation."

Agricultural History 56, no. 3 (July 1982): 503–15.

———. "Nature, Liberty, and Equality." *American Wilderness: A New History*. Edited by Michael Lewis. New York: Oxford University Press, 2007.

———. "Seeing beyond Culture." *Journal of American History* 76 (March 1990).

———. "Watershed Democracy: Recovering the Lost Vision of John Wesley Powell." Edited by Marnie Leybourne and Andrea Gaynor. *Water: Histories, Cultures, Ecologies*. Crawley, Australia: University of Western Australia Press, 2006.

Wright, Carl C. "The Mesquite Tree: From Nature's Boon to Aggressive Invader." *Southwestern Historical Quarterly* 69 (1965): 38–43.

Books

Allen, Dorothy Louise. *The Kemp Public Library: A History, 1896–1963*. Austin: University of Texas Press, 1965.

Anderson, Benedict. *Under Three Flags: Anarchism and the Anti-Colonial Imagination*. New York: Verso, 2005.

Archer, Kenna Lang. *Unruly Waters: A Social and Environmental History of the Brazos River*. Albuquerque, NM: University of New Mexico Press, 2015.

Barker, Eugene C. *Life of Stephen F. Austin, Founder of Texas, 1793–1836: A Chapter in the Westward Movement of the Anglo-American People*. Nashville, TN: Cokesbury, 1925.

Baugh, Virgil E. *A Pair of Texas Rangers: Bill McDonald and John Hughes*. Washington, DC: Potomac Corral, the Westerners, 1970.

Beasley, Ellen. *Historic and Architectural Survey, Wichita Falls, Texas*. Wichita Falls, TX: Wichita County Heritage Society, 1992.

Beesley, Claude A. *An Ever Rolling Stream: The Chronicle of the Parish of the Good Shepherd, Wichita Falls, Texas*. Wichita Falls, TX: s.n., 1964.

Benton, Minnie King. *Boomtown: A Portrait of Burkburnett*. Quanah, TX: Nortex Offset Publications, 1972.

Betty, Gerald. *Comanche Society: Before the Reservation*. College Station, TX:

Texas A&M University Press, 2002.

Bickers, Margaret A. *Red Water, Black Gold: The Canadian River in Western Texas, 1920–1999*. Austin, TX: Texas State Historical Association, 2014.

Bogener, Stephen. *Ditches Across the Desert: Irrigation in the Lower Pecos Valley*. Lubbock, TX: Texas Tech University Press, 2003.

Bowman, Timothy Paul. *Blood Oranges: Colonialism and Agriculture in the South Texas Borderlands*. First edition. Connecting the Greater West Series. College Station, TX: Texas A&M University Press, 2016.

Brown, David, ed. *The Wolf in the Southwest: The Making of an Endangered Species*. Tucson, AZ: University of Arizona Press, 1983.

Buenger, Walter L., and Robert A. Calvert, eds. *Texas Through Time: Evolving Interpretations*. College Station, TX: Texas A&M University Press, 1991.

Butzer, Karl W. *Archeology as Human Ecology: Method and Theory for a Contextual Approach*. Cambridge, MA: Cambridge University Press, 1982.

Carbyn, Lu. *The Buffalo Wolf: Predators, Prey, and the Politics of Nature*. Washington, DC: Smithsonian Books, 2003.

Collins, Michael L. *Tales of Texoma: Episodes in the History of the Red River Border*. Wichita Falls, TX: Midwestern State University Press, 2005.

Collins, Michael L., Dorothy Montgomery, and Joyce Hinds. *Inherit the Joy—Continue the Quest, 1890–1990: A History of First Christian Church, Wichita Falls, Texas*. Wichita Falls, TX: Humphrey Printing Company, 1990.

Cronon, William. *Nature's Metropolis: Chicago and the Great West*. New York: W. W. Norton & Company, 1991.

Cunfer, Geoff. *On the Great Plains: Agriculture and Environment*. College Station, TX: Texas A&M University Press, 2005.

Cunfer, Geoff, and Bill Waiser. *Bison and People on the North American Plains: A Deep Environmental History*. College Station, TX: Texas A&M University Press, 2016.

Darnton, Robert. *The Great Cat Massacre and Other Episodes in French Cultural History*. New York: Basic Books, 1984.

Douglas, C. L. *Cattle Kings of Texas*. Fort Worth, TX: Branch-Smith, 1939, 1968.

Douthitt, Katherine. *Romance and Dim Trails: A History of Clay County*. Dallas, TX: William T. Tardy Publishers, 1938.

Drago, Harry Sinclair. *Red River Valley: The Mainstream of Frontier History form the Louisiana Bayous to the Texas Panhandle*. New York: Clarkson-Potter, 1962.

Duty, Michael. *Wichita Falls: A Century of Photographs*. Wichita Falls, TX: Midwestern State University Press, 1982.

Earle, J. P. *History of Clay County and Northwest Texas*. Austin, TX: The Brick Row Book Shop, 1963.

Flores, Dan L. *American Serengeti: The Last Big Animals of the Great Plains*. Lawrence, KS: University Press of Kansas, 2016.

———. *Caprock Canyonlands: Journeys into the Heart of the Southern Plains*. Austin, TX: University of Texas Press, 1990.

———. *Coyote America: A Natural and Supernatural History*. New York: Basic Books, 2016.

———. *Horizontal Yellow: Nature and History in the Near Southwest*. Albuquerque, NM: University of New Mexico Press, 1999.

———, ed. *Journal of an Indian Trader: Anthony Glass and the Texas Trading Frontier, 1790–1810*. College Station, TX: Texas A&M University Press, 1985.

———. *The Natural West: Environmental History in the Great Plains and Rocky Mountains*. Norman, OK: University of Oklahoma Press, 2001.

Foreman, Dave. *Rewilding North America: A Vision for Conservation in the 21st Century*. Washington, DC: Island Press, 2004.

Foster, Morris W. *Being Comanche: A Social History of an American Indian Community*. Tucson, AZ: The University of Arizona Press, 1991.

Garrison, George P. *Texas: A Contest of Civilizations*. New York: Houghton Mifflin, 1903.

Gholson, Nick. *Hail to Our Colors: A Complete History of Coyote Football*. Wichita Falls, TX: s.n., 1999.

Goldberg, Gary, and Louis J. Rodriguez. *Midwestern State University in Photographs.* Wichita Falls, TX: Midwestern State University Press, 1995.

Greer, Flavis. *History of the Church of Christ in Wichita Falls, Texas, 1908–1973.* Wichita Falls, TX: Western Christian Foundation, 1973.

Guthrie, Woody. *Pastures of Plenty: A Self Portrait.* Edited by Dave Marsh and Harold Leventhal. New York: Harper Perennial, 1992.

Hagan, William T. *Quanah Parker, Comanche Chief.* Norman, OK: University of Oklahoma Press, 1993.

———. *United States-Comanche Relations: The Reservation Years.* New Haven, CT: Yale University Press, 1976.

Hansen, Nancy. *Wichita Falls: Where Enterprise and Opportunity Meet.* Wichita Falls, TX: Anniversary 100, 1982.

Hays, Samuel P. *Conservation and the Gospel of Efficiency: The Progressive Conservation Movement, 1890–1920.* Cambridge, MA: Harvard University Press, 1959.

Hendrickson, Kenneth E. *The Waters of the Brazos: A History of the Brazos River Authority, 1929–1979.* Waco, TX: Texian Press, 1981.

Hofsommer, Donovan. *Katy Northwest: The Story of a Branch Line Railroad.* Boulder, CO: Pruett Publishing Co., 1976.

Hollon, W. Eugene. *Beyond the Cross Timbers: The Travels of Randolph B. Marcy, 1812–1887.* Norman, OK: University of Oklahoma Press, 1955.

Hundley, Norris. *Water and the West: The Colorado River Compact and the Politics of Water in the American West.* Berkeley, CA: University of California Press, 1975.

Huser, Vern. *Rivers of Texas.* College Station, TX: Texas A&M University Press, 2000.

Isenberg, Andrew. *The Destruction of the Bison: An Environmental History, 1750–1920.* New York: Cambridge University Press, 2000.

Jackson, C. Emerson, and Gwendolyn McDonald. *The History of the Negro Wichita Falls, Texas 1880–1982.* Wichita Falls, TX: Humphrey Printing Company, 1988.

Jones, Sylvia Jo. *Wilbarger County.* Lubbock, TX: Wilbarger County Historical Commission, 1986.

Kavanagh, Thomas W. *Comanche Political History: An Ethnohistorical Perspective, 1705–1875.* Lincoln, NE: University of Nebraska Press, 1996.

Kelly, Louise. *Wichita County Beginnings.* Burnett, TX: Eakin Press, 1982.

Kerstetter, Todd M. *Flood on the Tracks: Living, Dying, and the Nature of Disaster in the Elkhorn River Basin.* Lubbock, TX: Texas Tech University Press, 2018.

Kilpatrick, Hazel. *A History of Floral Heights Methodist Church, Woman's Society of Christian Service, 1919–1965.* Wichita Falls, TX: Floral Heights Methodist Church, 1966.

Kindig, Everett William. *Midwestern State University: The Better Part of a Century.* Wichita Falls, TX: Midwestern State University Press, 2000.

Kindig, Everett William, and Jodie Moon. *A Brief History of Midwestern State University's Sikes House.* Wichita Falls, TX: s.n., 2001.

Kinter, Max. *Sacred Heart Parish: 100 Years of Growth and Service.* s.l.: s.n., 1992.

Kittinger, Roy. *The Formation of the State of Oklahoma, 1803–1906.* Berkeley, CA: University of California Press, 1917.

Kline, Benjamin. *First Along the River: A Brief History of the US Environmental Movement.* Boulder, CO: Rowman and Littlefield, 2000.

Laxson, Homer C. *Economic Survey of Wichita County, Texas.* Wichita Falls, TX: Bureau of Business and Economic Research at Midwestern State University, 1958.

Lewis, David Rich. *Neither Wolf Nor Dog: American Indians, Environment, and Agrarian Change.* New York: Oxford Press, 1994.

Liles, Deborah, and Cecilia Gutierrez Venable, eds. *Texas Women and Ranching: On the Range, At the Rodeo, and In Their Communities.* Texas A&M University Press, 2019.

Limerick, Patricia Nelson. *Desert Passages: Encounters with the American Desert.* Albuquerque, NM: University of New Mexico Press, 1985.

———. *Something in the Soil: Legacies and Reckonings in the New West.* New York: W. W. Norton & Company, 2000.

Loftin, Jack. *Trails Through Archer.* Austin, TX: Eakin Publications, 1979.

Longo, Peter J., and David W. Yoskowitz, eds. *Water on the Great Plains: Issues and Policies*. Lubbock, TX: Texas Tech University Press, 2002.

Lynn-Sherow, Bonnie. *Red Earth: Race and Agriculture in Oklahoma Territory*. Lawrence, KS: University Press of Kansas, 2004.

Malin, James C. *History and Ecology: Studies of the Grassland*. Edited by Robert P. Swierenga. Lincoln, NE: University of Nebraska Press, 1984.

Mason, Tyler Madeleine. *Riding for Texas: The True Adventures of Captain Bill McDonald of the Texas Rangers*. New York: Reynal and Hitchcock, 1936.

Masterson, V. V. *The Katy Railroad and the Last Frontier*. Norman, OK: University of Oklahoma Press, 1952.

McKay, Seth Shepard. *Making the Texas Constitution of 1876*. Philadelphia, PA: University of Pennsylvania, 1924.

McLean, Duncan. *Lone Star Swing: On the Trail of Bob Wills and His Texas*. New York: W. W. Norton, 1998.

Mech, L. David. *The Way of the Wolf*. New York: Voyageur Press, 1992.

Miller, Char, ed. *Fluid Arguments: Five Centuries of Western Water Conflict*. Tucson, AZ: University of Arizona Press, 2001.

———. *On the Border: An Environmental History of San Antonio*. Pittsburgh, PA: University of Pittsburgh Press, 2001.

Monbiot, George. *Feral: Rewilding the Land, the Sea, and Human Life*. Chicago, IL: University of Chicago Press, 2017.

Morgan, Jonnie R. *The History of Wichita Falls*. Wichita Falls, TX: Nortex Offset Publications Inc., 1931.

Morris, Christopher. *The Big Muddy: An Environmental History of the Mississippi and Its Peoples from Hernando de Soto to Hurricane Katrina*. New York: Oxford University Press, 2012.

Morris, John Miller. *El Llano Estacado: Exploration and Imagination on the High Plains of Texas and New Mexico, 1536–1860*. Austin, TX: Texas State Historical Association, 1997.

Nash, Roderick. *Wilderness and the American Mind*. Fifth Edition. New Haven, CT: Yale University Press, 2014.

Opie, John. *Nature's Nation: An Environmental History of the United States*.

New York: Holt, Rhinehart, and Winston, 1998.

Opie, John, Char Miller, and Kenna Lang Archer. *Ogallala: Water for a Dry Land.* Third Edition. Our Sustainable Future Series. Lincoln, NE: University of Nebraska Press, 2018.

Overton, Richard C. *Gulf to Rockies: The Heritage of the Ft. Worth and Denver Colorado and Southern Railways, 1861–1898.* Austin: University of Texas Press, 1953.

Paine, Albert Bigelow. *Captain Bill McDonald: Texas Ranger.* New York: J. J. Little and Ives Co., 1909.

Parfet, Ione. *The Diamond trail: Published on the occasion of the 75th anniversary Diamond Jubilee Celebration of Wichita County, Texas, 1882–1957.* s.l.: s.n., 1957.

Parker, Al. *Baseball Giant Killers: The Spudders of the '20s.* Quanah, TX: Nortex Press, 1976.

Pisani, Donald J. *From Family Business to Agribusiness: The Irrigation Crusade in California and the West, 1850–1931.* Berkeley, CA: University of California Press, 1984.

———. *To Reclaim a Divided West: Water, Law, and Public Policy, 1848–1902.* Albuquerque, NM: University of New Mexico Press, 1992.

———. *Water, Land, and Law in the West: The Limits of Public Policy, 1850–1920.* Lawrence, KS: University of Kansas, 1996.

———. *Water and American Government: The Reclamation Bureau, National Water Policy, and the West, 1902–1935.* Berkeley, CA: University of California, 2002.

Powell, T. J. *Samuel Burk Burnett: A Sketch.* Fort Worth, TX: Graves & Groves, 1916.

Reisner, Marc. *Cadillac Desert: The American West and Its Disappearing Water.* New York: Penguin Books, 1993.

Richardson, George Taylor. *An Economic Analysis of Range Improvement Practices in the Texas Rolling Plains.* Lubbock, TX: s.n., 1977.

Richardson, Heather Cox. *How the South Won the Civil War: Oligarchy, Democracy, and the Continuing Fight for the Soul of America.* Oxford: Oxford University Press, 2020.

Richardson, Rupert Norval. *The Comanche Barrier to South Plains Settlement: A Century and a Half of Savage Resistance to the Advancing White Frontier.* Glendale, CA: The Arthur H. Clark Company, 1933.

———. *The Frontier of Northwest Texas, 1846 to 1876: Advance and Defense By the Pioneer Settlers of the Cross Timbers and Prairies.* Glendale, CA: The Arthur H. Clark Company, 1963.

Ross, Charles P., and T. L. Rouse. *Official Early-Day History of Wilbarger County.* Vernon, TX: The Vernon Daily Record, 1973.

Scott, James C. *Seeing Like a State: How Certain Schemes to Improve the Human Condition Have Failed.* New Haven, CT: Yale University Press, 1998.

Shelton, Glenn. *Wichita Falls: A Lady with a Past.* Wichita Falls, TX: Western Christian Foundation, 1978.

Sherow, James Earl. *Watering the Valley: Development along the High Plains Arkansas River, 1870–1950.* Lawrence, KS: University Press of Kansas, 1990.

Spellmann, Norman W., and Betty B. Spellmann. *History of First Methodist Church, Wichita Falls, Texas: A Century of Faith, 1881–1981.* Wichita Falls, TX: Heritage Committee of First Methodist Church, 1981.

Spratt, John S. *The Road to Spindletop.* Austin, TX: University of Texas Press, 1970.

Steinberg, Ted. *Acts of God: The Unnatural History of Natural Disaster in America.* Oxford: Oxford University Press, 2006.

Swanson, Doug J. *Cult of Glory: The Bold and Brutal History of the Texas Rangers.* New York: Viking, 2020.

Taylor, William Charles. *A History of Clay County.* Austin, TX: Jenkins Publishing Co., 1972.

Tillman County Historical Society and Carolyn Maxwell. *A Diamond Jubilee History of Tillman County, 1901–1976.* Frederick, OK: The Society, 1976.

Turner, Frederick Jackson. *The Frontier in America History.* New York: Henry Holt and Company, 1921.

Tyson, Carl N. *The Red River in Southwestern History.* Norman, OK:

University of Oklahoma Press, 1977.

Webb, Walter Prescott. *Divided We Stand: The Crisis of Frontierless Democracy*. New York: Farrar & Rinehart, 1937.

———. *The Great Frontier*. Boston, MA: Houghton Mifflin Company, 1952.

———. *The Great Plains*. Boston: Ginn and Company, 1931.

———. *More Water for Texas: The Problem and the Plan*. Austin, TX: University of Texas Press, 1954.

———. *The Texas Rangers: A Century of Frontier Defense*. Boston, MA: Houghton Mifflin Company, 1935.

Welborn, C. A. *History of the Red River Controversy*. Wichita Falls, TX: Nortex, 1973.

Weniger, Del. *The Explorers' Texas: The Lands and Waters*. Austin, TX: Eakin Press, 1984.

White, Richard. *Land Use, Environment, and Social Change: The Shaping of Island County, Washington*. Seattle, WA: University of Washington Press, 1980.

———. *The Organic Machine: The Remaking of the Columbia River*. New York: Hill and Wang, 1996.

Williams, Andrea. *A History of Libby Fair Holland Library in Wichita Falls, Texas*. Denton, TX: Texas Women's University Press, 1980.

Williams, J. W. *The Big Ranch Country*. Wichita Falls, TX: Nortex, 1954.

———. *Old Texas Trails*. Edited by Kenneth F. Neighbours. Burnet, TX: Eakin Press, 1979.

Williams, Jack S., and Robert L. Hoover. *Arms of the Apacheria: A Comparison of Apachean and Spanish Fighting Techniques in the Later Eighteenth Century*. Greeley, CO: University of Northern Colorado Museum of Anthropology, 1983.

Williams, Lorene D. *A History of Lamar Baptist Church the First 75 years: February 11, 1912 through February 11, 1987*. Wichita Falls, TX: Lamar Baptist Church, 1987.

Wilson, Steve. *Wichita Falls: A Pictorial History*. Norfolk, VA: The Donning Co., 1982.

Wittfogel, Karl. *Oriental Despotism: A Comparative Study of Total Power.* New Haven, CT: Yale University Press, 1957.

Worster, Donald. *Dust Bowl: The Southern Plains in the 1930s.* New York: Oxford University Press, 1979.

———, ed. *The Ends of the Earth: Perspectives on Modern Environmental History.* New York: Cambridge University Press, 1988.

———. *Nature's Economy: The Roots of Ecology.* New York: Doubleday, 1979.

———. *Rivers of Empire: Water, Aridity, and the Growth of the American West.* New York: Oxford University Press, 1985.

———. *Under Western Skies: Nature and History in the American West.* New York: Oxford University Press, 1992.

Dissertations and Theses

Adams, Leann Cox. "Winning Hand: Burk Burnett of the 6666 Ranch." Master's thesis, Texas Christian University, 1969.

Anderson, Jahue. "An Environmental History of the Wichita River Valleys." Master's thesis, Texas State University–San Marcos, 2004.

———. "Red Earth, Salty Waters: A History of Environmental Knowledge in the Upper Red River Basin." PhD diss., Texas Christian University, 2009.

Barker, Olden Lee. "An Historical Account of the Red River as an Inland Water-Way." Master's thesis, University of Colorado, 1926.

Cranford, Norman Bayne. "The History of Sheppard Air Force Base." Master's thesis, Midwestern State University, 1965.

Duncan, Patricia Lenora. "Enterprise: B. B. Paddock and Fort Worth: A Case Study of Late Nineteenth Century American Boosterism." Master's thesis, University of Texas at Arlington, 1982.

Haley, Jack Dan. "A History of the Establishment of the Wichita National Forest and Game Preserve, 1901–1908." Master's thesis, University of Oklahoma, 1973.

Hayes, Harry Howard. "John Gerham Hardin: Philanthropist." Master's thesis, Hardin-Simmons University, 1940.

Kinnard, Knox. "A History of the Waggoner Ranch." Master's thesis,

University of Texas at Austin, 1941.

Loggie, Mary Basham. "Joseph Sterling Bridwell." Master's thesis, Midwestern State University, 1967.

Martin, Meredith Richards. "Samuel Burk Burnett: Old 6666." Master's thesis, Midwestern State University, 2002.

Morgan, J. Howard. "The History of Banking in Wichita Falls, Texas." Master's thesis, Southwestern Graduate School of Banking, 1964.

Morgan, Margaret Lee. "The History and Economic Aspect of the Wichita Valley Irrigation Project." Master's thesis, Southern Methodist University, 1939.

Neely, Lloyd. "History of Wichita Falls: From Frontier Settlement to City." Master's thesis, Southern Methodist University, 1962.

Sandefer, Marguerite. "The Development of the Oil Industry in Wichita County." Master's thesis, University of Texas, 1938.

Smith, Clint Leland. "A History of Call Aviation Field." Master's thesis, Midwestern State University, 1970.

Thompson, Gerald L. "Rainfall Interception by Mesquite on the Rolling Plains of Texas." PhD diss., Texas Tech University, 1986.

Van Horn, Gladys. "The History of the Roads in Wichita County, Texas." Master's thesis, University of Texas at Austin, 1936.

Novels

Bissinger, H. G. *Friday Night Lights: A Town, a Team, and a Dream.* Boston, MA: Addison-Wesley, 1990.

McMurtry, Larry. *The Last Picture Show.* New York: Liveright Publishing, 1966.

———. *Lonesome Dove.* New York: Simon & Schuster, 1985.

Sinclair, Upton. *Oil!* New York: Albert and Charles Boni, 1926.

DISCOGRAPHY

Clark, Guy. "Desperados Waiting for a Train." *Old No. 1*. RCA, 1975.

———. "Red River." *Cold Dog Soup*. Sugar Hill, 1999.

Guthrie, Woody. "Dust Bowl Refugee." *Dust Bowl Ballads*. Victor, 1940.

———. "I Ain't Got No Home in This World Anymore." *Dust Bowl Ballads*. Victor, 1940.

———. "So Long, It's Been Good to Know Yuh." *Dust Bowl Ballads*. Victor, 1940.

Marchman, Houston, and the Contraband. "Wichita Falls." *Tryin' For Home*. Blind Nello Records, 2000.

McMurtry, James. "Out Here in the Middle." *Saint Mary of the Woods*. Signal Hill, 2002.

FILMOGRAPHY

Boom Town. Directed by Jack Conway. Beverly Hills, CA: Metro-Goldwyn-Mayer, 1940.

Giant. Directed by George Stevens. Burbank, CA: Warner Brothers, 1956.

Hell or High Water. Directed by David Mackenzie. Santa Monica, CA: Lionsgate, 2016.

The Last Picture Show. Directed by Peter Bogdanovich. Culver City, CA: Columbia Pictures, 1971.

Red River. Directed by Howard Hawkes. Beverly Hills, CA: United Artists, 1948.

Red River Valley. Directed by B. Reeves Eason. Los Angeles, CA: Republic Pictures, 1936.

Red River Valley. Directed by Joseph Kane. Los Angeles, CA: Republic Pictures, 1941.

Stagecoach. Directed by John Ford. Beverly Hills, CA: United Artists, 1939.

There Will Be Blood. Directed by Paul Thomas Anderson. Hollywood, CA: Paramount, 2007.

INDEX

CPSIA information can be obtained
at www.ICGtesting.com
Printed in the USA
LVHW100437070423
743672LV00006B/314